AMERICA'S LOST PLAYS

V

TRIAL WITHOUT JURY
and Other Plays

VI

THE LAST DUEL IN SPAIN
and Other Plays

A series in twenty volumes of hitherto unpublished plays collected with the aid of the Rockefeller Foundation, under the auspices of the Dramatists' Guild of the Authors' League of America, edited with historical and bibliographical notes.

BARRETT H. CLARK

GENERAL EDITOR

Advisory Board

ROBERT HAMILTON BALL, QUEENS COLLEGE

HOYT H. HUDSON, PRINCETON UNIVERSITY

GLENN HUGHES, UNIVERSITY OF WASHINGTON

GARRETT H. LEVERTON, FORMERLY OF NORTHWEST-
ERN UNIVERSITY

E. C. MABIE, UNIVERSITY OF IOWA

ALLARDYCE NICOLL, YALE UNIVERSITY

ARTHUR HOBSON QUINN, UNIVERSITY OF
PENNSYLVANIA

NAPIER WILT, UNIVERSITY OF CHICAGO

Trial without Jury

& *Other Plays*

BY JOHN HOWARD PAYNE

EDITED BY CODMAN HISLOP
AND W. R. RICHARDSON

WILDSIDE PRESS

ACKNOWLEDGMENTS

THE editors wish to express their gratitude for the encouragement and help extended to them by President Dixon Ryan Fox of Union College, Professors Burges Johnson of Union College, Allardyce Nicoll of Yale University, Hyder E. Rollins of Harvard University, R. G. Noyes of Brown University, to F. A. Smith and Helmar L. Webb, Librarian of Union College, to T. H. Ralston, and to the many others who have given generously of their time and advice.

They would like to thank Mrs. Lillian A. Hall, of the Theatre Collection, Harvard University, and Colonel Thatcher T. Payne Luquer for allowing them to use their extensive collections of the manuscript plays and letters.

PREFACE

T HE eleven plays by John Howard Payne in the series of America's Lost Plays are divided between two companion volumes. The first volume is entitled *Trial without Jury and Other Plays by John Howard Payne* and the second *The Last Duel in Spain and Other Plays by John Howard Payne*.

CONTENTS

Acknowledgments   v

Preface   vii

John Howard Payne   xi

Trial without Jury; or, The Magpie and the Maid   1

Mount Savage   55

The Boarding Schools; or, Life among the Little Folks   91

The Two Sons-in-Law   113

Mazeppa; or, The Wild Horse of Tartary   163

The Spanish Husband; or, First and Last Love   205

JOHN HOWARD PAYNE
1791-1852

I

On January 17, 1813, the "American Roscius," John Howard Payne, sailed from New York City on the *Catherine Ray* for Liverpool. At twenty-one he found himself putting off for a man's world with little more than the tattered remnants of his American reputation as a child actor to sustain him. He had, however, an enormous self-confidence, a desire to excel on the London stage, and letters which were keys to England's stiff locks.

Payne's charm made him welcome at once. Peter Irving and Henry Brevoort introduced the handsome young actor to their wide circle of friends; William Roscoe presented him to John Kemble, Coleridge, and Southey. Payne's eyes, however, were on the stage; he had come to take his place with Kean and Cooke and Macready. The management of the Theatre Royal, Drury Lane, finally agreed to present this eager American; on June 4, 1813, the playbills of Drury Lane announced the tragedy of *Douglas* in which Norval was to be played by "a Young Gentleman"—who had actually made his début in this part in New York City four years earlier.

From this well received performance until his last stage appearance in Birmingham, in May 1818, Payne played the major theaters of England and Ireland; Rolla, Hamlet, Romeo, Norval, were applauded, but with less and less enthusiasm. The romantic-looking boy was growing into a rather stoutish, short man whose figure lodged uncomfortably in the hero's costumes. Reluctantly the old rôles were put by for the then humbler one of the playwright, the theater hack, the literary agent whose productions for the London managers were often rewarded with neglect or with outright theft.

Payne's transition from actor to playwright was not a difficult one. He had been as precocious an author as he had been an actor; before he left America his second play, *Lovers' Vows,* an adaptation of Mrs. Inchbald's and Benjamin Thompson's version of Kotzebue's *Das Kind der Liebe,* was published in Baltimore. He had been proprietor and editor of a New York theatrical paper, *The Thespian Mirror,* at the age of fourteen. And now, with that questionable facility which marked so much of his work, he again turned to adapting foreign plays to the English stage.

In the early months of 1815 Payne was in Paris, frequenting the rooms of the French tragedian, Talma, and enjoying the "free list" of the National Theatre. At this time he made an adaptation of a current Paris success, *La Pie Voleuse,* which he may have shown on his return to London to Douglas Kinnaird, chairman of the managing committee of Drury Lane.

French "successes" were what the English theaters fattened on. Although Drury Lane was unable to use Payne's adaptation, its managing director saw in Payne a source of supply for those usually ephemeral plays which his audiences were demanding. Would Payne return to France as literary agent for Drury Lane until such time as the committee could "bring him out" in some suitable rôle? Payne would, and did, after having made arrangements for the disposal of the *Trial without Jury; or, The Magpie and the Maid* to Henry Harris, manager of Covent Garden.

The return to Paris was definitely the return to the literary life for Payne. On February 1, 1816, Drury Lane was producing *Accusation; or, the Family of Anglade,* a production which was staged ten days after the receipt of the manuscript, an unprecedented event, according to Thomas Dibdin.

From this time on, Payne's literary star described an erratic course. The Drury Lane committee, for various reasons, among them poor houses and managerial fickleness, grew cool toward its new Paris agent. Payne complained of the neglect of his "system organized by which every accessory to pieces which might be desirable, could be completed in four days." What of his extensive collection of "novel prints of costume" and the "original music" bought from the leader of the Emperor of Austria's band and the several adaptations already submitted to the theater?

Receiving, unaccountably, little satisfaction from Drury Lane, Payne arranged to devote his "system" to the services of its great rival, Covent Garden. For £50 its manager, Harris, was to receive a "free translation." If the play was wanted for production, the adaptation was to cost 200 guineas. Harris also agreed to bring Payne out in suitable parts, for Payne was still dreaming of applause and great rôles in 1817. For the next two years he acted as correspondent for Covent Garden, hoping for, but never finding, enough support for the resumption of his acting career.

On December 3, 1818, Drury Lane produced Payne's *Brutus; or, The Fall of Tarquin,* perhaps his greatest success as a playwright, although it was damned by many critics as outright plagiarism. In spite of their attacks, the play had a tremendous run from which everyone seems to have profited but the adapter.

In February 1819, Payne, disgusted with his treatment at the hands of the London managers, undertook the direction of the Sadler's Wells theater.

Because of bad financing and a "poor season" the venture landed its proprietor in "Naked Boy Court," an unwelcome debtor-guest of Fleet Street Prison.

And here he stayed, toying with the idea of a spelling book on a "familiar plan," occasionally pawning articles of clothing for food. And then, one day, rather mysteriously, he received a packet of three plays, one of which, *Thérèse* by M. Victor, he immediately adapted and sold to Drury Lane where it was successfully produced on February 2, 1821.

Paris was the best place for a recent resident of the Fleet whose creditors were far from satisfied. Here on the Rue St. Pierre, Payne refurbished his "system," sent over to R. W. Elliston at Drury Lane such pieces as *Love in Humble Life* and *Adeline* and grew enthusiastic over plans for an English summer theater in the French capital. Elliston, wrote Payne to Washington Irving in March 1821, "was to pay me for a week's work and then employed me three months without pay in the bargain."

Here the old Irving association was renewed, and continued with varying degrees of warmth for many years. Irving, in 1821, agreed to do what he could to forward Payne's fortunes with the English publishers and managers, although his efforts were attended with little success. In 1822, on Irving's advice, Payne discontinued sending plays to the unreliable Elliston, and began to write for Charles Kemble, the new manager of Covent Garden. The year 1822 was a "good" year; at the end of it he wrote to his brother, Thatcher, in New York: "I have earned about £500 by pieces uniformly successful. I have ceased to be vain about these trifles, and they generally go forth anonymously, or are ascribed to some of the old London authors." There were plans for a *Faustus,* a *Sappho,* an *Alfred the Great,* and a *Camille* during this year.

On May 8, 1823, Covent Garden produced *Clari, The Maid of Milan,* with music by H. R. Bishop. Here occurred the song "Home! Sweet Home!." For this not-too-successful operetta and two plays, *Ali Pacha* and the *Two Galley Slaves,* Payne received £250.

From August 1823 until the spring of 1824 Washington Irving and John Howard Payne combined their literary fortunes, living together, when Payne was not in London trying to sell their manuscripts, at 89 Rue Richelieu, where, for a time, Peter Irving also lived. Although Irving's desire to bolster his purse by writing for the theaters was unfulfilled, he and Payne, and occasionally Peter, collaborated on perhaps ten adaptations before Washington Irving returned to more productive fields. *Charles the Second, Married and Single,* and *Richelieu* were acted with some success. After 1824 Irving continued to help Payne with an occasional "coup de plume," as he phrased it, but the literary partnership was dead.

On August 16, 1825, Payne made the surprising and to him, bitter, revelation to Irving that the newly widowed Mary Shelley had confided to him her increasing regard for the popular author of the *Sketch Book* and *Bracebridge Hall*. To Irving it was apparently a matter of indifference, to Payne it meant the end of what he had hoped was to have been a personal romance; it meant the abrupt return to the realities of dunning creditors and literary "trifles."

To forward the sale of these "trifles," Payne arranged, during the summer of 1825, only at Irving's request, to prepare fifteen plays for Stephen Price, an American theatrical agent who was directing the fortunes of Drury Lane, and who had recently been persuaded by Irving that Payne was not the irresponsible hack his enemies had painted him as being. The Irving-Payne correspondence for the period mentions *Red Riding Hood, Mazeppa, Peter Smink, 'Twas I,* and *Maid of Erin,* plays for which Irving made suggestions. In January 1826, a selection of plays, *Mazeppa* and *The Spanish Husband* among them, was offered to John Fawcett, the actor-manager at Covent Garden who had made "Captain Copp" famous in the Irving-Payne *Charles the Second. Richelieu* and *La Dame Blanche* were also sent to Fawcett. Price, complained Payne, was now forgetting to pay for the ten pieces he held; in February, however, "six full pieces" went out to Price "on the new account."

Payne, always ready to try some fresh venture, established in London, in October 1826, a critical theatrical paper, *The Opera Glass,* which ran until March 1827. A serious illness at this time brought an end to the journal and to his plan to accept the management of a theatre in London and one in Paris.

Payne's career from 1827 until 1832, when he sailed for America, is still somewhat obscure. In December 1830, Irving noted in his journal that Payne "fresh and fair as a rose" was about London, trying to interest him in a new comedy. He undoubtedly continued to produce pieces for the London theaters, among them, in the spring of 1830, *The Spanish Husband,* and two years later, *Woman's Revenge.*

In July 1831, however, the shadow of poverty deepened; on the fifteenth Payne wrote to an unnamed correspondent that, "ill in my bed, I am sinking to ruin for want of £50." On June 15, 1832, he wrote again that he was about to leave England for Portsmouth on the *S.S. President,* and added, "I am so perplexed for resources as not to know how I am to manage to get to the ship."

Of these hurried, frustrated years of theatrical allegiance, Payne wrote, just before he sailed, that they had "only been prolific in experience. If my resources are diminished with them; if I have gained no renown, I have gained what is better—a disregard for the sort of renown of which I was in ardent pursuit; if I go back to the home of my ancestors almost like a prodigal, I go with the certainty of the prodigal's welcome and with the treasure of the prodigal's wisdom."

On July 25, 1832, Payne arrived in plague-ridden New York, intending to return to England in September or October. He remained in America, however, comforted for a time by the enthusiasm with which he was received everywhere. Benefits were given him in New York, Boston, and in several other American cities. His playwriting career was apparently over, although he made a few sporadic attempts to interest producers in such manuscripts as *The Italian Bride* and *Romulus*.

The years until his death on April 9, 1852, while serving his second term as American consul at Tunis, were filled with visionary literary schemes and maneuvering for political appointment which usually ended in stalemate. This unfulfilled career of our first outstanding dramatist and these last ineffectual years are more clearly understood, perhaps, when we read his own self-analysis, made to Mary Shelley in 1825; "I know [mine] is not the kind of mind likely to be understood and still less so to be valued and therefore more at home out of the world. It is better than I am, if you can understand the paradox, and it is only when events divert me from its first suggestions that it becomes wounded and perplexed. . . ."

Payne, "wounded and perplexed" as he often was, diverted too easily from the expedient course, went to London at a time when the stage no longer exhibited great drama.

Low standards of taste, unfair treatment of authors, and the popularity of the so-called illegitimate theater allowed for little development of a substantial dramatic literature. The unabashed sentimentalism of the audience had resulted in the substitution of tears and sensationalism for the pity and terror formerly aroused by a great character's weakness; and sympathy, for the ridicule once directed at the unreasonable man. The playwright's very struggle to keep alive was bitter, for both the managers and publishers, unfettered by copyright laws, bid low for his work. The market for legitimate tragedy and comedy was restricted to the poorly managed patent houses, Drury Lane and Covent Garden. The far more popular but illegitimate farces, burlettas, and melodramas were produced at the minor theaters for a vulgar and unruly mob deaf to the subtleties of characterization and situation.

Payne, limited by his own desire "to seek renown," and by the physical and spiritual inadequacies of the theatre, soon adjusted himself to serve the popular taste. He learned how to satisfy the overwhelming interest in current French successes, adapting them with unusual speed for the uncritical London audiences. Although he wrote in the preface to *Thérèse* that the drama of action was inferior to the "literary work" whose merit lies "in what it said, and the manner of saying it," he nevertheless continued to adapt "actable plays" in great numbers and without apparent affront to his literary conscience. As a result, the emphasis in his plays is on action; his characters are seldom natural. In his dramas he is very much in the spirit of the time in his use of the romantically remote and unreal; in most of his lighter plays one finds a realistic treatment of manners and setting.

Payne's originality is extremely limited. In company with Thomas Dibdin, Milner, Moncrieff, Planché, and Pocock, however, he holds a relatively high place as a representative of the age in which the demand for novelty spurred the playwright to produce derivative drama.

II

MANUSCRIPT HISTORY

The seven Harvard manuscripts have been added to the Theatre Collection of the University by purchase and donation. Their history is obscure. It seems likely that the majority of them were among Payne's effects which were carelessly dispersed following his death in Tunis, in 1852.

The Luquer manuscripts were among the Payne items which escaped dispersal, in 1852. On March 9, 1864, William Cullen Bryant, at the request of Mrs. Lea Luquer, Payne's niece, opened a correspondence with Amos Perry, American consul at Tunis, designed to effect the return of the Payne memorabilia which was still to be found at the consulate. On May 27, Mr. Perry informed Mrs. Luquer that the preceding consul, William Chandler, had unfortunately permitted the scattering of many of Payne's papers; on September 10 of this year Mr. Perry forwarded to Mrs. Luquer those papers which remained, including among them four manuscript plays which were inherited by Mrs. Luquer's son, their present owner, Colonel Thatcher T. Payne Luquer.

AIM AND METHOD

In order to conform with the aim of the series of America's Lost Plays, that of presenting to the public a readable version, the editors have adopted the following methods. Payne's spelling and punctuation have been standardized and modernized. Modern typographical conventions have been used in the printing of stage directions; and standardized abbreviations of the names of the speakers of dialogue adopted. At times Payne, without crossing out what he first wrote, offers one or more variants; the reading that seemed best has been chosen. The texts of two acted plays, *The Spanish Husband*

and *Woman's Revenge,* which are extant in the Lord Chamberlain's collection and which upon collation seemed superior were used. Any illegible readings in these two texts were replaced by legible passages from the Harvard texts. Additions, such as those of casts of characters, or settings, etc., or occasional words or phrases necessary for completing the meaning, are marked: [ ]. Conjectural emendations, for instance, of illegible words or passages, or of inconsistencies, are marked: < >. Whenever possible these emendations have been supplied from Payne's sources.

TRIAL WITHOUT JURY;
Or, THE MAGPIE AND THE MAID

TRIAL WITHOUT JURY;
Or, THE MAGPIE AND THE MAID

THE autograph manuscript of *Trial without Jury; or, The Magpie and the Maid* is in the Harvard collection.

This melodrama, dated August 1815, was completed about three months after its source, Caigniez and D'Aubigny's *La Pie Voleuse, ou La Servante de Palaiseau*, was performed at the Théâtre de la Porte St. Martin, April 29. So popular was the French play that at least four English adaptations were made, three of which were acted late in the summer of 1815 and eventually printed: Arnold's *The Maid and the Magpye; or, Which Is the Thief?*, brought out at the Lyceum, August 28; *The Magpie; or, The Maid of Palaiseau*, commonly attributed to Thomas Dibdin, Drury Lane, September 12; and Pocock's *The Magpie, or The Maid?*, Covent Garden, September 15. The fate of the fourth version, Payne's, is not wholly clear; but it seems likely that it was never acted. Evidently in August Payne sold it to Harris of Covent Garden, who then laid it aside in favor of Pocock's play; however, Pocock may have been allowed to consult his competitor's version. Payne undoubtedly alludes to the sale when, in the letter to the subcommittee of Drury Lane, April 29, 1816, in which he reviews his dealings with Kinnaird, he tells of a conversation with him during the preceding August about "a piece" that had just been bought "in a liberal manner by Mr. Harris." Of Pocock's play the reviewer in *The Theatrical Inquisitor* for September writes enigmatically that a share in its production "is said to be due to Mr. Payne, the American Roscius—*thereby hangs a tale.*"

Consequently there is a split of opinion over the question of authorship. Apparently in the belief that Pocock not only had access to Payne's play but is greatly indebted to it, G. Harrison (*The Life and Writings of John Howard Payne*, Philadelphia, 1885, pp. 80-1), Colonel T. T. P. Luquer ("Writing a Play in a Debtor's Prison," *Scribner's*, January 1921, p. 80, n. 19), A. H. Quinn (*A History of the American Drama from the Beginning to the Civil War*, New York, 1923, pp. 168-9, n. 1), and the *D.A.B.* all ascribe to Payne the play acted at Covent Garden, September 15, 1815. *The Magpie, or The Maid?* acted on this date, like many other plays of the time, is billed anonymously, but the cast is that of Pocock's version printed later, and it is to Pocock that Genest (*Some Account of the English Stage*, Bath, 1832, VIII, 539) and Allardyce Nicoll (*A History of Early 19th Century Drama, 1800-1850,* Cambridge, 1930, Vol. II, p. 374) attribute it. Mrs. Lillian A. Hall (*Harvard Library Notes,* December 1935, p. 89), who briefly reviews these opinions, concludes that Payne's play was never performed.

The most convincing evidence, a comparison of the two plays, which seems to have been overlooked by the critics, reveals similarities so slight as to suggest that Pocock's version is mainly an independent adaptation of the French. Both Pocock and Payne change most of the French names; and two of the altered names in both versions are alike. On the other hand, Pocock, using different phraseology throughout, writes with more spirit than Payne, and he shortens his version somewhat through the omission of many wordy passages, thus speeding up the movement of the action. In general, Payne's work suffers somewhat by the comparison, for he seems to have lacked as yet the ability of his slightly more experienced competitor.

[PAYNE'S] FOREWORD

Everybody has heard of the expiatory Mass of the Magpie, which was in ancient times performed at Paris in atonement for the error committed by some judges who had passed sentence of death on an unfortunate female servant, unjustly charged with thefts which had been committed by a magpie. Though the period and circumstances of the famous trial are variously related, its authenticity is unquestionable. It does not appear likely that this religious ceremony would have been founded without an adequate motive. The prevailing tradition is that the theft consisted of spoons, forks, and pieces of money, which were discovered when it was too late in a gutter, where the bird had successively concealed them. This last form of the story is the one we have adopted.

CAST OF CHARACTERS

The Justice of Palaiseau

<Mr.> Gregory, *a rich farmer of Palaiseau*

Henry, *his son*

Everard, *a soldier, father of Rosalie*

Francour, *comrade and friend of Everard*

Coody, *the godson and servant of Farmer Gregory and his wife*

George, *a young villager and servant of the Justice*

Durmont, *a jailor*

Isaac, *a Jew*

<Mr.> Anthony, *the Justice's clerk*

Nannette, *the wife of Gregory*

Rosalie, *maid of the farmhouse at Palaiseau*

A Magpie

Soldiers, Villagers, etc.

THE SCENE PASSES AT PALAISEAU IN FRANCE

ACT I.

SCENE: *A farmyard at Palaiseau. On the left is the entrance to the farmhouse. On the right, a tuft of trees. One of these trees projects from the side wing beyond the rest and sustains an osier cage with a magpie in it, the cage door hanging open. At the back of the stage is a hedge, through the center of which a rustic gate opens on the farmyard. Beyond this hedge appears a little hill and picturesque mountains in the distance.*

MAGPIE. [*Calls*] Coody! Coody!

COODY. [*In the farmhouse*] Coming! Coming! [*He enters, wiping his mouth with the back of his hand*] Hang these people! One has not even time —hey! Nobody here! Stop a minute—here comes Miss Rosalie! It was she perhaps. Oh, she's a lovely creature! Only to think, that such a gentle-man-nered, modest being should be servant maid in a farmhouse! It's a downright *sin,* so it is! Hum! she's here. [*Music. Rosalie descends the hill with a basket under her arm*]

ROS. Ah, Coody! You there!

COODY. Was it you, Miss Rosalie, who called me just now?

ROS. Me! No.

MAGPIE. Coody! Coody!

COODY. [*Turning round*] Aha! Have I caught you, my deary? It's the magpie! That cursed magpie! She's always making herself merry at my expense.

ROS. [*Laughing*] Ha, ha, ha! It is hard to say which is the most ridiculous of the two: you or the bird. But how does this happen, Coody? You are such an old acquaintance of hers, that, by this time, you ought to know her too well to be deceived.

COODY. 'Od's bodikins! She's one of those animals that one may know forever and never get acquainted with. I should like to have seen you in my place just now. I was settling some bottles in the cupboard. I hit upon one in which there was left a little of that capital wine which our master and mistress keep for their own private use. Now I hadn't the remotest notion in the world of drinking the wine—no, nothing further from my thoughts; but I had a kind of ticklesome curiosity just to feel a touch of its fine flavor upon the tip of my tongue. And lo! Miss Rosalie, just at the very moment the bottle got into the neighborhood of my lip, that devil of a magpie sets up an infernal hue and cry, "Coody! Coody!" [*Mimicking*] Oh! 'Twas a miracle that it didn't fly into fifty pieces as I sat it down again, the little squaller threw me into such a quandary!

Ros. [*Laughing*] Yes, and you well deserved it for your tricks. Ha! Ha! Ha!

MAGPIE. Yea! Ha! Ha!

Coody. [*Threatening the Magpie*] Oh! I'll make you keep your tongue between your teeth, that's what I will, Madam Blackjacket! I can't think how it happens that running about every day as she does, on the roofs of all the houses in the village, she has not met with some brave cat before now, to save me the trouble of inflicting justice on her myself.

Ros. Oh, but she has woman's weapons! She can scratch, bite, and scold. These are found, in general, I believe, to answer pretty well.

Coody. That's all one. If she was a good beast and worth anything some ill luck would have long ago happened to her as it always does to me, but there—as they say, "Naught's never in danger," and 'tis her own very deviltry that saves her. She's malicious, cunning, greedy, and she chatters. O Lord! She chatters like—like—like a magpie!

Ros. But pray don't forget that she has at least one good quality. She frightens country bumpkins that are not over trustworthy from doing mischief, and what they ought not. Good bye, Coody! Whenever you want to be your master's wine-taster again, beware of Maggy! [*Exit, laughing. Music*]

Coody. [*Alone*] Yes, indeed, I will. I'll take care of that. Now in the name of sense, in the name of sense, I say, what could have put it in my godmother's head to take such a favorite as that into keeping? Such a chattering, noisy, but Mrs. Gregory herself is somewhat given to chattering, and "Birds of a feather—" Oh, you cunning devil! [*He goes up to the cage and teases the Magpie. Enter Nannette, speaking to someone on the outside*]

NAN. Come, come, Jack! Bestir yourself! Sweep the great parlor clean! Get everything ready to lay the cloth! [*To herself*] It is now five o'clock, and our good son Henry will soon be here. But where is Coody?

Coody. [*With a shout*] Eh! eh! You wicked brute!

NAN. Hey-day, hey-day! What's all this?

Coody. Oh, the dickens, godmother! Your magpie has bit my finger!

NAN. She did right. Why did you provoke her?

Coody. [*Menacing the magpie*] You shall pay for that trick, Miss Chatterbox!

NAN. Run, Coody! Fetch the great table, and set it under the trees. We shall have our supper there.

Coody.   So we are going to see Master Henry once more! And what's better yet, they say he brings a full discharge from the service with him.

Nan.   Ah, yes, Coody! And so he does, the dear boy returns this evening. He has been a soldier for six long years, and it will now soon be eighteen months since we have seen him. But, thank Heaven, he comes this time never to quit us again.

Coody.   O! What fun we shall have in listening to his stories about battles, and cannon balls, and broken heads, and—

Nan.   Make haste! Make haste with the table lest you get a broken head of your own. [*Pushing him*] Go, go! [*Coody prepares to go. Music. Enter Gregory, rolling a barrel*]

Greg.   This way, Coody! Lend a hand here!

Coody.   Stop, stop, godfather! [*He runs to assist Gregory. Music*]

Nan.   Good Heavens! Are you out of your senses, husband? What do you want to do with that thing?

Greg. [*To Coody*]   Let it stand there. Good! That's right. Now all is as it ought to be. Thank you, my lad! [*To Nanette*] There isn't a drop too much in it, wife! Consider all the young folks of the village are coming to rejoice at the return of our son, and if we would have the day's sports go off swimmingly, why we must furnish good wine, sure, to set 'em afloat.

Coody.   And besides that, consider, godmother, that I shall have fiddlers here to set the girls and boys dancing, and my fiddlers must drink. Drink to the fiddler is like resin to his bow.

Nan.   The table, Coody! Come, come, the table!

Coody.   Ready, godmother! All ready. [*He brings the table, and is arranging it during the rest of the scene*]

Greg.   Well, good wife! Is everything prepared? Have you forgot nothing?

Nan.   Forgot! Forgot! A puzzle-head like you might forget indeed. 'Troth matters would go on prettily in the house if I hadn't an eye to everything.

Greg.   Oh, as to that, dear Nannette, one must allow that for activity, cleverness, and vigilance, there isn't your match in all Palaiseau. You only want one thing, my dear, a temper a little more—

Nan.   Hey!

Greg.   No, I mean a little less—

Nan.   A little more—a little less—Mr. Gregory, you're a fool!

Greg.   Thank you, my dear!

Nan.   He talk about my temper! I defy you to find a wife with more gentleness, more patience, more—[*To Coody who laughs while listening to them*] Hey-day! What are you about, hey! You'd better stand laughing there, and neglect your table, indeed! Look at that Coody! He has not done yet! Must I come to you at last? Oh yes, yes! I see I must do everything, absolutely everything—not a soul in the house to give me any help!

Coody.   Oh, godmother! How can you say that! La me, women are never satisfied. They're always riding the free handle to death. I do nothing! I who from morning to night never have breathing time, and there's pretty Miss Rosalie, too, who scarcely allows herself a moment to eat, drink, or sleep. I suppose you think she does nothing neither, hey?

Nan.   There's another pretty dawdle, too, Miss Rosalie, as you call her.

Greg.   Come, come, you have a prejudice against that dear good girl. You don't render her what she deserves.

Nan.   The dear good girl can do well enough without my praises. She gets more than her share from other people.

Greg.   Nay, nay, good wife! For the two years that she has lived with us, has she ever given you reason to complain? Has she not fulfilled her duties with a punctuality, a gentleness?

Nan.   Oh! As to that, she has too much of your gentleness. I can't bear a girl who is obedient to the least sign, who hardly allows one time to give an order before it is executed. I can't bear it. [*Pointing to Coody*] Stop, stop! Look at yonder ninny who a hundred times a day drives me mad with his awkwardness and blunders. Well, well. In one respect he pleases me, even he, that sawney there! He gives me a chance of talking, he always waits to hear what one has to say, and when he makes me angry I fetch him a box o' the ear, and there's an end of the matter, and that's what I like. None of your mawkishness—your gentleness for me. I like to see a young woman of spirit like myself. It does me good to bustle and fly into a rage once and a while. It keeps me in exercise. I require it. It helps the circulation of the blood, and at such times I am healthy to a charm.

Coody.   Thank ye, kind godmother, but if it's the same thing to you, I am not over and above anxious to be your doctor in that way.

Nan.   Yes, and there's another thing. She is too often told that she is pretty. It is nothing, but "Charming Rosalie" here, and "Beautiful Rosalie" there—high and low, up to the very Justice himself! Truly, I believe, Heaven forgive me! that the old dotard is seriously in love with her.

Greg.   Faith, and I think so too! I believe there's some truth in that.

Nan.   Look you, all this will end in turning her brain with a self-conceit which won't at all become her place. It is an honest knockabout, and not a fine lady that one wants upon a farm.

Greg.   Not so fast, wife. Rosalie does not come to us as a servant. You well know our agreement with my sister in Paris, who recommended her. Rosalie's family is respectable. She is well educated. Her father, Granville, is descended from wealthy farmers like ourselves, therefore she is our equal. If poor Granville's misfortunes forced him to enlist as a common soldier after the death of his wife, ought his daughter to be reproached for it?

NAN. Well and good, I don't deny a word of what you say, but it's for the future that I tremble. A young girl, you know, who has a little beauty—oh, I hate to see pretty women in my house!

GREG. [*Laughing*] Right enough, my dear! It is rather ticklish. [*Pulling out his watch*] Oho! Gone half past five, and our son's letter promises that he'll be with us about six.

NAN. Then listen, Gregory, I will just take a glance to see how matters are going on down below, and run back to fetch you. Then we'll go up the hill together, and Henry will be in our arms a quarter of an hour the sooner for it.

GREG. An excellent plan that! With what pleasure we shall behold him again, the dear boy! I say, Nannette, the next thing we shall have to do, I suppose, will be to think of marrying him, and getting him well settled, aye?

NAN. Yes, yes! We'll see about that.

GREG. I have a scheme in my head already, but—

NAN. Oh, I see your drift! Gently, my good man, that's my business. [*Calling*] Rosalie! [*To Gregory*] Yes, yes! The settling of Henry is my concern, not yours, for I mean that he shall marry—

MAGPIE. Rosalie!

GREG. Ha, ha! Do you hear mag? One would imagine that bird was possessed! 'Fore Heaven, she has dived into the very plan!

NAN. Yes, indeed, but I would have you know that I think just as little of her opinion as I do of yours. [*Enter Rosalie*]

ROS. Did you call me, madam?

NAN. Yes, my girl! I want you to lay the tablecloth, while I get the napkins and basket of plate ready, and mind, take good care! Don't a second time—Remember Mr. Gregory's birthday. It will now be a fortnight on St. John's day, when the silver fork was lost.

ROS. Oh, make yourself easy, madam! I will be very careful. This tiresome fork has given me such misery! I am sure it has cost me more bitter tears than I ever shed before in all my life.

COODY. That fork was surely bewitched! Now did not we ransack over and over again, every cranny in the house for it! The devil must have run off with it, I'll take my oath of that!

GREG. Poh, 'tis nothing! The woman's beside herself to think so much of a trifle! Prithee, Nannette, let us hear no more of it. The silver fork, nothing but the silver fork has been dinging in our ears for more than a week past. I am sure they may be said to have paid dearly enough for it by this time.

Nan. So, so, and I'm always talking about it, am I? Good truth! I have not even thought of it for this long while. Follow me, Coody, you are wanted. [*To Gregory*] Don't be impatient, my good man, in two minutes I shall be with you again. [*Exit into the house, followed by Coody. Music*]

Greg. What's the matter, Rosalie? You seem out of spirits.

Ros. It is nothing, only Mrs. Gregory—she is still harping on—

Greg. Pshaw, pshaw! That doesn't concern you.

Ros. Pardon me, Mr. Gregory, it concerns me deeply. They always wish to make it appear that if I had been careful, that unfortunate fork never would have gone astray.

Greg. Never mind, my dear, never mind. Who can answer for—But let's quit this, and talk about my son, our dear Henry whom we expect every minute. I hope that subject does not make you unhappy, does it?

Ros. [*Embarrassed*] Oh, no, certainly, it makes me—Mr. Henry is such a charming youth! Who can avoid being interested for him? So good a son, so kind-hearted a man! He is a perfect portrait of yourself, Mr. Gregory.

Greg. A little flattered, perhaps; but stay: since your regard for me makes you feel such a warm interest in my portrait, I have half a mind to make you a present of it.

Ros. Yes, sir, but—you know—

Greg. Dear Rosalie, I know all! Henry conceals nothing from his father. You are a sweet, amiable, well educated girl. Your father is poor, but he is noble-hearted and honest, and those qualities lift the poor man to a level with the peer. But I'll say no more.

Ros. Heavens! Can I have understood you rightly? But Mrs. Gregory—

Greg. Oh! let her bluster. What can we do better than give her her way? Blustering is her element! She would die if she didn't scold. But after all, she's good at bottom. All's right enough hereabouts. [*Putting his hand to his heart*] Hope, child, hope! Everything shall be settled properly.

Ros. Dearest benefactor! This generosity—[*Enter Nannette with a basket of plate*]

Nan. Come, Gregory! All's ready.

Greg. As soon as you please, my dear!

Nan. [*To Rosalie*] Here, Rosalie, take the basket, and I hope, this time, there is no need of recommending it to your special care.

Ros. No, madam, I have too much interest—

Greg. Rosalie, we are going to meet Henry—[*Enter Coody*]

Coody. [*Speaking as he enters*] To meet Mr. Henry! That's right! And I too, I'll go meet Mr. Henry! [*He puts down something he has brought, then scampers out and scrambles up the hill*]

Greg. Goodbye, till we meet again, my child! Make yourself happy. We—

Nan. [*Pushing her husband*] There, my dear! There, that's enough, in all conscience. 'Od's my life! What's the matter with the people? They're all too civil by half! [*They go out and ascend the hill*]

Ros. [*Alone, laying the table*] Good Mr. Gregory! He bids me hope! And Henry we are to meet again! How everything this day conspires to make me happy! My father also! I shall soon fold him in my arms! Yes, his regiment will soon arrive in Paris, and he will then obtain a furlough to come and see me. Oh, I am all rapture! He says too, that he has received the money I sent him from my little savings; and he is so thankful, though 'twas so very little! Oh, that I could have sent him more! [*Music*]

Is. [*Behind the scenes*] Knifes! Fine knifes! Chewels! Fine lace! Chentlemen and ladies, come puy! Come puy!

Ros. Aha! There's the Jew, I declare! The Jew who never fails to pass a few days every year in our village. I remember I bought something of him last year, but if he thinks I shall do the same this, he'll find himself mistaken. I sent all that I possessed to my father, and I don't regret it, no, I am *sure* I don't.

Is. [*Appearing behind the hedge*] Chentlemans and ladies! Puy mine fine chewels, mine lacesh, mine knifes, mine scissors! I sells, I puys, I parters. Come, come, come, puy, chentlemans and ladies! Puy! Puy! Puy!

Ros. [*To Isaac as he enters*] Nothing is wanted here, my good man! Mr. and Mrs. Gregory are both gone out.

Is. But do, Miss, only pehold! vot pretty tings I bringsh all new from Parish!

Ros. Pray leave me. I don't want anything today, I tell you.

Is. Don't be fexed, don't be fexed, miss! Some oder time den, some oder time. I peg you tellsh Mr. Gregorysh and Madame Gregorysh that I vil be dil domorrowsh in de Tavern of de Vite Horse, if they need shome of my little nicknackeriesh.

Ros. Very well, I won't forget it.

Is. Mine cracious, mine gentle miss, good-bye! [*Music. As he goes out*] Knifes! Fine knifes! Chewels! etc., etc.

Ros. He's gone at last. So much the better. [*Coody is seen capering down the hill*]

Coody. Miss Rosalie! Miss Rosalie!

Ros. Ah, there comes Coody! Doubtless to announce—

Coody. [*Entering out of breath*] He's come! He's come! Coody was the first that saw him!

Ros. And have you indeed seen him, my dear Coody?

Coody. Seen him! That I have, and I'm proud of it! "How are you, Coody?" says he, when he met me, just so—just in that way, "And my dear Rosalie?" "She longs to see you again, Mr. Henry," says I. Then he catches me by the fist and gives me such a shake. "Thank you, Coody!" says he, "You're a good fellow, Coody!" [*Looking at his hand*] I should have been quite charmed with the compliment, if he had not squeezed so hard.

Ros. [*Aside*] Oh, Henry! Then I am not deceived! [*A strain of music*] What is it I hear there?

Coody. Hear? Why, my fiddlers, to be sure! And here come all the villagers, lads and lasses that went out to meet him! All in their holiday clothes, to welcome Mr. Henry home. Oh, you'll see presently! There! there! Look, look! Only to think what a crowd!

Ros. [*Perceiving Henry descending the hill accompanied by Mr. and Mrs. Gregory and all the villagers*] Henry! Oh, Heavens! the transport! I can scarcely breathe! [*Music. Enter Henry, Nannette, Gregory, and villagers, descending the hill. Henry, discovering Rosalie, springs from the crowd and reaches the gate at the same moment with Rosalie, who runs to meet him*]

Hen. Dearest Rosalie!

Ros. Ah, Henry!

Greg. [*Coming up with Nannette and the villagers*] Come, come, bustle here! Let's have something to eat.

Nan. Henry, your walk must have given you a good appetite. Are you hungry?

Hen. Why, tolerably, mother, tolerably! I think I shall do some credit to your feast.

Greg. And aren't you thirsty, my boy? [*Going towards the table*] You shall drink a cup to stay your stomach.

Hen. No, at table, if you'll permit me.

Greg. Well, well! Just as you like.

Nan. Dispatch, dispatch! Why Rosalie, have you nothing to do, pray?

Greg. A moment's patience, wife! Haven't we help enough without her? Bless me! give 'em time, at least, to ask one another how they do.

Nan. Well and good, but it frets me—

Greg. [*Endeavoring to gain time for them to converse together*] Wife! I have only one word to say: are you glad to see our son in good health and high spirits?

NAN. Truly, a pretty question! Do you hear, Henry? Your father asks if I am glad to see you! Glad? No, I am not glad, I am transported, I am bewildered, out of my wits with joy!

HEN. Oh, my dear mother! Let me again embrace you.

NAN. Oh, yes, my child, yes! Ten times over! [*She embraces him*] My dear Henry!

GREG. [*Wiping his eyes*] Zounds, that's right!

NAN. [*To the farm boys who are bringing the service*] Well, well, you louts there! Will you make haste and be done? [*She goes to the table to give orders*]

Ros. [*To Henry*] And have you ever thought of poor Rosalie?

HEN. My love! Rosalie was never absent from my thoughts.

GREG. [*To the villagers*] There, my good friends, is a cask of wine, waiting to be drank up to the health of our worthy Henry.

VILLAGERS. That's right! Huzza! That's right, Mr. Gregory!

GREG. [*Pointing to the barrel*] Coody! Broach that jolly boy and bleed him—gadzooks! bleed him without mercy.

COODY. Till he's a dead man, godfather? Shall I?

GREG. Aye, aye, that's right. [*Turning to Henry*] So we have got you again, my boy! Fire and faggots! I'm ten years the younger for it. [*In a low voice*] Well, and what do you think of our little Rosalie now?

HEN. Lovelier than ever, father! But my mother—

GREG. Hush! We'll talk about that some other time!

NAN. All's ready. Let us get round the table. Oh, bless me! where's my head? There's the Justice! Mustn't we wait for him?

GREG. No, Nannette, he told me just now he wasn't sure of being able to come.

NAN. Well, just as he pleases.

HEN. Ah, tell me, mother, where's my dear uncle?

NAN. Your uncle? Alas! For this month past the gout has confined him to his chamber, where he growls and swears. Oh, it would make you tremble to hear him. Faith, but for that you might be sure of his not failing! He loves you so dearly! But you shall go and see him tomorrow.

HEN. This very evening, mother.

GREG. 'Ods life, and so we will! That's better yet. Come, come to table, Henry! There's your place, by the side of your mother. Rosalie, here! If the Justice comes, he'll put himself there. Mr. Exciseman, come this way! And you, merry Tom, sit down, sit down! [*Addressing the country people who are near. Music. Those who are invited take their places*]

GREG. Coody, take good care of—

Coody. Make yourself easy, godfather! [*Showing the fiddlers who are drinking*] Look, do you see the scrapers tuning up? Will you give the young folks leave to—[*He signifies that they want to dance*]

Greg. Ecod, that's just what I wanted! Dance away, young ones, dance away! Henry, here's your health! [*He drinks with Henry; Nannette and Rosalie do the same*] Come, my children, let's all be merry! Damn it, let's all be merry! [*Music. Grand pastoral ballet. At the end of the dance all rise from the table*]

Greg. Well done, my lads and lasses, well done! Now, we'll go into the orchard, and there, under the apple trees, you shall dance as long as your legs will carry you! Coody, bring the cups and jugs! When they are empty, there's the spring.

Coody. Done, godfather! Done! Everybody! follow Coody! [*Exeunt Coody, dancers, fiddlers, etc.*]

Hen. [*After they have retired*] Father, before dark, let me run and embrace my uncle.

Greg. Good, my son! I'm sure the sight of you will drive away my dear brother's gout, but we'll go along with you. What say you, wife?

Nan. Oh, I'm ready! Rosalie, child, you'll stay behind. You know what you've got to do.

Ros. Make yourself perfectly easy, madam.

Hen. [*To Rosalie*] Dearest Rosalie, we shall not be long away.

Ros. Adieu, Henry!

Greg. Take my arm, wife!

Nan. Do you walk on. [*Taking his arm*] This is the arm I shan't quit. No, not for the whole evening. [*Music. Gregory and his wife and son go out by the gate of the hedge. While they disappear in the plain, Everard is seen on the hill descending toward the front, and constantly looking with a disturbed and anxious air on every side. Music*]

Ros. Now let me hasten to put up the silver plate, lest Mr. Gregory may say a second time that—[*She collects the things on one side of the table, and is counting them*] Oh, Henry! How I love you! [*Music. Everard, having an old surtout coat with a military vest under it, and a hat drawn down over his eyes, enters hesitatingly*]

Ev. This must be the farm.

Ros. [*Her back to Everard*] Very well, the number is complete. [*Music*]

Ev. Powers of mercy! Is not that my daughter? Could I but speak with her alone!

Ros. [*Beginning to replace the plate in the basket*] Oh, was there ever a more charming youth!

Ev. It is she!

Ros. [*Continuing*] And just now, in a whisper, at this very table, how fervently he swore to make me happy!

Ev. To make her happy! Poor girl, and I this moment come. [*Hiding his face with his hands*] Merciful Heaven! [*Music*]

Ros. [*Turning, terrified*] Ha! What man is this? He's weeping. [*Approaching timidly*] Friend, may I ask—

Ev. [*Discovering himself, and with agony*] Oh, my dear child!

Ros. Father! [*Music. She throws back on the table the last piece she was about to replace in the basket, and rushes forward on her father's neck*]

Ros. And is it you, my father? Oh, unexpected joy!

Ev. Hush, Rosalie! We must not be heard.

Ros. Ah! You fear, after this long parting, my transports will be so extravagant—

Ev. I command you to be silent.

Ros. To be silent! Nay, quick, explain the mystery.

Ev. Then listen to a tale of horror! Last night our regiment arrived at Paris. I solicited a furlough of five days that I might fly to embrace my child. My captain, perhaps from whim, perhaps from the necessity of conforming to higher orders, refused it. I urged, he replied harshly; I dared to reproach him with cruelty in terms, far, doubtless, from prudent. Irritated by my audacity, "Wretch!" cried he, lifting his cane above my head. Infuriated by this remorseless insult, I forgot for an instant the subordination which a soldier owes to his superior. I drew my saber. Had not my comrades sprang forward to the rescue, he might have sunk before me, a sacrifice to my wrath!

Ros. Father!

Ev. You will indeed tremble, Rosalie, when you shall learn that this enormous fault is a crime which military law punishes with death.

Ros. Great Heaven!

Ev. I need not say that the order for my arrest has been already given. But thanks to some friends, I have escaped! The worthy Francour, one of my dearest comrades, who belongs to Paris, sheltered me among his relations, where I passed the night. With the remaining portion of the money you last sent me, dearest child, I bought the dress in which I am now disguised, and this morning, at the break of day, the faithful Francour conducted me to the Gate of Paris, where we parted in tears and without a hope of ever seeing each other again.

Ros. Oh, my father! Cherish yet the hope—

Ev. No, my girl. That cannot be. The War Council were this morning to assemble, and at the moment when I speak, the sentence of death will have been already pronounced. The law is absolute.

Ros. Nay then, remain with us, my father! Where else can you find so much safety as when guarded by your daughter? Mr. Gregory, his wife, his son, will all, I'll answer for it—

Ev. What dost thou say, my child? Never will I endanger the benefactor of my daughter! No, no! This village is too near Paris. I shall inevitably be discovered in it. Hear me, Rosalie! Since I have been fortunate enough to meet you thus alone, promise, swear, never to reveal, to any creature breathing, either my imprudence or my condemnation.

Ros. What! Not even to Mr. Gregory?

Ev. Not even to Mr. Gregory. I conjure thee, by all that is most sacred, if thou wouldst save thy father, if thou wouldst snatch him from the horrors of despair, guard thyself from revealing his fatal secret. Dost thou promise?

Ros. I swear it.

Ev. It is for your own sake, my dear child! that I exact the promise. You have confided to me your hopes. Henry and his relations must be kept ignorant of the misfortune of your father. They could not link themselves with the family of a felon! Concealment will be easy. In the regiment I am only known under the name of Everard. Here, I am only known under my real name of Granville. The condemnation of the poor soldier, Everard, will excite nobody's curiosity, and even such friends as may chance to hear of it, how far will they be from conceiving that the unfortunate offender could be Granville?

Ros. Oh, my father! If it be true that nothing can save you but flight or eternal exile, all happiness has flown from me forever! I will abandon this spot, I will pursue your destiny, I will hang upon your steps; always by your side, I will only breathe that I may watch over your security, that I may shelter you from danger, that I may hide you from pursuit; and if I am denied the power of averting the fatal blow [*Bursting into tears*], oh! then still will I cling to you and die with grief, receiving upon the scaffold the last sight of my father!

Ev. Noble-hearted child! [*Pressing her to his bosom*] No, no! Heaven preserve me from accepting this pious sacrifice! To fly together is to double the difficulties of success, to render escape almost impossible. Alone, more easily may I shun the dangers which you dread. By proceeding at night only, through winding paths, and sleeping in the woods, I may soon gain and pass the frontier. Should I once reach it, a letter will assure you of my safety. But —-should it be otherwise—

Ros. [*Rapidly*] No! No! You will write to me, my father! I feel the presentiment that you will! [*Music*] Good Heavens! Some one approaches! It is the Justice!

Ev. Cruel interruption! I had yet to ask thee—it is indispensable—where can I conceal myself?

Ros. Conceal yourself, that is impossible—he is here! Stay! Seat yourself at the corner of that table, and strive to keep your uniform out of sight. [*Music. Everard closes his coat and places himself at the farthest extremity of the table. Enter the Justice, stopping at the gate of the hedge*]

Jus. Oho! There she is! I saw, from a distance, Mr. and Mrs. Gregory and their son going towards the green. I come, then, in the very nick of time, to find the charming Rosalie by herself.

Ros. [*To her father, pouring out the wine, and pretending not to see the Justice*] Come, my good man! Take this glass of wine. It will put you in good breath, and you will be able to get forward on your journey.

Jus. [*Approaching*] Good day! Good day, my pretty dear!

Ros. Your servant, Mr. Justice.

Jus. Who is this man?

Ros. Oh, a poor traveller. How you would have pitied him. When he came in, he could hardly stand. I have invited him to rest awhile and take something to drink.

Jus. That's right, that's right, my child! Always charitable and compassionate! Give drink to the thirsty, and you follow one of the first precepts. [*Taking her hand*] Eh! Eh! Eh! I too, I have a tormenting thirst, my little dear! If you will extend the same—

Ros. [*Moving towards the table*] Why did you not speak before, Mr. Justice? Permit me—

Jus. [*Detaining her*] No, no, you don't comprehend. The thirst which torments me—[*Checking himself*] Ah, but I must not frighten her by getting on too fast.

Ros. [*Going to Everard*] Well, my good man! Are you refreshed? [*In a whisper*] Pretend to sleep. [*Returning to the Justice*] You wish, doubtless, to speak with Mr. and Mrs. Gregory. They have just gone out with Mr. Henry.

Jus. In fact, I came to express my regret at not having been able—but they will come back, and I am not at all pushed for time. [*Everard composes himself so as to have the appearance of sleeping, but from time to time he lifts up his head to hear and see what is going on*]

Ros. Pardon me, Mr. Justice, I can't stay with you. I must be going to and fro. You see for yourself that everything is yet in confusion on the table; so, believe me, have the kindness—

Jus. No, chick! I won't have the kindness to lose so good a chance for—but that man—is he going to stop there a century? You ought—

Ros. Do you not perceive that he is asleep? Oh, let him—let him sleep on. Indeed, he requires it.

Jus. [*To himself*] Oh, If he sleeps, that's very well. [*To Rosalie*] My dear Rosalie! I have been waiting this long while for a moment to find you alone, that I might declare—come, don't be angry. [*Everard raises his head*]

Ros. Let me tell you, sir, this conversation is improper—is disagreeable—

Jus. Oh, the little slyboots! These girls! These girls! This is always their reply: "Leave me, sir, this conversation is improper—disagreeable!" Eh! Eh! Eh! Confess the truth, rogue! Your little self-love exults to see that even a Justice could not resist your charms and is forced to declare his submission. Yes, dear Rosalie! I love thee, I adore thee to distraction!

Ev. [*Aside*] Insolent!

Ros. [*Aside*] How to free myself—

Jus. [*Aside*] She is agitated, I think. Good, good! So much the better. [*Aloud*] Come, my lovely angel! Tell me that this modest embarrassment is the effect of your disposition to reward. Tell me—[*Music*] Hey! What! Hey! What the devil does my servant want? [*Enter George*]

Geo. Mr. Justice! Your clerk, Mr. Anthony, in the fear that you might not come home soon enough, sends you this packet. It is very urgent, he says.

Jus. [*Aside*] Confound his thick pate! [*Aloud*] Hem! Hem! Who brought it?

Geo. A courier from the War Council.

Ros. [*Aside, with horror*] The War Council!

Jus. Let us see, then, let us see. Leave me, George. [*Exit George. Music*]

Ros. [*Aside*] A courier from the War Council! Should it chance—

Jus. [*Searching his pockets*] Hey? Well? My spectacles! Where the devil are my spectacles? Goose that I am! Come, I've left 'em at home. Let us see if I can do without them. [*He attempts to read, holding the paper far from his eyes*] "Mr. Justice"—hum—hum—"Description of the person, Soldier—Everard—"

Ros. and Ev. [*At the same moment*] Heavens!

Jus. It's a settled point! I can't read without spectacles. But it's only the description of some deserter. It will do to employ her. Eh! This way, my dear Rosalie! Since you are here, do me the favor to read this for me.

Ros. I! Why don't you go home with it?

Jus. 'Tisn't worth the trouble. You read, I pray you.

Ros. [*Aside, taking the paper, trembling*] Is all hope extinguished? [*Reading*] "Mr. Justice, I forward you the description of a soldier of the Regiment of Champagne" [*With an altered tone and broken voice*], "condemned to death this morning by the Council of War."

Ev. [*Aside*] I was sure of it!

Ros. "His name is—"

Jus. A mere trifle! Zounds! If one is to be miserable thus for every—go on! Go on! [*Aside*] How charming she is with that little air of tenderness! Truly, the more I look—

Ros. [*Aside*] Oh Heaven! Should I proceed with it, all will be lost! "Forty-two years, five feet, eight inches—"

Jus. What, can't you read?

Ev. [*Aside*] Unhappy child!

Ros. The writing is so bad—

Jus. How! Bad? I thought it charming. [*Searching in his pockets*] If my spectacles—

Ros. [*Rapidly*] Permit me. [*Aside*] Heaven inspires that thought! [*Aloud, reading*] "His name is Everard, aged twenty-four years—" [*Everard listens with emotion*]

Jus. Hey! Quite a young man!

Ros. [*Appearing to read*] Height—six feet, one inch.

Jus. The devil! That's a loss to the service! Proceed.

Ros. [*As if still reading*] Eyes, blue; hair and eyebrows, auburn.

Jus. Aha! He must be an Adonis, that fellow!

Ros. [*Aside*] At least he will gain time to fly.

Jus. Hair and eyebrows, auburn. What next?

Ros. [*In continuation*] Uniform, white; facings, blue. [*Looking toward her father, who has black gaiters*] Gaiters, white. [*Reading*] "Neglect no pains, Mr. Justice, to arrest or cause to be arrested, the above named deserter if he passes within your jurisdiction. Subjoined are copies of the present description."

Jus. [*Taking the packet*] Aye, aye, for the different parts of the district. I'll send them off tonight. [*He turns round, and Everard has only time to resume his position*] Let's see. Who knows now, but by chance—[*Music. Calling Everard*] Friend!

Ros. [*Aside*] Heavenly powers!

Jus. [*To Everard, who pretends to wake*] Do me the favor to come this way. [*Everard approaches, his back averted, his hat drawn down over his eyes. The Justice slaps him on the shoulder*] Take off your hat.

Ros. [*Aside*] I sink with terror!

Jus. [*To himself, examining Everard*] Twenty-four years, six feet, one inch, auburn hair! [*Laughing violently*] Ha! Ha! Ha! A beautiful Adonis, this fellow, indeed! [*To Everard*] Take yourself off, friend! [*Rosalie expresses by action her joy at the escape. Music*]

Ros. [*Aside*] I breathe! [*Approaching her father*] Good-bye! Pleasant journey! Pleasant journey, good man! [*Low and rapidly*] Till he is gone, conceal yourself there. [*She points out to him the trees at the right, where Everard goes and hides himself*]

Jus. [*Gathering up his papers*] Faith, soldier Everard! Young and handsome as you are, I pity you, if your unlucky star throws you in my way.

Ros. But, Mr. Justice, if you would only suffer me to finish my work—

Jus. Willingly, my angel! But on one condition: that you promise to satisfy my love, and grant me, as the pledge of it, only one, single, pretty little kiss—

Ev. [*Reappearing at the edge of the wing*] Damnation! I—[*Music. He retires suddenly on a signal from his daughter*]

Jus. Hey? [*Looking about anxiously*]

Ros. [*Aside*] He has betrayed himself!

Jus. [*Examining on every side*] Some one spoke—

Ros. [*Aside, perceiving the magpie on a branch*] Ah! [*Aloud, pointing to the magpie*] Look! There's the intruder, Mr. Justice!

Jus. Oh! 'Twas Mrs. Gregory's infernal magpie! How cursedly provoking! But, Rosalie, don't forget the condition on which I promised to depart. [*He attempts to kiss her*]

Ros. [*Repelling him indignantly*] Sir!

Jus. The devil! You have too much pride, my dear! That little princess-like air of yours will make me die with laughter! Come, you can't frighten me. I am positively determined—

Ros. [*Repelling him*] Stop, sir, or I shall—[*Everard shows himself again and seems ready to spring forward*]

Jus. [*Laughing*] How! How! Threats! Zounds! I should like to see who dares to interfere with me!

Ros. [*Looking towards the wood which conceals her father*] Some one who knows how to punish your audacity.

Jus. What's that I hear?

Ros. [*With firmness*] Let me counsel you, sir, to retire.

Jus. [*Angry*] Indeed! Is it to me you talk in this style?

Ros. Yes, Mr. Justice, even to you.

Jus. [*Furious*] A servant maid dare to treat me thus! Me! Chrysostom Athanasius of the Rock, Justice of Palaiseau! Ungrateful girl! Dost thou not fear my wrath? Thinkest thou I want the penetration to divine the cause of this contempt! It is Henry that you love, it is Henry that you hope, perhaps— farewell, most beautiful! Tremble to learn hereafter at your cost what it is to insult a Justice! [*He goes out grumbling between his teeth*] A servant maid! Oh! It is an—[*Exit the Justice, raving with fury. Everard comes forward. Music*]

Ev. Wretch! And I have been forced to sit tamely here and not punish the indignity!

Ros. Calm yourself, my father! Had I not trembled for you, I could easily have stopped his insolence. I had only to call, and instantly—but, we are alone. Let us not lose the precious time. Finish. You had something more to ask of me. Speak.

Ev. Listen, my child! It remains for me to ask—I am penniless.

Ros. Merciful Heavens! And at this moment I have not a single farthing!

Ev. I know it well. You have too lately sent me all you had! Alas! Of all my past wealth, this only remains to me. It is—it is a—a silver spoon, the last relic of a long-stored legacy left to your poor mother by her much-loved parent, and which that best of women used, even to the day I lost her.

Ros. [*Taking the spoon, kissing it, and weeping*] My poor mother!

Ev. I did hope to preserve it as long as I lived, for it is dear, most dear to me. But imperious necessity compels. Hasten then to sell it for me tomorrow morning at the latest; but above all, my child, remember, and be secret. Some distance hence there is an old willow which has been hollowed by time—

Ros. I know it well.

Ev. Place in the hollow of that willow the money you may get for it. I shall pass the night in the thickest part of the wood. Contrive so that tomorrow, at daybreak, I may find the money in the willow—

Ros. At daybreak! Will it be possible? But stay [*To herself*], that Jew, who came here just now—[*Aloud*] Father! Perhaps this evening—yes, do not wait till daybreak to visit the old willow.

Ev. That will be better still; oh, much better! Adieu, dear child! Heaven grant this may not be the last kiss of your unfortunate father! [*Music*]

Ros. [*Throwing herself into his arms*] Oh, my father! [*Everard tears himself from her arms with difficulty and departs. Rosalie conducts him to the hedge, where she embraces him again*] Adieu! Adieu, my father! [*Music. Rosalie throws herself on her knees. The father ascends the mountain. While she is kissing her hand to him as he slowly disappears, the magpie jumps upon the table, takes the silver spoon, and flies off with it. The curtain drops upon the picture*]

ACT II.

SCENE: *A room in the farmhouse. At the top of the stage, a door and two latticed windows, looking into the street of the village. The windows have shutters. A buffet and straw chairs. A basket of plate. On the table several piles of plates, some glasses, etc. In one corner of the room hangs the magpie's cage, with the bird in it.*

The day has just broken. At the rise of the curtain the stage lights are yet low, the shutters closed; but it is evident by the door, which is open, that it is day on the outside.

Rosalie, alone, at the door, looking out.

Ros. That provoking Jew! He has really gone! Is he not ashamed to offer me so little? What can my father do with such a trifle? But time presses. If the Jew does not return, I must run after him and take anything he chooses to give. But, look! It is broad daylight! First let me open the shutters, and then I'll go—[*She goes on talking while she is opening the shutters. As they open, the lamps gradually rise, and the stage becomes entirely light*] Why wasn't that vile Jew at his inn last night? If my father does not find the money, what will he do? Will he wait till night and then put himself on the way? Surely it will be so! For he will doubtless know it has been impossible. Ah! The Jew comes back! I'll engage he offers me something more. [*Enter Isaac*]

Is. Young voman! I can kive four three-shilling pieces. I cannot kive a shingle farthing more.

Ros. Twelve shillings! That's not one-third of its value. I must have stolen the spoon to let it go for that.

Is. Dot's not my pusiness.

Ros. What an insult!

Is. Vell, miss, very vell! I—I gives vive pieces.

Ros, No, no, you may take yourself off.

Is. Vell, child! I co— I co—[*Makes a few steps*]

Ros. [*Aside*] Nay! It is time to finish—

Is. [*Returning*] Den, tou art young, and tou art pretty, and pecause vor dat, I gives de zix.

Ros. There, then take it. [*Delivering the spoon*]

Is. Oh, vicked girl! You crudges mine boor profits! [*Aside*] I vas nigh do give sheven. [*He draws three six-shilling pieces out of a little bag*]

Ros. [*Impatiently*] Make haste! Someone may come, and I do not wish—

Is. Dot's chuste! I parfactly unterstand. [*Counting*] Vun, doo, tree, dere, mine pretty! Dere—[*Looking in her hand*] Dere be tree big pieces, hey?

Ros. Yes, yes, three pieces of six shillings. Away, quick, away! [*Coody appears at the window outside*]

Coody. Hey-day! What's she doing there, with that—

Is. Coot-pye, young woman!

Ros. Good-bye, good-bye! [*Pushing him*] Ah! [*Perceiving Coody*] Coody! Is that you? [*Exit Isaac*]

Coody. [*Entering*] What's all this, Miss Rosalie? By what chance—

Ros. [*Putting the money in her pocket*] I wanted a little pocket money, and have been selling to this man—

Coody. Ah, I know, some trinket or other, some—

Ros. Yes, which was not of the least value to me just for the moment.

Coody. I'll wager now he's got it for next to nothing. For, they are so Jewish, these Jews! It would have been much better for you to have told me of it. I could have lent you the money.

Ros. Oh, my friend! Could I have wished—

Coody. Stop now. Is it that I have not my little thingummy? I can't say, exactly, how much I've got, because it is yet in my own private box, but for you, Miss Rosalie, zounds! In half a minute I would have made it fly into a thousand pieces!

Ros. Thank you! But now, leave me, Coody. I have so much to do this morning—

Coody. Yes, yes, and haven't I too? [*Nodding*] Bye, bye, Miss Rosalie! [*He goes out running and singing*]

Ros. Now to place this in the old willow. Oh, my poor father! [*Music. Rosalie runs towards the door and is met by Henry, who brings her back*] Ah!

Hen. Dearest Rosalie!

Ros. Already risen, Henry! [*Aside*] What's to be done?

Hen. I could not close my eyes. The pleasure of meeting my family, the joy of finding my Rosalie still tender, still faithful, the intoxicating hope of soon calling her my wife, these delicious reflections have agitated me to such a degree the whole night long, that I have not been able to catch one moment of repose. And you too, dearest Rosalie—

Ros. Ah, Henry! I have not slept more than you, but—

Hen. And wherefore? You are pale, dejected. Those eyes—you have been weeping, dearest Rosalie!

Ros. Nay, believe me—[*Aside*] Oh, the unfortunate who now awaits for me!

Hen.   But, your agitation—Rosalie, some hidden grief—

Ros.   No, no, nothing is the matter. But I must away! Dear Henry, till we meet again—

Hen.   [*Detaining her*]   One moment only—stay! I guess the cause. My mother has done something to disturb—

Ros.   Your mother! [*Aside*] Let him believe so. [*Aloud*] Your mother, Henry—ah! I greatly fear that she never will consent to receive as her child the daughter of a poor and humble soldier.

Hen.   And what am I? I too am an humble soldier. Is there a station more glorious than his who nobly devotes himself to the sacredness of his rights and the honor of his country, and who swears that the last drop of his blood, if requisite, shall be consecrated to their defense? But listen, Rosalie: my mother loves me so much, that I am sure she is incapable of doing anything to make me wretched.

Ros.   Nevertheless, I tremble. [*Aside*] The hour elapses—

Hen.   Stay, here comes my father, who will confirm what I have said. [*Enter Gregory*]

Greg.   Aha! Together already! Very well, my children! [*Shaking hands with his son*] Good morning, Henry! Good morning, my boy!

Ros. [*Aside*]   How much it costs me to dissimulate with them!

Greg.   What time is it now?

Hen.   Faith, I believe it is not far from six o'clock, father.

Ros. [*Aside*]   Six o'clock! It will be too late!

Greg.   Zounds! I have been playing the sluggard, I! Well, it's your fault, my boy! One sleeps well when one's heart is light.

Hen.   Then everybody is not alike, for I haven't slept a wink.

Greg.   Ecod! That's astonishing. But at your age I myself—eh! eh! eh! One must confess that this love is a terrible alarm clock.

Ros. [*Aside*]   If I could escape while—[*She gets softly to the door*]

Greg.   Isn't it true, my dear Rosalie? Zounds! What are you doing there, three miles away from us? Come hither, it regards you, what I am saying here. Come, come! Quit the melancholy look. It will never do for my daughter to be melancholy. [*Taking one arm of each and passing it under his own*] Listen, listen to what I tell you. We must this day begin a regular attack on Mrs. Gregory concerning your marriage, my children!

Hen. [*With joy*]   To the charge, father! To the charge!

Ros. [*Aside*]   Alas!

Greg. [*To Rosalie*]   Don't be afraid, little fool! [*To Henry*] At first she'll cry—oh, me! How could you think of such a thing? She will say so. She will say so. Well, leave her to let off her fireworks. When all is over, then we'll talk, we! When I say *we*, it is you, Henry, that I mean shall begin.

HEN. And why not yourself, father?

GREG. Not I, zounds! That would be spoiling everything! I know Nannette well; the best wife in the world! But when I am the first to start a thing, it is enough to make her frantic from downright opposition. In fine, Providence has willed it thus, and there's no remedy. [*Rosalie softly disengages her arm, without perceiving it*]

HEN. Well, father, I *will* speak first.

GREG. That's right. Through the love she bears thee, thou wilt do better than anybody else; and after that we'll set about to convince her that Rosalie, poor as she is, has a hundred times more recommendations for a good wife than—[*Music. At this moment Rosalie, who had gained the door escapes, running*] Hey-day! hey-day! Where the deuce is she running to? [*Calling*] Rosalie! Rosalie! Ah, good! There comes my good woman, leading her back to us.

HEN. This is strange! This anxiousness to depart—[*Music. Enter Nannette, leading back Rosalie*]

NAN. Where are you running to so fast? Is it that you can find nothing to do where you are? Ah, good morning, Henry! How are you, my child?

HEN. Charmingly, mother, but you—

NAN. [*Looking all around her*] Well, well, my boy! Eh! But, good Heavens, Rosalie! How in the world do you spend your time? These plates, these glasses, everything is yet—oh, this is terrible! Only look! Miss must leave everything˙helter-skelter, at sixes and sevens here, to run nobody knows where, forsooth! It's shocking! Who ever saw—[*To Gregory and her son*] Hey! What are you gaping at one another for? Have you nothing better to do than to stand there and overlook *my* house affairs?

GREG. Oh, well, wife! Well. I'm going, I'm going—

NAN. So much the better. [*She begins to settle some things in the buffet*]

ROS. [*Aside*] Well then, for the present I must abandon it!

GREG. [*Low, to his son*] Henry! We'll put off the attack. You see the sky is stormy. We must wait for the first ray of sunshine. [*Aloud*] Come, Henry! Help me to get in those heaps of wheat sheaves that passed the night in the courtyard, because last night—Marry! It's healthy work! [*Low*] Don't mind. Let her have her full swing.

HEN. But Rosalie—

GREG. She's used to it. Come, let's be off. [*Music. They go off. As they go out, Nannette catches a sign made by Rosalie to Henry*]

NAN. Hey? What are they whispering to one another about? Rosalie, you know something of it, perhaps?

Ros. I, ma'am!

NAN. Hum! There are projects which some people would conceal from some people, but if some people think to overreach other people, some people will find themselves mistaken. Thank Heaven, I have neither a tongue likely to grow rusty for want of use, nor a head to be guided by a bridle, not I! But, be that as it may, you, Miss! help me to settle everything in its place. I hope we had confusion enough yesterday. Come, arrange the plates, the glasses. Where's the silver plate-basket? [*Rosalie showing it on the buffet*]

Ros. There, madam.

NAN. It is good that I examine it. [*She counts the plate and talks alternately, while Rosalie takes from the table to the buffet several piles of plates*] I must confess they gave Henry a charming welcome. Poor Lucas! He took a jolly dose of it! And his wife too, didn't she chatter? Dear me! Here are the eleven forks, all right. How can people be such gabblers? That's past my comprehension. [*She counts the spoons*] One, two, three—and the young girls—seven, eight—how they enjoyed the dance! Ten, eleven! How is this, there are only eleven? I counted wrong, without doubt. [*Counting a second time, at first in a low voice, but rising as she gets to the last numbers*] Nine, ten, and eleven! Come, come, come! One spoon wanting!

Ros. How? A spoon! [*She goes to count*]

NAN. Marry, count them yourself. There were only eleven forks in all. There they are; but we ought to have twelve spoons.

Ros. [*Counting*] Ten, eleven! I don't find any more. I have, notwithstanding, taken the strictest care of them.

NAN. But not enough, it seems. However, let us see, let us see. Now, search, look under the table, behind the buffet, inside of it, outside of it, everywhere. [*Rosalie searches*] In truth, it's incredible! What could it have done with itself? [*Calling at the wing*] Gregory! What are you about there? Come here, quick! Come here. Hallo! Coody! Run, look under the trees where we supped; search well! See if you can find a spoon there. [*Music. Enter Gregory*]

GREG. What's the matter? What's the matter? Wife! What are you saying about a spoon?

NAN. Yes, my dear! There's a spoon gone now! Well, Rosalie! you don't find it?

Ros. No, madam, I search for it in vain! Oh, Heavens! Oh, Heavens! What a miserable, luckless thing!

NAN. Doubtless, doubtless, bad enough. Two articles of so great value in less than a fortnight! This is most extraordinary.

GREG. Let it rest. Let it rest. We shall find the spoon.

NAN. That man's calmness will be the death of me! But you don't foresee the consequences. Yes, but this time things shan't pass off as they did last. I'll have it inquired into.

GREG. There you begin again! Must everything be thought stolen that goes astray in a large house like ours?

NAN. No, no, it is much better in your opinion to look upon things as mislaid which you know to have been stolen. But, however, that is the very way to—[*Enter Coody, running*]

COODY. Godmother! I have looked all about and about, searched under all the trees, Lord bless ye! There's no more of a spoon to be seen there than there is now on my hand. But now I know the whole affair!

NAN. Well?

COODY. The spoon has gone to look after the fork!

GREG. Idiot!

NAN. Not entirely, not entirely that, neither, husband! What he has just said—[*To Coody*] So! You have looked sharply?

COODY. Sharply! Why now do ever I look otherwise? Let me alone for that; and George, too, the Justice's man, who bid me good day as he passed by, he looked about with me, and found—

NAN. Found what?

COODY. Why, that it was all labor in vain!

GREG. Confound ye! Was it necessary to tell the whole story to that babbler, George?

COODY. Natural enough! George asked me what I was doing there, and I—I told him.

NAN. There is no harm, not the least harm, that the Justice should know. Besides, as for me, my opinion is that the same accident could not happen twice running, without—in fine, you'll never get it out of my head that the spoon was not stolen, just as the fork was stolen; but who is the thief?

MAGPIE. Rosalie! Rosalie!

ROS. Great Heaven!

NAN. Hey! What strange voice was that?

COODY. There's the devil at his tricks again!

GREG. [*Laughing*] Ha! ha! ha! Look! look! There's your dark oracle! From thence came your mysterious voice! It is poor mag, who, as usual, will be talking, like her betters, she doesn't know what. Ha! ha! ha!

COODY. Now only to think of that devil's limb!

NAN. At any rate, it is very strange.

GREG. How now, how now, Rosalie! You are weeping? Are you a fool? You know us but very little, if you fancy we are capable of attending to what a chattering bird—[*Rosalie, still weeping, points to Nannette*] My wife? No, no, you mistake. Nannette has too much reflection, she has too much judgment, justice, and good sense to—isn't that true, my dear?

NAN. [*With an air of doubt*] Certainly, my dear! I am far from giving any weight to—a fine question! One must be a—no, no! I accuse nobody, but I am free, Mr. Gregory, to suspect everybody.

COODY. Suspect everybody! Oh, not so fast, godmother! For I am somebody, or the deuce is in it, by the—

NAN. Simpleton! No one speaks to thee!

COODY. Simpleton as much as you like, that does not in the least offend me. One may be a simpleton and honest at the same time, but if anyone said to me that I was a—I won't even pronounce the word, it is so vulgar—by the living jingos, I—I can't!

ROS. [*Mournfully*] Ah, Coody! Do you not perceive that it is not to you Mrs. Gregory alludes? No, no, I see but too well! Just Heaven! It may be possible—[*Music*]

GREG. Let us be silent. The Justice comes this way.

NAN. Ah, very well! So much the better. [*Enter the Justice*]

JUS. What is the bustle now, my children? What is this that George has been telling me about a spoon that has been also stolen from you? But, be quiet, be quiet. I have sent orders to my clerk, Anthony, to come and meet me here. It is absolutely indispensable to—

GREG. Not at all, by no means, Mr. Justice! I have none but honest persons in my house, and I am sure I am robbed of nothing—

JUS. However—

NAN. My husband does not know what he is saying. We have a silver spoon less this morning than we had last night. We must find out what is become of it. The Justice will therefore have the kindness to exercise here the duties of his office.

JUS. Judiciously spoken, Mrs. Gregory, very judi—how should all this be? A fortnight ago, it was a fork, and today—why it is but too evident that the crime exists, and there is a repetition of it. We will straightway interrogate every individual and draw up a formal declaration—

GREG. Oh, no! Oh, no! Mr. Justice! It is not worth while. I won't have paper spoilt for such a trifle.

NAN. Then I will. Mr. Justice is in the right. There is no harm in making a slight examination, if it were only to know what we ought to think. If the criminal happens to be detected, well then, we are no Turks, and we shall consider what is best to be done.

Jus. What is best to be done! Oh, the most trifling thing in the world! The thief must be hanged, and there is an end of the matter!

Coody. He calls that a trifle! 'Tis a pity he wouldn't try it for his own amusement!

Greg. [In a whisper to Nannette] Do you see—do you see, now, Nannette, of what you will be the cause, if—

Nan. Oh, let me alone, let me alone! The Justice is only joking, don't you see that?

Jus. [Looking towards the street] How now? Will this clodpate of mine never come? [Perceiving Rosalie] Aha! You are there, Miss Rosalie! I will bring you a few more descriptions to read, you acquitted yourself so cleverly with the last.

Greg. Hey? What's all that?

Jus. Oh, a piece of ill-timed pleasantry which Miss Rosalie here yesterday allowed herself. [In a stern voice] Let me tell you, young woman! that it did not become you quite as well as you may imagine.

Ros. Your pardon, Mr. Justice! It would become me still less to have endangered the safety of an unfortunate. [Music]

Jus. Ah! Here comes Anthony at last. [Enter Anthony] Draw near, Mr. Anthony! We have business on our hands here. [Whispers to Anthony] Have you summoned the guard? [Anthony answers in a whisper] At hand? And George with them? Very well! Very well! [Aloud] Mr. and Mrs. Gregory! Do me the pleasure to be seated.

Greg. But, Mr. Justice—

Nan. Come, come, my dear! I am curious to see what measures the Justice will take for the detection—sit down then. [Music. She sits down. Gregory takes a seat by her side. The Justice places himself at the corner of the table, and Anthony in the middle, where he prepares his paper and writing materials]

Jus. [To Anthony] Write the preamble. This day, and so on—[To Nannette] We will begin by questioning those of your family who are here present.

Coody. Question away, Mr. Justice! I'm not afraid, by jingo!

Ros. Not I, certainly, Mr. Gregory.

Jus. [To Anthony] You have written? Good. Continue. Before me personally appeared Nannette, wife of William Gregory; and the aforesaid Nannette declares, that there was stolen from her about fourteen days ago, one silver fork, and that on this day, she, the said Nannette, has been robbed by the same thief, of one silver spoon.

NAN.   I said no such thing, for I know nothing at all about the matter.

JUS.   Patience, patience! These are the forms of law. Now tell us, Mrs. Gregory, who is the person charged in your house with the care of the silver plate?

NAN.   Rosalie.

JUS.   Oho! Is it you, pretty Mistress Rosalie? [*Aside*] Bravo, Mr. Justice! Now for your revenge! [*Aloud*] Write: A very strong presumption against the said Rosalie.

ROS.   Against me, merciful Heaven!

JUS.   Her family name?

NAN.   Granville.

GREG.   Stop, stop, Rosalie cannot be answerable—

JUS.   [*Coolly to Anthony*] Rosalie Granville.

GREG.   But, wife, why the devil don't you speak?

NAN.   The Justice understands very well that I do not, on that account, affirm that it is she—

JUS.   No, you do not affirm it. But whereas Rosalie was in your confidence, and charged especially with the care of your silver plate, on Rosalie the first suspicion must naturally rest.

COODY.   That's a specimen of—argument, Mr. Justice! if of nothing else—

JUS.   Hey?

COODY.   Oh, dear! I don't say that to vex you. But it seems to me, although, as all the world says, I'm but an idiot, that if I were to argue after that fashion—

JUS.   Silence! [*To Anthony*] So, write down that Mrs. Gregory—

ROS.   What, madam! And can it be possible that you do not contradict— [*To herself, weeping*] Oh, wretched Rosalie! [*Music. She takes out her pocket handkerchief to wipe away her tears, and the money which she received from the Jew drops out on the floor*]

NAN.   Hey-day! What's all that?

ROS.   [*Hastily picking it up*] It is mine, madam, mine.

NAN.   Yours? And we know that it is no later than eight days since you sent all your money to your father.

GREG.   That is true, Rosalie! That is very true, girl! Whence comes—

ROS.   Oh, Heavens! And you too, Mr. Gregory? I swear by everything most sacred that this money is truly mine.

GREG.   I believe you, I believe you. But I could wish to know—

JUS.   A new and strong circumstance in aggravation. Write down—

Coody. Stop a minute, stop a minute, Mr. Anthony. Write down, if you please, nothing at all. This money belongs certainly to Miss Rosalie, and I know where she got it.

Greg. Oh, speak then, Coody!

Coody. It is a Jew. You know him very well. Him that they call Isaac, he lodges at the sign of the White Horse. Well now, I saw him this morning give that very money to Miss Rosalie for some trinkets she sold to him.

Jus. A Jew! We have it. We have hit the right nail on the head!

Nan. Well, husband! Is the thing clear now?

Greg. Rosalie? Has Coody told the truth?

Ros. Yes, Mr. Gregory! But in the name of Heaven, do not imagine—

Nan. Then let her tell us what she could have sold for this sum. It was not her cross, for that still hangs at her neck.

Jus. An excellent observation, Mrs. Gregory.

Ros. [*Aside*] My cross! Oh, Heavens! Why did I not think of it before? I would have parted with that more willingly than—

Jus. Murder will out. Come, there's no doubt left. The Jew has bought the stolen article. Hand me that money, pretty fair one! [*Aside*] This comes opportunely enough to fee the clerk.

Ros. What? Rob me of my last resources! [*Falling on her knees*] In mercy, Mr. Justice! restore the money to me. Its destination is sacred. It is honestly and truly mine. That which I sold belonged to me. I had the right of parting with it. Take pity on my despair. I am innocent.

Jus. Excuse me, my little darling! You might perhaps have been drawn out of the scrape, but the Jew—oh! the Jew does you immense harm. A bad affair, my child! A domestic robbery, criminal matter, and, unhappily for you, the Grand Judge, who is on his circuit, is expected daily at Palaiseau. This affair will go on briskly—

Coody. Oh! but we'll know what to say to the Grand Judge—

Jus. Write down that Coody declares having seen Rosalie Granville receive from the Jew Isaac, the sum of eighteen shillings in payment of the fork and spoon of Mrs. Gregory.

Coody. It is not that, it is not that which I said. Fire and faggots, Justice! Don't try to twist and turn my words, or I warn you that I won't put my cross to your scribble and scrawl.

Jus. We can do very well without that, my friend, by a simple declaration: This witness affirms that he has never learned to write.

Coody. [*Disconsolate*] This witness! There! I thought to justify the poor girl by bringing up the Jew, and I have twisted matters into a snarl ten times worse than ever!

Jus. [*Aside*] They vex me! [*To Anthony*] Write away.

Greg. Stop, Justice! You have a manner of dictating—what the devil! Wait a moment. There is wanting yet, as it appears to me, an essential witness, Isaac the Jew!

Jus. Certainly, certainly. But we must begin.

Greg. By hearing the Jew.

Coody. Right, godfather! I'll scamper to the White Horse, and if the Jew be still there—

Jus. Coody, I command—

Coody. Pooh! pooh! Let me alone! I committed a blunder, and I'll make up for it. [*Exit running*]

Ros. [*Aside*] Oh, my father! And I have sworn, sworn never to divulge!

Greg. [*Observing her*] Rosalie! Perhaps the Jew will come.

Ros. Oh! Let him, let him come quickly!

Greg. [*Whispers to Nannette*] Do you hear, Nannette?

Ros. [*Aside*] If he shows the spoon, it will be evident, and I am saved! [*Music*]

Hen. [*Without*] Nay, let me see who dares accuse her!

Ros. [*Shuddering*] Henry!

Hen. [*Running in*] Father! What's this I hear? My darling Rosalie accused of crime!

Ros. Oh, Henry! Believe them not!

Hen. No! my beloved, no! I cannot thus far wrong the innocent, whose sweetness, intelligence, and nobleness of soul, even more irresistible than her beauty, have triumphed o'er my heart!

Nan. What's that you say, son?

Hen. Yes, mother, yes! She is the object of my love! She is destined to be my wife!

Nan. Do I stand on my head or my heels? What, Henry, can you intend? But you are not yet acquainted with what has passed. You don't know that this girl—

Hen. Mother! I know but one thing. Rosalie is innocent. I'll answer for it with my life!

Ros. Henry! You read my heart.

Hen. [*To the Justice*] You may retire, sir! Your presence is no longer necessary.

Jus. [*Rising*] But, Mr. Henry—

Hen. Away with your scribbling mummery, and be advised. Do not excite my rage!

Jus. [*Raising his voice*] Mr. Henry, things can't go on thus. Justice will have its course, and whereas there are already proofs—

Hen. Proofs! They are false! Is it not so, my father?

Greg. At least I hope so.

Jus. Mr. Anthony, read for Mr. Henry the article relating to the money found on the accused, also concerning the Jew Isaac, who gave it to her this morning as the price of the sale made to him.—Read, read!

Hen. Indeed, indeed, Mr. Justice, these are glorious proofs!! Because Rosalie desired to dispose of some trinket, belonging to her, doubtless to assist the unfortunate, for I know her heart, and because it chanced that a piece of the plate was missing on the self-same day, you dare to assume that she has stolen and sold it! Oh, Justice, Justice! Tremble lest you augment the number of those too famous judgments, the offspring of error and precipitation, whose innocent victims have received no other recompense, but the sad renown which consecrates their memory.

Jus. Mr. Henry, it is not for you to lecture me. You are a party interested —come, come, sir, if you were not in love with Rosalie—

Hen. Oh, sir, would to Heaven that your motives in pursuing were as pure as mine in defending her! But I have room to think.

Nan. Hold your tongue, sir! [*To the Justice*] Mr. Justice, Henry is in love. It is a certainty, and afflicts me deeply, very deeply, but I am just. What he has said concerning hasty judgments seems to me very rational, and I declare to you it would pain me more to have the girl suspected wrongfully than ever to see her the wife of my only son.

Greg. Perfectly well said, wife! Now that's what one may call talking to the point.

Jus. Softly, my friends! Be persuaded that I do not wish any more than you to find her guilty, but let her explain to us. Draw near, Rosalie, and answer me! Draw near, I say, nearer yet! [*Low*] Disdainful charmer!

Ros. [*Recoiling rapidly*] Nay, Mr. Justice, ah!

Jus. [*Interrupting her*] Hush, wait for my interrogatives! And tell me— [*Enter Coody*]

Coody. Here he is, here he is! Come in, come in, Mr. Isaac! [*To Rosalie*] Miss Rosalie, here is where withal to make up for everything! [*Enter Isaac. Music*]

Is. Ah, to devil! De chustice here, and they was not let me know—

Hen. Ah, well! Approach, Mr. Jew, and tell us quickly—

Jus. A moment, Mr. Henry! It's my business to question the man. [*To Isaac*] Your name—your profession?

Hen. What is that to the purpose?

Jus. [*To Henry*] I beg your pardon. [*To Isaac*] Answer!

Is. Mine name ish Solomon Ishaac. I carrysh on de leetel drade. I bysh from ones. I shells to uddersh, and alwaysh wid de goot conscience.

Jus. Do you know this young girl?

Is. I does, Mishter Chustish.

Jus. What has she sold you this morning?

Is. [*Hesitating and looking at Rosalie*] Hey, hey! A shilver, a shilver—

GREG., NAN., and COODY. [*Together*] A silver—what?

Jus. [*Aside*] That is most fortunate!

Is. A shilver spoon.

HEN. What says the wretch!

Ros. Henry, the truth!

HEN. Merciful Heavens!

Jus. Well, you hear him?

Ros. [*To Isaac*] Show the spoon I sold to you.

Is. Wid all mine art, but imposhible, mine lufly damsel! Because I zold it, I zold it to one of my travelling comrades, and he got avay vid it dat very moment, and he ish now very var from dish, very crate way off. Oh, I know not where, but he ish zone.

Ros. [*To herself*] Then I am lost!

HEN. [*To Isaac*] You are an imposter!

Is. Ah, shir, mine tear shir!

Jus. [*To Anthony*] Are you writing down everything?

GREG. Rosalie, where did you get that plate? Come, reply! Who gave it to you? For, certainly you had none of your own.

Ros. Good Mr. Gregory, I cannot. Do not question me. I ought to, I must be silent.

COODY. [*Aside*] O Lord, see, another blunder of my stupid noddle! What the deuce did I bring the Jew for?

Jus. [*Signing an order*] There, gentlemen! The crime is proved, and Rosalie is guilty.

HEN. [*Aside*] I am thunderstruck!

Jus. [*Calling at the door*] George, advance! [*Music. Enter George*]

Ros. [*Aside, while the Justice is speaking to George and giving him the order he has just signed*] Oh, depth of humiliation, and still to tremble for my father! Great Heaven, is there aught more?

NAN. Now, Gregory, from my soul I pity her.

Jus. [*Approaching*] Good, they are there! Come, my pretty child, I am sorry for it, but you must go to prison.

ALL. To prison!

GREG. Listen to me, Justice, that cannot be—

Jus. Yes, Mr. Gregory, but it must be. It is too late.

HEN. [*Stopping the Jew, who strives to escape unseen*] Stop, sir!

Is. [*Affrighted*] Pon mine honorsh, 'tish imposshible—

HEN. I command you!

Is. If it vil pleash you den, vid all mine art! [*Turning aside with a malicious grin*] Eh! [*Music. A guard appears at the door with George. The villagers are in crowds without, pressing forward to gaze through the windows*]

Jus. [*To the guard*] Guard, conduct this girl to prison! [*Music*]

HEN. [*Stopping the guard which approaches*] Hold, Justice, for one instant! [*To Nannette*] Haste, Mother, bring hither one of your pieces of plate!

NAN. Yes, son! [*She runs to fetch one. Music*]

HEN. [*To the Jew, who approaches*] Describe minutely the form and weight of what you purchased.

Is. Vid all mine art. First, it vas bretty eavy, and I pade von very grate shum for it.

HEN. Plain or ornamented?

Is. Ornamented? I can't shay to the contrary.

Jus. Ornamented, now we shall see. [*Aside*] Better and better!

HEN. Had it a cypher?

Is. A shypher? Shtop!

Ros. [*Aside*] Good Heavens! The initial of Gregory and Granville are the same!

Is. True, true, a shypher! I remembersh vel, de lettersh chee!

HEN. G? You are deceived!

Is. No, no, it vash a chee, a veritable chee!

Ros. [*Aside*] Fatal coincidence! [*Nannette brings a silver spoon, and gives it to Henry. Henry hands it hastily to the Jew*]

HEN. Examine, wretch, compare them, and pronounce! [*Music*]

Is. Yesh, yesh, de zame ting, parfectly alike!

HEN. [*In despair*] All hope is lost!

Ros. I expire! [*Music*]

NAN. Oh, Heavens! Oh, Heavens!

COODY. My knees are getting weak! I can hardly stand!

GREG. It is in vain to deny it. There is a mystery at the bottom of all this—

Jus. Come, come! To prison! [*Pointing to the Jew*] And her accomplice with her!

Is. Nay, put, Mr. Justice! Upon mine knees, I peg—

Jus. To prison! [*Aside*] Now she's in my clutches!

Ros. [*Weeping*] Henry! Henry!

Hen. [*Distractedly*] Rosalie! I loved, adored you—go! You have destroyed my happiness, for—I love you still! [*Throwing himself in his father's arms*] Father! Let me die!

Ros. Henry! I am very unfortunate, but I am not guilty.

Hen. Then prove it, Rosalie!

Ros. It is impossible. [*Henry remains stupefied with despair*]

Jus. Come, come, we delay too long! Conduct them!

Ros. Dear sir! Madam! You abandon poor Rosalie! You believe her guilty. [*Aside*] Oh, my father! [*Music. Aloud*] Henry, I am innocent! I am innocent! [*Music. The guard, conducting Rosalie and the Jew, pass through the crowd of villagers, who open to make way. Nannette remains, her face hidden by her handkerchief. Gregory holds his son, who strives to follow Rosalie. Coody is inconsolable, and the curtain falls*]

ACT III.

Scene 1: *A Gothic hall. On one side is a door, the irons of which announce that it communicates from the hall to the prison. Enter Rosalie and Durmont.*

Dur. [*Coming out of the prison, and addressing Rosalie, who follows him*] Come, come, my sweet girl! Come and breathe a purer air in the hall. [*Music*] I'll take it upon myself to bring you for a quarter of an hour out of your dark, unwholesome dungeon.

Ros. [*Appearing*] A thousand thanks!

Dur. This hall is somewhat more agreeable and not less strong, for nobody comes in here or goes out, but by my permission, and the windows are well grated. And really, I could not help taking compassion on you.

Ros. Indeed you are very kind.

Dur. Now I will leave you here. If you want me, knock at that door. [*Seeing her wipe her eyes*] Come, come, do not weep! [*Aside*] What a fine fellow I am! [*Wiping an eye*] Have I lost my senses? If anybody should see me now! Hum! Blubbering becomes a jailer to be sure! [*Music. He goes out by the door at the extremity of the stage. Rosalie seats herself by a table*]

Ros. Oh, my father! What will become of him, when a second time he shall be disappointed of the money of which he so much stands in need?

But should he learn that his daughter sinks beneath the most disgraceful of accusations! Frightful apprehension! Ah, that he might fly before it is possible for him to hear of my calamity! And yet that cannot be unless before this day shall end, he finds in the old willow—[*Perceiving her gold cross*] Ah, this cross! But how contrive to sell it? How send him the value? Mr. Gregory? Henry? No. They would require explanations which I cannot—no, no! I must think no more of them! [*Rising*] Coody! whose friendship for me is so strong—yes, he alone can blindly and without demanding that I should unfold the mystery, render me this important service. Let me ask the jailer. [*Music. She knocks three times at the door. Durmont appears*]

Dur. What's the matter, Miss Rosalie?

Ros. Mr. Durmont, can you inform Coody, the godson of Mrs. Gregory, that I wish to speak with him?

Dur. Hum! I can't exactly tell. However, I risk nothing in letting him know. When he's here, we shall see. I will endeavor—[*Music. A knocking at the outer door*] Who is there? [*Running to look through the wicket*] Oh! oh! It's Mr. Henry.

Ros. [*With emotion*] Henry!

Dur. [*At the wicket*] Impossible, Mr. Henry! I have orders from—

Ros. My dear friend! I entreat—

Dur. Wait, he's looking for something. [*At the wicket*] Ah! You have a passport! That's another case! Let us see, let us see. [*He takes at the wicket a piece of gold and examines it*] Very well. It is perfectly in rule. This passport will free you everywhere. [*To Rosalie*] Be satisfied, Miss! The passport is for the whole family of the Gregory's. [*Music. He opens the door for Henry and goes out. Enter Henry*]

Hen. My beloved!

Ros. Ah, Henry! Then you have not yet abandoned me?

Hen. Pardon my weakness, dearest Rosalie! But the idea of the crime with which I saw you charged, the force of the presumptions which darken over you, and which you yourself refuse to dissipate, have broken my heart, troubled my brain, bewildered my reason. I would wish instantly to rejoin my regiment, bid an eternal farewell to my home, and blindly court death in battle. Yet I could not depart without once more seeing you, without questioning you myself, without diving into your very soul in the hope of discovering—answer me, Rosalie. Are you guilty?

Ros. [*With dignity*] Henry, no!

Hen. But by what fatality—

Ros. I can prove nothing, summon nothing, show nothing in my defense. I must be silent. I must implore the aid of Heaven and lament the mistakes of man!

Hen. You cherish then a secret whose development might justify you! And you refuse to confide it to the friend of your soul, who would exult this very moment to make his life a sacrifice for yours!

Ros. Dearest Henry, add not to my misery and despair. The secret you demand is not my own; besides, at this moment, how could I serve myself by speaking? I have only one witness to invoke, but he is an unfortunate, who could not be believed. That wretched sufferer would destroy himself without saving me. Nay, instead of being heard as a witness, he might be punished as an accomplice! No, no, I must be silent. Duty, prudence, and my oath require it.

Hen. [Aside] I know not what to think. [Aloud] Rosalie! The Grand Judge has just arrived. Your persecutor, the Justice—my father has told me all—that hateful Justice, now denounces you at the tribunal. Perhaps you know not with what frightful rapidity the judgments of this court are pronounced and executed! It is possible that this very day—

Ros. I shall be condemned. Alas! The time may come, perhaps, when my innocence will be proclaimed, when the whole world will pity me, when men will solemnly celebrate their repentance for the error to which you see me about to be made a sacrifice. But in the day of triumph poor Rosalie will be no longer there!

Hen. You make me shudder. [Aside] No, no, it cannot be. Those tones of truth and candor, sure pledges of sincerity, never could be feigned!

Ros. Henry! Permit me to ask you one question, and answer me with all your native frankness.

Hen. Speak, dearest Rosalie!

Ros. My friend, if I fall a victim, what will you think of me?

Hen. [Firmly] That you are innocent.

Ros. Merciful Heaven! I shall not die then without a consolation!

Hen. Be persuaded, too, that my father partakes of my conviction. Even my mother—

Ros. Mrs. Gregory—[Sighing] Alas!

Hen. I know how you must feel towards her; but forgive her, my Rosalie. Since it has past, she has done nothing but weep over your misfortune.

Ros. I do forgive her.

Hen. Now, whilst I am yet speaking with you, she has gone with my father to the Justice, to try to soften him. My unhappy parents will leave no means untried. [Enter Durmont]

DUR. Very sorry to interrupt you, but it is necessary that the young woman returns into her prison. The Justice orders me to say that he is coming to interrogate her once more, before he submits his proceedings to the Judge—

Ros. Henry, farewell!

HEN. Dearest Rosalie, adieu!

DUR. I hear a noise below. Perhaps it is the Justice. Go in, go in, quick! [*Rosalie and Henry embrace in despair. Music*]

Ros. [*With a stifled voice*] Adieu! [*When she gets to the door, she runs back, embraces Henry, and is torn from his arms by the jailer. Durmont makes her go in and shuts the door on her*]

HEN. Should this meeting have been our last! Oh! that fear—

DUR. Hey? Mr. and Mrs. Gregory! Good faith! If they come to see poor Rosalie, it is impossible for me to let them at this moment. [*Enter Mr. and Mrs. Gregory*]

HEN. [*Going to meet them*] Now, father! Of the Justice?

GREG. We have not been able to see him, but they told us he was coming here, and if Mr. Durmont will permit us to wait for him—

DUR. Willingly. Stay in this hall. He will be obliged to pass through it. [*Music. Exit Durmont. Henry points out the prison door, and the characters form a picture before it*]

GREG. [*Pointing to the door of the dungeon*] Is the poor child there?

NAN. [*In a melancholy tone*] She is even there! And it is my fault!

GREG. Well, my son! Have you spoken to her?

HEN. Yes, father! And I am more than ever—oh, my mother!

NAN. I hear thee, Henry. [*To Gregory, who makes a sign to his son to be silent*] No, my dear! It is not his reproaches which afflict me; it is those of my own heart. Yes, I have been wrong, frightfully wrong. I ought not to have—yet for all that, Heaven knows I never wished the poor girl harm! Unhappy impetuosity! Fatal prejudice! Whither have you brought me?

HEN. Give me your forgiveness, mother! Despair has driven me almost to madness.

NAN. First teach me how to forgive myself for having suffered the Justice to commence his infamous proceedings. Oh! If they shall have reason to say that I caused the death of Rosalie, be sure, my son, I never can survive it!

GREG. Come, come, my dear Nannette! Do not give up all hope yet. We'll talk to the Justice, entreat him to stop the proceedings, and neglect no means of winning him to our wish.

NAN. Yes, Gregory! Ask what you will, there is no sacrifice I would not make to save her! And now, Henry, let me tell you, after weighing well everything which is brought against her, I am no longer able to persuade myself that she is guilty.

HEN. Mother! You inspire me with new life! No, no, she is not guilty.

GREG. Has she divulged to you the secret which appeared to overwhelm her?

HEN. No, father. Some imperious duty, I know not what, prevents her, yet still I know her to be innocent.

NAN. But I cannot divine for what earthly reason she persists.

GREG. Hear me, wife, if duty obliges her to be silent, she is the more to be pitied for it, but someone comes. Doubtless it is the Justice. Leave us, Henry.

HEN. Father, you are right! I could not promise to smother my indignation, but if he resists your offer and your prayers, then let him tremble! [*The Justice appears at the door at the back of the stage*] He shall hear me vindicate the holy cause of innocence; he shall hear me divulge, with a voice of thunder, the hidden and disgraceful origin of the rancor of his resentment.

JUS. [*Advancing*] Mr. Henry.

GREG. and NAN. [*Together*] Merciful Heavens!

HEN. Mr. Justice, you have heard me? I am glad of it, sir. Guilt may triumph for a while, but its hours are numbered. When Heaven's lightnings are reserved, it is that their explosion may be more tremendous. Expect the day of retribution, sir! That day will come! [*Exit. Music*]

JUS. That young man forgets himself, madam! You ought to—

NAN. In mercy pardon him, Mr. Justice. He is in despair. He knows not what he says.

GREG. Yes, indeed, Mr. Justice, Henry will be the first to ask your pardon, if you will listen to our demand.

JUS. · What demand do you mean? Tell me what it is.

NAN. Stop your proceedings for Heaven's sake! Throw your papers into the fire, Mr. Justice, I implore you. Do not let us be the death of a fellow creature for a miserable spoon.

JUS. My dear madam, it is quite too late! It is no longer in our hands, but in the hands of the King—the country. The Grand Judge has already [taken] cognizance of it. If I should withdraw a proceeding of which he will not fail to demand an account at my hands, he would charge me with prevarication, if not with compounding a capital crime, and in obliging you, I should destroy myself.

GREG. Mr. Justice, I cannot think so. Nothing would be easier than to gain time, so let the reports about it die away little by little, and before long it will be entirely forgotten.

Jus. You have settled matters very comfortably, it seems!

Greg. We will make any sacrifice.

Nan. Yes, we will pay anything which may be required. I don't say that for you, Mr. Justice, but if there are expenses to defray, if there are measures to take which may be costly, or men to be feed highly to hold their tongues, don't inconvenience yourself, take our money, plate, jewels, everything, we will sacrifice all to save this unhappy girl!

Jus. Once more it is impossible. Cease to make offers which you have spoken. I have understood you, Mrs. Gregory, but be assured, the Justice of Palaiseau is not a man to be seduced by the vile allurements of gold, or to betray his duty for—

Greg. Mr. Justice of Palaiseau, duty at least commands you not to be precipitate. This affair merits deep investigation. There is an obscurity throughout it, which, if you are not careful, may, sooner or later cause you bitter regrets.

Ju. I am not afraid of that, my judgment never deceived me.

Greg. Except, perhaps, when blinded by your lust.

Jus. Sir!

Nan. Nay, Mr. Gregory—

Greg. [*Growing warm*] Pshaw, leave me, Nannette! Is it not plain that the Justice might have seen the innocence of our dear Rosalie, could she have ceased to be innocent for him? But she spurned his advances with the contempt they merited. It is this which animates our pure apostle of the laws, the man whose judgment never yet betrayed him to wreak so eagerly that damned revenge which he strives to hallow by the sacred names of duty and of justice.

Jus. [*Enraged*] Mr. Gregory, tremble, sir, lest I force you to repent—

Nan. [*Throwing herself on her knees*] Nay, sir, have pity—

Greg. [*Roughly raising his wife*] Damnation, wife, do you wish—No! Let offenders kneel, you claim your rights. Then stand erect, and make those rights respected. Nannette, follow me! [*Exit followed by Nannette in despair. Music*]

Jus. I choke with rage. Both father and son to venture the audacity. Well! Their dear Rosalie shall feel it. [*Calling*] Durmont! [*To himself*] At least, however, after having maturely weighed her situation, this disdainful beauty—[*To Durmont, who enters*] Bring Rosalie! [*Durmont retires*] No, no, it never shall be said that a low servant maid with impunity—[*Music*] But she comes! Let me hasten to hide my agitation. There then, why is it that she appears more lovely now than ever? [*Music. Rosalie appears, with perfect calmness. Durmont retires*]

Jus. Come hither, Rosalie! [*Aside*] Let me breathe a moment. Those insolent Gregorys have disturbed me to such a degree—

Ros. [*Aside*] He has my life, what more can he desire?

Jus. [*Getting gradually more composed*] Rosalie, hear me! You see me in despair. The Grand Judge has arrived; he is about to pronounce irrevocably upon the statement which appears against you. I wish to save you, although it will now be very difficult, since the proceedings are so far advanced. As to the rest, believe me, the resentment I affected to feel at your offensive disdain, was meant to be limited to a momentary punishment, but I must frankly admit I was far from conceiving that you were really criminal.

Ros. Criminal, and you now believe me criminal, Mr. Justice?

Jus. Yes, surely I do. But I did not think so till after the testimony of Isaac the Jew. It was a thunderbolt and certainly unexpected.

Ros. Everything combines to criminate me I admit, yet I am innocent.

Jus. I wish to think so, but listen, dear Rosalie, you may still expect everything from my anxiousness to serve you. Yes, I am resolved, I wish this very day to open the gates of your prison.

Ros. Mr. Justice, I have no wish to leave it till I am freed from the imputation of a crime so shameful.

Jus. Oh, I understand that very well too, Rosalie! [*Taking her hand*] Yes, yes, my charming girl, I would have you go out of it as white and innocent as a dove, I would—

Ros. [*Withdrawing her hand with haughtiness*] Leave me, sir!

Jus. Reflect, Rosalie, your life's in danger.

Ros. That life is worthless without honor.

Jus. No doubt, no doubt. My intention also—

Ros. Is not to be mistaken. Leave me, I command.

Jus. Well then, ungrateful, since you refuse to owe me the slightest obligation—[*In a loud voice*] I—I leave you. The Grand Judge will decide your destiny; in less than an hour you will appear before him. [*Music. Exit Justice. Enter Durmont*]

Dur. Miss Rosalie, Coody is here. I am going to bid him enter, but I can't answer for it that I shall be able to leave you long together, besides—

Ros. Enough, let him approach, and leave us, Mr. Durmont.

Dur. Come in, come in, Coody. [*Enter Coody*] There! [*He points to Rosalie and goes out*]

Coody. [*Approaching mournfully*] There she is, poor girl! There she is!

Ros. [*Aside*] Oh, yes, I can rely on him!

Coody. [*Faltering and sobbing*] Miss Rosalie, it is I.

Ros. Coody, you can render me a great service but promise to do what I shall ask without addressing me a single question, without seeking to discover the reasons why I entrust you with the charge.

Coody. I do promise, miss.

Ros. You have seen them this morning deprive me of money which was lawfully mine, and of which I stand in the most pressing need.

Coody. Yes, yes, the clerk took it and that's pretty nearly as bad for you as if it was lost.

Ros. Well then, my good Coody.

Coody. I see how it is. You want to replace the money. You needn't say a word more about it. All my little hoard, I am sure, is entirely at your service.

Ros. [*Unclasping her cross*] No, Heaven shield me from imposing on that good heart! I only ask you to lend me a sum equal to what I lost, and that you will then take it to the place I shall describe. There is my cross, which is worth at least—

Coody. [*Repelling her hand*] Softly, softly, let us understand one another. Where must I leave this money?

Ros. Do you know at the outlet of the village, a little on one side of the Paris road, there is an old hollow willow—

Coody. Know it indeed. Why 'twas there when I was a little tiny boy I—

Ros. Well in that tree I intreat you to deposit the money before the close of day.

Coody. [*Astonished*] What, in the hollow of that old willow? In the tree?

Ros. Yes, that stands on the bank beside the stream.

Coody. Yes, yes, I know, but lord 'a mercy, that's the drollest bank to deposit one's money in I ever heard of. However, if you wish it.

Ros. Oh, yes, Coody, yes, but pray, pray let no one see you, and above all do not loiter near to look for the person who may come and take it.

Coody. This is droll! It is then—

Ros. You have promised to ask no questions.

Coody. You're right. I will hold my tongue, and keep my curiosity to myself.

Ros. You swear it?

Coody. I swear it. Oh, I'll be as quiet as a lamb. I'll wager it is a good action that I'm helping you to do there, for whatever these black rascals may say, you don't know how to do any other. Now mind what I tell you. Before one hour let the person come and see if I haven't done it properly. [*Going*]

Ros. Coody, you forgot the cross.

Coody. No, I forgot nothing at all. Keep it, miss, I won't take it.

Ros. If you refuse, I will not accept your service.

Coody. Ah, I defy you! Now I know what I ought to do, I don't need your permission.

Ros. Coody, will you hear me? Think, my friend, that tomorrow or perhaps today this ornament will have ceased to be of value to me.

Coody. No, no, don't believe that, Miss Rosalie. It is not possible. Keep your cross.

Ros. Well then, dear Coody, as a remembrance of my friendship I pray you to accept it. Can you refuse me now?

Coody. [*Ready to cry*] No, no, as to that, it's all right. [*Taking the cross*] I'll take it and it is worth a hundred times more to me than its value. [*Weeping*] I'll never part with it as long as I live, Miss Rosalie.

Ros. Stop, my friend! Hold! When you see Henry, give him this ring. It is braided with my hair. Tell him—that till my latest sigh—[*She cannot finish what she would say*]

Coody. [*Crying*] But, but, go on, go on, miss! You—you—you—yes, yes —I'll give it to him. I'll tell him, but I must go, for if I stay much longer— Farewell, Miss Rosalie!

Ros. [*Grasping his hand*] Adieu, my good friend! Do not forget.

Coody. [*Sobbing*] Oh, as to that, you may be perfectly sure—only time enough—to go and look for him at home. Yes, you might—[*Going out*] Poor Coody, poor Coody! [*Exit, weeping. Music. Enter Durmont and soldiers*]

Dur. [*Mournfully*] Miss Rosalie, they come to take you before the Judge.

Ros. I am ready. [*To the soldiers*] Conduct me. [*To herself*] Oh Heaven, oh Heaven! Is there no longer hope? [*Music. The soldiers conduct Rosalie who traverses the stage addressing her timid prayer to Heaven. Exeunt*]

Scene 2: *At the right a steeple and part of the church. Towards the top of the steeple, a small scaffolding for the repairs of it. A cord is firmly fastened to it by one end, the other is carelessly thrown on one of the posts of the scaffold-ing. At the left, in the distance, is the door of the village courthouse, from which there is a descent of many steps. Beyond the courthouse is a street, and another street which passes across the stage behind the church. In front, also on the left, is a rustic porch, which encloses the farm of Gregory. In the back-ground a sentinel, who appears and disappears alternately behind the door of the courthouse. Enter Francour, alone.*

Fran. I cannot meet anyone to point out the Justice's house, or Gregory's farm, hang it! I hope Everard, who was so anxious to visit his daughter, is not gone yet. With what pleasure would his comrade, Francour, embrace him now! However it is not likely he can be very distant, and one may be able—good! The door opens, now I shall certainly hear—[*Enter Coody through the little door to the left, counting the money in his hand*]

Coody. Just so, it's quite right. Now to stow it quickly.

Fran. Friend, have the goodness to tell me which is the farm of Gregory, and which the house of Justice?

Coody. The farm, Mr. Soldier? Stay, look, if you don't wish to make a long roundabout, there, there is the gate of the enclosure, and you may—

Fran. No, the Justice's first.

Coody. Hey, the Justice's! Turn down that street, the first door to the right, painted yellow, with a knocker in the form of a serpent, next to the Judas' head. Farther down, in the same street, you will see the other gate of the farm. [*Exit Francour. Music*]

Coody. I'm sure he won't find anybody, for every one is at the courthouse to see the trial. Ah, yes, I must hasten to execute Miss Rosalie's commission. I have just smashed my money-box. [*Striking his pocket and making it sound*] And I've got it all here! I haven't reckoned how much, but that's all one. There's the eighteen shillings for the old willow. When one begins by doing a service, the account is always settled afterwards. [*Everard appears at the back*] Oh, that poor Rosalie! Is it possible they could have the heart—no, no! Heaven will take pity on her. Well, here I scamper! [*He runs off to the right. Music*]

Ev. [*Advancing*] Heavens! Was it not my daughter's name which that peasant uttered with an air of pity? But what of that? Why should I alarm myself? There are, doubtless, other Rosalies in the village. And yet I cannot drive away this uneasiness. Since yesterday she has not come to—I am at a loss what to think. Ah! so well I know her heart, that unless some insurmountable obstacle had arisen, she would at least have let me hear from her. But what obstacle could arrive? Unless some accident has happened to the dear child—I must see her once more. I know the risk I encounter by entering openly into the village, but no matter; it must be so. Let me hasten to the farm. Oh, Heavens! The sentinel! How can I pass him? [*Looking towards the right*] Ha! Here comes a peasant. Perhaps he may be able—[*Enter George, who runs across the stage from the right*]

Ev. [*To George*] Friend, will you render me a service?

Geo. Willingly, sir, if it is in my power.

Ev. As I don't wish to walk so far as the farm of Mr. Gregory, you would oblige me by going to acquaint—

Geo. To the farm of Mr. Gregory? Lord! Only enter by that gate which stands open, cross the inclosure, and the house is before you.

Ev. If so, I'll go myself. Thank you, friend! [*He approaches the gate*]

Geo. I don't suppose you'll find Mr. and Mrs. Gregory at home. They are most likely—that is, they are in great trouble today, but try, try—

Ev. [*Returning*] In trouble? In trouble? What about?

Geo. Unluckily, their maid, a pretty girl, called Rosalie—

Ev. Rosalie! What has happened to Rosalie?

Geo. What no one would have suspected. Poor unfortunate girl! She is at this moment [*Tossing back his hand in the direction of the courthouse*], awaiting to be condemned!

Ev. Almighty Powers! What has she done?

Geo. Why, truly, she has robbed her master and mistress.

Ev. Robbed! It is impossible!

Geo. Ah! May be; but for all that, it's true.

Ev. Some horrible deception.

Geo. I beg your pardon. All the village is below there in the courthouse. I'm going to see if it will soon be over. [*Going*]

Ev. Stop! Answer me. Is it truly Rosalie—

Geo. [*In going out*] Yes, yes! Rosalie Granville! [*Exit. Music*]

Ev. Granville! Powers of mercy! No! My daughter never could so descend—I fly to be convinced. [*Seeing the sentinel*] Nay, far from me be now all thought of personal security! Let them arrest me! Let them take my life—what matters it to me! Rosalie was my only comfort! If I have lived to see my child's disgrace, I have already lived too long. [*Looking toward the side wing*] Do I deceive myself? Francour! What does he here? [*Enter Francour, at the back, on the left*]

Fran. How provoking! No Justice to be found! They told me—what do I see? Everard! [*Running towards him. Music*]

Ev. Francour! What brings you hither?

Fran. Rejoice, comrade! Rejoice! I bring your pardon.

Ev. [*With a wild and gloomy air*] Pardon—to me—for what?

Fran. [*Showing the papers*] Yes, yes, my friend! Here is thy pardon, and here a letter to the Justice! Be gay, my boy! The danger is all over! Our officers petitioned the King, and your Captain, who was generous enough to confess that he provoked you wrongfully, took charge of the petition, presented it, urged it, and behold! the signature of the King!

Ev. [*Who has not been attending to Francour*] No, I cannot believe she could be guilty. Oh, let me hasten to be convinced.

Fran. [*Holding him*] Hey! What? Why, what the devil's the matter with you, my friend? Does my news drive you mad with joy? I hope you are not—

Ev. [*Mournfully*] Joy, joy for me! Oh, Francour! You bring me life, when my child—ah! That is indeed a death blow! Leave me. [*He attempts to go*]

Fran. Your daughter? Stay. Where are you going to?

Ev. To Gregory, to hear him exculpate or confirm—leave me, I am in agony! [*Music*]

Fran. Everard, I cannot quit thee! [*He follows Everard, who goes out precipitately by the gate of the inclosure. Enter, Coody, alone, returning, from the right*]

Coody. I have just put the money in the old willow tree! Now that's all over, I am curious a bit to see how much my little fortune may amount to. And every shilling of it, I am sure, would I give from the bottom of my heart, if I did but know who in the world I could go and give it to, to do that poor girl any service. It would be a long reckoning. Let us sit down here. [*He seats himself on a stone bench, hard by the gate of the inclosure, and counts his money*] One, two, three—Oh, gemini! I'm richer than I thought. And all these little pieces too. One, two—aha! Look at this pretty half-crown! All brand new. Rosalie gave me that one day when—you 'bide by yourself, Mr. Half-crown! You must be put with the cross. [*Puts it aside*] Poor girl! I hear her yet: "Adieu, my good friend!" Perhaps the last words she will ever say to me! No, no! It would be too bad to think that! [*He wipes his eyes. At the same moment the magpie appears at the gate of the inclosure*] Eh, eh, Mag! What do you do here, miss? That cursed, unlucky looking bird follows me everywhere! Come here, and I'll—[*The magpie returns into the inclosure*] That's wise! You've done well to hop in there. Don't come back, if you know when you are well off. [*Enter George*]

Geo. What's that, you, Coody?

Coody. What's that, you, Georgy? Well, what news, Georgy? What news? Have you been to the court?

Geo. Aye, indeed, have I. Poor Rosalie! They were reading her sentence—

Coody. Why, is she condemned?

Geo. To death, dear Coody!

Coody. [*Rising and gathering up his money*] But that's an abomination, that! Stop, Georgy! I'd give all that I'm worth in the world, to have that damned Justice—[*While he speaks, the magpie gets on the bench, takes the half-crown piece in her beak, and retires*]

Geo. Look, Coody! Look there!

Coody. Stop, thief! Stop, thief! Why the devil didn't you stop her? [*After the magpie has retired with the half-crown, Coody, thinking to catch the magpie on the tree, as he exclaims: "Stop, thief! Stop, thief!", mounts on the bench, and, endeavoring to ascend, he assists himself by a projecting branch, behind which the magpie is concealed. By thus drawing the branch downwards, the magpie is discovered with the half-crown piece in her beak. As he exclaims: "Why the devil didn't you stop her?", he attempts to seize her with his right hand, when the magpie flies off into the belfry. Music]* Mag! Mag! The brute! She has carried off my bright half-crown piece, all brand new! 'Od Zookers! A piece I wouldn't have given for—

GEO.   Well, that would be a trick worth laughing at, if one could laugh just now at anything! She's off, look as you like. Upon my life now, that was a good joke of Mag's! 'Twas worth the half-crown, all the money, I'll be hanged if 'twasn't, I say, Coody! See how one's money flies. Oh, excellent! Ho! Ho! Ho!

COODY.   Excellent, d'ye call it? Oh yes, I dare say! A pretty thing to laugh at, indeed! [*To the sentinel, who stops and laughs*] And you, Mr. Mumchance! with your damned, goodnatured grin, how would you like it, I should be glad to know? Hey! Look! There! See how she mounts up, the arrant thief! There! Now she's near the scaffolding—now she's lighted there. Stop! Now if I could scramble up so high, I might find my little bright boy there. Let us see. [*He attempts to push open the belfry door*] Good! The workmen who are mending the steeple have left it open. Softly, softly. Now, Mag, if I catch you, you shall pay for your sins, you may take my honest word for it. [*Exit into the belfry. Music*]

GEO.   Ha! Ha! Ha! He thinks the magpie'll wait for him. I say, Coody! "A bird in the hand" you know! Ha! Ha! Ha! [*The people come out of the courthouse and assemble in the back*] Hey! They're coming out of the courthouse! It's all over with poor Rosalie! [*Enter Mr. and Mrs. Gregory and Henry*]

HEN.   Oh, tell not me! I will proclaim it everywhere. 'Tis the very mockery of justice!

GREG.   Be calm, be calm, my son! You destroy yourself and expose us all.

NAN.   Let us retire, Henry, I implore you!

HEN.   The barbarians have condemned her! They refused to hear me! Oh, father! Had you known how my soul was at that moment harrowed up with misery, rage, and indignation!

GREG.   Believe me, Henry, my indignation is equal to yours. But compose yourself; in mercy, let us retire.

HEN.   No, I will once more see her.

GREG.   Has she not received your last farewell? Nay, follow us. Retire, I supplicate, I command! Regardless boy! Obey thy father!

HEN. Oh, misery! [*Music. Gregory drags Henry in at the gate of the inclosure. Nannette follows*]

GEO. Poor young man! Good Lord! Here comes the unfortunate, surrounded by a guard! Ah, they conduct her to the place of punishment! Poor Rosalie! Poor Rosalie! [*Enter guards, who range the people in the background. Rosalie, in the midst of the guards, descends the steps of the courthouse and goes slowly towards the street which turns behind it. She is preceded and followed by villagers. She casts her eye towards the church and seems to solicit from the guards permission to pause one moment near it*]

ROS. [*Kneeling before the portal*] Powers of mercy! Inspire me with firmness, and take pity on my father! [*She rises, proceeds, and disappears. The crowd follows her. Music all the while. Coody, on the scaffolding above, is seen drawing something from a hole in which he has thrust his arm*]

COODY. Ho, there! 'Od's bodikins! Stop 'em all, Georgy! Somebody there, stop 'em! Stop 'em! Rosalie is innocent! Look here! Look here! See what I've got here! [*He rings the bell violently. Mr. and Mrs. Gregory and Henry run in*]

GREG. What's this? What has happened?

NAN. What now? What now?

COODY. [*Ceasing to ring*] This way, this way! Come up here, everybody! She is innocent! Rosalie! She is innocent!

HEN. What do I hear? [*Some villagers run to the courthouse*]

GREG. [*Calling*] Coody! Coody!

NAN. Tell us, Coody! Tell us, quick—

COODY. Oh, godmother! Ah, Mr. Henry! Run! Run, and tell them there's your spoon and your fork, and my brand new half-crown, godmother! Here they are [*Throwing them down*] and the magpie is the thief!

HEN. Just Heaven! Come, Father, let us fly! [*Music*]

GREG. Ah, gadzooks! Let's run and show—let's run—let's run, my boy! [*Overjoyed, he seizes the spoon and fork and runs out with Henry. Coody begins to ring again. Enter the Justice*]

JUS. Hey! How! What? What's this alarm rung for?

NAN. Mr. Justice, you see me mad with joy! Rosalie is innocent. And her father, who has just arrived at the farmhouse in an agony of despair—yes, yes, Mr. Justice, my silver is all found! Oh, 'tis a happy day! [*The villagers return from the courthouse*]

JUS. How! How! Your silver—your spoon and fork, say you?

GEO. Yes, Mr. Justice! The sentinel and I, we are witnesses that it was Coody who found it there in the belfry!

JUS. Incredible! [*The villagers from the courthouse run to meet Gregory*]

Coody. [*Looking out*] Huzza! There they are! Make way there! Here comes Miss Rosalie! 'Od's bodikins! They're bringing her in triumph. That's what she deserves! [*Music. Coody throws down the end of the cord which <lay> on the scaffolding. Enter Rosalie, Mr. Gregory, Henry, villagers, guard, etc. Henry, Gregory, and two villagers bring Rosalie on a car hastily formed of branches with their leaves on. Around at the front of the stage, she descends*]

Greg. Mr. Justice of Palaiseau, you may go to the devil, sir! The Grand Judge has interposed his authority! Your victim's here, sir! [*Taking her under his arm*] We have rescued her out of your clutches.

Coody. [*Preparing to come down by the cord*] And it was Coody that brought it all about! By jingo, this is the first good thing I ever did, and I'll make the most of it!

All. Bravo, Coody, bravo!

Jus. Silence! Silence! It is necessary that some one should explain—

All. Rosalie is innocent! Rosalie is innocent! [*Enter Everard, followed by Francour, from the inclosure*]

Ev. My child! My child is innocent!

Ros. [*Flying into his arms*] My father! [*Music*]

All. Her father! [*The characters form a picture*]

Jus. Hey! [*Regarding Everard*] But, is not that—

Ev. Yes, Mr. Justice, I am Everard!

Ros. [*Terrified*] Just Heaven!

Jus. In that case, Mr. Soldier, I have an order—

Fran. To leave him unmolested, Mr. Justice! [*Presenting a paper*] Read.

Ev. [*To Rosalie*] Rosalie! It is my pardon. [*Rosalie expresses her joy*]

Jus. True, it is his pardon.

Ros. Oh, my father! [*To Henry*] That was my secret, Henry! [*Turning*] But where is Coody?

Coody. [*Sliding down by the cord*] Here he is, Miss Rosalie! Here's Coody, here!

Nan. Dear child! I have done you wrong. But a daughter pardons everything in a mother. Then be my daughter, Rosalie, and forgive me. [*Rosalie and Henry embrace*]

Greg. Good, wife! good! Thank you for having spoken before me.

Jus. [*Aside*] The happy boor! I must be off, I can't bear this.

Coody. Stop, Mr. Injustice! Not so fast. If your malice is sorry for having lost all its trouble [*Pointing to the steeple*], get up there, sentence Mag—she deserves it. Hang her, or for want of a better subject, hang yourself, and the devil will have his due. [*Enter a messenger and an officer from the court. The former gives Henry a paper and bows*]

HEN. How! From the court? From the Grand Judge! My father, 'tis for you! [*The messenger speaks to the Justice, whom he detains*]

GREG. For me, boy? Let it be read aloud.

HEN. Here is an order under the seal of the Judge himself, for immediately suspending the Justice from the duties of his office, and securing him for the purpose of a strict inquiry into the causes of his "culpable proceedings in the matter of Rosalie Granville!"

COODY. What, you'll have to pay off your old scores at last, will ye?

HEN. And here, my father! "In consequence of which said suspension, it is the pleasure of the Court that Aubert Gregory be appointed to exercise in his stead the Magistracy of the Village and District of Palaiseau."

ROS. Kind Heaven! Thou art ever just and watchful! [*To Gregory*] Oh, let me, let me be the first to offer you the affectionate obedience of those hearts which surround you, the kindest, best of masters, of fathers, and of friends!

EV. [*Addressing the Justice*] Go, disgraced and unhappy man! Go, hide yourself from the scorn and indignation of the world. Yet know, that notwithstanding the pangs you have inflicted on a father, or the persecution heaped on his distracted child, that father can so far award his pity, that it shall be his task to solicit for you a mercy which you never yet have shown.

HEN. Take him away.

JUS. I burn! I suffocate! Oh that my curses could crush—could overwhelm! Damned, damned disgrace! Irreparable ruin! [*Exit, guarded by the officers. The villagers follow him with groans to the door, waving their hats*]

GREG. Well, now, my friends! Let us proceed to the farm, and celebrate the happy result of this eventful day with draughts of native wine. There we will wish happiness to Rosalie, to Henry, and all around them, and talk over the important lesson we have just received: never on light grounds to criminate our fellow creatures, nor weakly surrender ourselves to the dangerous delusion of trusting to appearances.

HEN. Come, my Rosalie! Let us hasten to welcome in the happier hours that may await us, and may the conduct of our future lives testify our best gratitude to Providence for their impressing us with the inspiring truth that there is no extreme of danger and affliction which can justify despair! [*Music*]

CURTAIN

MOUNT SAVAGE

MOUNT SAVAGE

THE manuscript of *Mount Savage*, in Payne's hand, is in the Luquer collection.

The Solitary of Mount Savage; or, The Fate of Charles the Bold, a romantic melodrama, which was billed anonymously, was brought out on May 27, 1822, and revived several times, at the Surrey, where it served to mark impressively the beginning of Watkins Burroughs's career as actor-manager. It seems likely that this is Payne's play, and A. H. Quinn (*A History of the American Drama from the Beginning to the Civil War,* New York, 1923, p. 455) attributes it conjecturally to him, although Allardyce Nicoll (*A History of Early 19th Century Drama, 1800-1850,* Cambridge, 1930, Vol. II, p. 526) lists it as anonymous. Unfortunately the licenser's copy, which might be of considerable help, is missing; and the only evidence is the coincidence in the use of the source, and the allusions in both the playbill and in the lengthy review in *The Drama* for June which suggest either Payne's play or one remarkably like it.

Payne's *Mount Savage,* as Allardyce Nicoll (Vol. I, p. 82) writes of *The Solitary of Mount Savage; or, The Fate of Charles the Bold,* is an adaptation of Pixérécourt's *Le Mont Sauvage, ou Le Solitaire,* acted for the first time on July 12, 1821, in Paris at the Gaîté, and printed later in the same year. Pixérécourt's play attracted immediate attention in England, for on November 24, 1821, at the Olympic, appeared Planché's version, *Le Solitaire; or, The Recluse of the Alps,* which according to *The Drama* for January 1822, was extremely popular. Payne in his translation follows Pixérécourt closely, for he introduces only one slight change, a short passage of pathetic dialogue in Act II.

The names of all but two of the dramatis personae in the playbill are like those in Payne's manuscript: in the former Count de Palzo appears as Prince de Palzo; and Eloi, a gardener, as Grampus, a change from the French original that might have been made in order to avoid confusion with the name of the heroine, Elodie. The production aroused the reviewer to superlatives, for it was "so excellently got up" that it became a "universal favorite." In the text one finds the same ingredients as those that the reviewer singles out for praise: the struggle between the mysterious but beneficent hero and the base ingratiating villain for the hand of the virtuous heroine that takes place before the romantic background of the Alps, with the most astonishing stage effects especially the devastating explosion of the mine at the close.

CAST OF CHARACTERS

THE UNKNOWN, *surnamed the Man of Mount Savage*

THE BARON DE HERSTALL, *proprietor of the priory of Underlach*

COUNT [DE] PALZO, *a rich Venetian lord, in the service of René, Duke of Lorraine*

MICHIELI, *lieutenant of the Count <de> Palzo, and his confidant*

ELOI, *gardener of the priory*

A child of five or six years

ELODIE DE ST. MAUR, *an orphan, niece of the Baron de Herstall*

MARCELINE, *an old countrywoman, nurse of Elodie*

THE SCENE PASSES IN SWITZERLAND NEAR LAKE MORAT

ACT I.

[SCENE:] *The parlor of an old monastery in ruins. The back is entirely formed of three large ogive windows of colored glass, but so broken that it is easy to see through them in the most distinct manner Mount Savage, covered with fir trees, larch trees, and whose ridg<e>, surmounted by eternal snows, is lost in clouds. On the swell of the hill, on the point of a perpendicular rock, rises a humble cottage. On the right, a road in the rock conducts to the arch of an old brid<ge>. Snow falls abundantly. [Enter] Eloi, Marceline, villagers and young girls.*

ELOI. Just like the old women! Always hating to see the young ones merry-making. Pray, what could we do better than dance, till this cloud blows over?

MAR. Idiot! I ask no better.

ELOI. Hallo! You going to dance! You! Oh ho! Mother Marceline going to dance!

MAR. And pray why not, Mr. Impudence! You are rather young to criticize my actions. No, sir, no, I don't want to dance. There's a time for all in their turn. I give up that pleasure to the young and pretty girls. But I'm going to sing—

ELOI. Some doleful ditty, no doubt. Well! I'll sing too.

MAR. So you may.

ELOI. Oh, no, I mistake. You want to sing the praises of your favorite, the man of Mount Savage. That bear—unknown bear—that nobody knows!

MAR. At any rate, better sing the praises of somebody than repeat the stuff and silly stories that you and your like utter every day.

ELOI. Good! Good! They that love me, come to me.

MAR. They that love me, hear me. [*The lads assemble at the right around Eloi, and the lasses around Marceline. Marceline and Eloi begin together*]

ELOI. Oh, I'll not be the first to give up. [[*Sings*]]

> To these heights do not approach
> If you have prudence;
> You will find death here,
> Believe my experience.

<MAR.> The fool! His experience! Wouldn't one say from that he has been dead three or four times? [[*Sings*]]

Listen not to such tales;
Believe in me, my talk, my age.
The benefactor of the country
Lives upon the Mount Savage.

ELOI. [[*Sings*]]

Fly the man of Mount Savage.

Now my turn. [[*Sings*]]

There, every evening, every morning,
There is the tumult of the devil.
There is of phantoms, of hobgoblins,
A most frightful assembly.

MAR. [[*Sings*]]

Respect this pious recluse;
He has in his humble hermitage
Only his virtues for companions.
Such is the man of Mount Savage.

ELOI. [[*Sings*]] Fly the man of Mount Savage. [*At each couplet of Eloi a part of the lads have quitted him, ridiculing him, and approached to Marceline. At the end of the second, he finds himself altogether deserted. Angry, to Marceline*] I'm sure you must be paid for talking good of him.

MAR. And you for talking lies. If that's the case, you work well for your money.

ELOI. In short, have you seen him, the benefactor, the angel—

MAR. Never.

ELOI. Like everybody else.

MAR. When I say never, I mistake: I have had a glimpse at him—

ELOI. From a distance, wrapped in a black mantle, isn't it? Come, mother Marceline, you may talk as you will. People don't hide themselves when they do nothing but good. [*The windows, pushed by an impetuous wind, open with a great clatter. The sky is overcast; the rain falls in torrents. A rumbling announces the shock of the elements. The thunder, the lightnings, come to add to the disorder of the scene*]

MAR. Oh ho! This is getting serious. Everything announces a hurricane. Run to your little cottages, my friends. Very likely you may be wanted in them. In any case, your absence may make your families uneasy.

ELOI. Come, mother Marceline, no animosity. Take my arm—

MAR. Thank ye, my lad. I shall wait here till the storm's over. If I should be in any danger, I'll give you notice by tinkling the bell that's all ready there in the chapel.

ELOI. Come, friends, let's run to our cottages—

ALL. Goodbye, mother Marceline—

MAR. Goodbye, children, goodbye. [*All depart right and left. Marceline comes and sits down on an old bench at the right*] Ah, Heavens! What weather! May no accident happen—[*Elodie is seen to traverse the background outside, from right to left, running. In one hand she holds her bonnet, drawn close under her chin to protect herself from the snow. In the other she bears a pretty basket. She enters the parlor by the left. She stamps her feet and shakes her bonnet*]

ELOD. At last I've got to a shelter.

MAR. What! You, Miss? In this frightful weather!

ELOD. Yes, good Marceline. You know I'm not afraid.

MAR. True—you've given more than once proofs of a courage, of a firmness, that one never could have suspected in a young person so mild, so modest—

ELOD. I left the priory an hour ago to go, according to custom, to visit some of the neighboring cabins—

MAR. Above all those of the poor. You are so charitable, so compassionate—

ELOD. The weather was calm, the sky serene, and I wished to profit by it, to offer, this day, to the poor Lisbeth—

MAR. The daughter of the old herdsman? [*From time to time Elodie regards, towards the left where she stands, an old niche in which was formerly placed the statue of a saint, and where now appears a lute*]

ELOD. This basket of <willow>. It contains little; but 'tis my own work, and I feel assured that she will set some value on it.

MAR. I doubt if there is a family two leagues round that ain't indebted to you for some kindness. They've named you the "Angel of the Valley."

ELOD. To love to do good, is, I believe, all the secret of happiness. [*During this dialogue the tempest seems to get calmer*]

MAR. What is it, pray, which draws your attention on this side?

ELOD. [*Aside*] Ought I to tell her? [*Aloud*] 'Tis that—I am astonished to see my lute here. [*She points to the old niche*]

MAR. Didn't you put it there then?

ELOD. No. Last night I was singing, seated near the bridge, when an old man, bowed under a heavy load, passed by me. I hung my lute on the arch of the torrent; I ran towards the poor man and assisted him to regain his cabin. When I quitted him, it was night, and I re-entered into the priory. This morning my first care was to return to the arch of the torrent, but my lute had disappeared.

MAR. And you cannot divine—

ELOD. [*Hesitating*] Why—no—

MAR. Well, then, I—I'll dare to wager that I know who put it in that niche.

ELOD. [*In the same manner*] And who do you suspect?

MAR. Who? That strange man that knows everything, sees everything, don't show himself to anybody, and never lets escape a chance of rendering a service or doing a good action: in one word, the Solitary of Mount Savage.

ELOD. The Solitary—

MAR. Isn't it he, that already charged me, six months ago, to restore to you that girdle that you had dropped on the border of the lake?

ELOD. [*With interest*] Then you have seen this mysterious personage?

MAR. 'Twas night. I only remarked his form, but I could not distinguish his features.

ELOD. [*Thoughtfully*] 'Tis astonishing—

MAR. His ample vestment appeared to me black—

ELOD. Black? 'Tis so—

MAR. Now for your turn, can you have met him?

ELOD. Marceline, I must avow the truth. Can I have a secret from my good nurse? I have thought I remarked for a long time that I was observed, followed in all my walks, by a mysterious being, invisible. Strange noises, unexpected sounds come to trouble my meditations or my studies, to such a degree, that, seized with secret terror, I dare but rarely venture out of the gardens of the priory. Nevertheless, I alarm myself wrongfully, no doubt, and no harm is meant against me. On the contrary, the words which strike my ear are tender, the voice which pronounces them is mild; it has an expression which penetrates my heart. For some time past above all, the advice that I received announce[s], on the part of him who gives it, a true solicitude. Doubtless he exaggerates the dangers that I run and which only exist perhaps in his imagination; but I am not the less touched by the motive which impels him to watch over me. In fine, shall I tell it to you, my good Marceline? There is, in my ideas, in my heart, a vague—an uncertainty, which distracts me. Ah! How happy I was then, when I was calm!

MAR. Not a doubt, child, not a doubt. The Solitary takes a particular interest in you.

ELOD. [*Going thoughtfully to take her lute and finds a paper attached to it*] What can this be? [*Reads the slip*] "For the Orphan of St. Maur." This hand is unknown to me. Can it be—

MAR. Read, miss—

ELOD. Ought I—

MAR. Why not? The billet is not sealed.

ELOD. [*Reads*] "White Dove of the Valley, a vulture hovers o'er thee; dread his blood-stained talon." What can mean—

MAR. There's one thing positive. Some danger threatens, and the Solitary knows it—

ELOD. But the Solitary himself, who is he?

MAR. That nobody knows. [*The tempest, which had appeared to relent, revives and increases to a frightful pitch of terror. The waters of the lake are prodigiously agitated. The lightnings <flash>. The thunder <bellows>. The trees are uprooted and fall with a crash. One of them overturns in its fall and draws with it a little cottage placed on the bend of the hill and the ruins of which are precipitated in the lake. A woman, dishevelled, appears on the mountain and shrieks in despair*]

WOM. My child! My child! [*She is on the brink of the rock*]

ELOD. Unhappy woman! Run. Oh, wretched, wretched mother!

MAR. I'll fly for help! [*Exit by the right. Elodie is going to go out by the opposite side, when a man of lofty figure descends from the summit of the left hand mountain, sees the disaster, pauses on the rock, throws [from] himself the black mantle which envelopes him, and plunges in the waves*]

ELOD. Behold him! What courage! What generous devotedness! Will he be able to save him? [*All the mountain is covered with villagers run thither and who give token of the most lively interest. Elodie gazes without, at the left. The tempest is horrible. The Unknown enters rapidly by the left and gives the child to Elodie*]

UN. Noble orphan, finish my work: restore this child to his mother, that she may receive it from the hands of innocence. [*Going*]

ELOD. But who then are you?

UN. [*Returning and with a grief-swollen accent*] The man of adversity.

ELOD. [*Making a step towards him*] Explain—

UN. Fly, angel of the valley. Approach me not. My presence announces death—[*Elodie, amazed, unmovable, dares no further to question. He goes out. Villagers, at the head of whom is the mother of the child, run in by the right. The child cries: "My mother!" He disengages himself from the arms of Elodie, who restores him to the poor woman. She covers her child with kisses and presses him to her heart*]

MAR. [*Arriving after them*] God be praised, here he is safe and sound.

ELOI. That is, 'pon my word, very lucky. Who is it that saved him?

ELOD. The Solitary!

MAR. There!

ELOI. <Is he then everywhere?>

MAR. Yes, everywhere that there is good to be done. Now mock me again, Mr. Incredulous. [*Enter the Baron de Herstall*]

BARON. Well, my children, what has happened? They talk of disasters. If there are any unfortunate, conduct them towards me, or rather, guide my steps towards their cottages; all that I possess belongs to them.

ELOD. My uncle, thanks to the Unknown, all is repaired. This child was about to perish in the waves. He plunged thither to restore it to its mother—

BAR. The thanks which he deserves have doubtless been given to him.

ELOD. He has not given us time. After some enigmatical words he disappeared.

BAR. Inconceivable man!

CHILD. [*Showing a purse*] Look what he put into my hand.

ELOD. A purse!

MAR. He forgets nothing.

BAR. Hold, my child, [add] this to it. [*The mother and the child kiss the hands of Elodie and of the Baron, then depart with the country people*] With so many qualities which command interest and affection, what motive can determine this singular man to live in an absolute retreat and to encircle himself with a mystery impenetrable? His actions announce a mighty soul; and nevertheless, spite of myself, I conceive suspicions—

ELOD. Ah, my uncle!

BAR. Why fly the eyes of man? Why only please himself amid forests and rocks? Why render inaccessible the approaches of his dwelling? It is not thus that the pure man should trace his path in the world. Virtue walks without a veil; mystery is not made for her. The mortal without reproach loves to let his heart to be read into; he fears not the light; he neither hates nor flies his fellow beings—

ELOD. The Unknown of the mountain hates not his fellow beings, since, compassionate to their sufferings, he has shown himself often their preserver. He flies them not, since he appears everywhere where the accents of grief and despair are to be heard. Why then suspect crime, where everything announces virtue? Perhaps he has experienced great chagrins—

BAR. Thy candid soul cannot imagine ill, and nevertheless it is encountered at every step we make in life. In proportion as we advance, the illusions of youth disappear, the charm vanishes, to leave to be seen, too often, man under the aspect the most sad, the most fatal—

ELOD. My good uncle, that misanthropy is a natural consequence of the frightful misfortunes which have overwhelmed your existence. But is it not necessary to conclude from it—

BAR. Yes, most frightful, without doubt. After all the evil men have done me, I cannot conceive that I can have the weakness, the meanness, ever to like them again. There is one, above all, whose name and memory makes me shudder with horror: the Duke of Burgundy!

ELOD. Why recall him to mind?

BAR. Why? To nourish my hatred, to augment it, if it be possible! Oh, the monster! My Irena, only and cherished daughter, has perished, victim of the frantic love he had conceived for her; and soon the grief of this loss snatched from me the best of wives. And thou, dear Elodie, what has made thee an orphan? Is it not he? Is it not this ferocious prince? Has he not struck with his homicidal skill, his best friend, thy father, the Count of St. Maur; and the same blow, has it not caused to descend into the tomb thy unfortunate mother? Ah! Everything here speaks to me of this sanguinary man, worthy emulator of the ferocious Louis XI. The bones of our brave mountaineers covered the plains of Granson. 'Tis on that fatal peak, 'tis on the summit of that rock that I have seen to roll at the bottom of the torrent the heads of the victims of his barbarity.

ELOD. Heaven, to punish him, without doubt, has wished that in his turn he should perish miserably.

BAR. 'Tis true. But this scourge of his subjects, this butcher of his friends, was treated after his death as if he had lived well. His ashes were the object of the greatest honors! Ah, my Elodie, for thy repose, for mine, may the great of the earth never approach these valleys. [*There is heard without, at the left, the sound of trumpets*] What can that be?

ELOD. [*Going to look at the back*] I see glittering afar lances, shields, and helmets. Numerous warriors descend the mountain.

BAR. What would they have with us? What leads them in this land, now so peaceable—[*Eloi runs along the edge of the lake outside. At a sign of the Baron he mounts on the bridge and meets Michieli, with whom he re-descends and <whom he conducts> to the Baron*]

MICH. [*Apart, seeing Elodie*] 'Tis she. [*Aloud*] Baron, the Count de Palzo, my master, General in the service of Lorraine, charges me to offer you his respectful homage and to demand of you permission to traverse your domains.

BAR. The recommendation which attaches itself to the name alone of the brave Duke René renders it my duty to grant it. Eloi, run to meet the General, and guide him hither. [*Exit Eloi*]

ELOD. [*Low to Marceline*] Marceline, it seems as if I had already had a glimpse of that man. See how he examines me—

MAR. [*Low*] So he does.

MICH. [*Apart*] That angelic creature fully justifies the violent passion my master has conceived for her and the resolution which he has taken to carry her off—

ELOD. To escape his stare, which displeases me, let us go and carry my basket to the good Lisbeth. Come with me, Marceline.

MAR. I consent, miss.

ELOD. [*To the Baron, who has come down to the fore part of the stage*] My Uncle, be not unquiet, I will presently rejoin you at the priory.

MICH. [*Apart*] 'Tis in vain she flies me. She will not be able to escape me.

BAR. Go, my child. [*He embraces her. She curtsies to Michieli and goes out by the left with Marceline. The sound of the trumpet comes nearer. The mountain, the parlor, the borders of the lake are lined with curious spectators. A numerous and well armed troop conducted by the Count de Palzo, descends the mountain and ranges on the edge of the lake. The Count and some officers only enter the parlor. Michieli loses himself adroitly in the crowd and goes out on the same side as Elodie*]

COUNT. Baron de Herstall, retired from the court, a happy occupant of this tranquil valley, you are become a total stranger to politics.

BAR. True, my lord, and I felicitate myself on it.

COUNT. Then you know not, of course, that Louis XI has established pretensions on Lorraine, that already he has taken possession of Barrois and prepares to march on Nantes. The Duke René awaits succor from the Emperor. He assembles on all sides soldiers to defend his territory. Honored by his confidence, invested with an eminent rank in his army, I am charged by him to come to solicit reinforcements from the Helvetian Republic. My mission has obtained all the success that could be hoped from it. I conduct to René a numerous and war-worn troop; but I should have thought myself wanting in all the respect due to the Baron Herstall, one of the most principal and most ancient lords of the land, if, passing so near his domains, I had neglected to see him, and to take his orders for the court; 'tis an attention for which the Duke René will feel indebted to me infinitely.

BAR. I am proud of the great honor of receiving the Count de Palzo, the friend of my sovereign. Formerly I sought and knew the illusions of glory. I have shone in camps. If age and unheard of misfortunes had not annihilated my strength, I would not hesitate even now to buckle on again my old armor and to march with you to the defense of René. Alas! I am reduced to form wishes for the success of the cause. It is just, no doubt; but I too well know that 'tis not the good right that carries it. Come, Count, deign to follow me to the priory. I hope to possess you in it yet some days.

COUNT. Impossible. The interest of René suffers me not to retard my march.

BAR. At least till tomorrow.

COUNT. Be it so. Pray go before and conduct yourself <and> my knights toward your dwelling. A second column follows me and must instantly arrive. I go to await to indicate to it the route it must take and to give to the chief some instructions.

BAR. Think that I shall see you again. I would not lose any one of the short moments you grant to me.

COUNT. Brave, loyal, hospitable, such are the qualities to which all agree you are entitled. I see the Baron de Herstall is worthy of his fame. Knights, follow the noble old man. I shall arrive at the priory nearly as soon as you. [*He extends his hand to the Baron in token of friendship. The Baron goes out at the left hand, preceded and followed by a numerous throng. Curiosity detains till then the country people, who do not weary themselves in regarding a spectacle so new to them. Michieli re-enters by the left*]

COUNT. Ah, well—well—Michieli?

MICH. My lord, I tracked the orphan to the entrance of a hut which they told me belonged to the herdsman of the valley. She cannot long remain there; and doubtless we shall not delay to see her.

COUNT. Have you posted guards around the neighborhood?

MICH. The success which has crowned various enterprises of this sort undertaken in your service at Venice and elsewhere is a guarantee to you of my address. All my precautions are taken. From this moment the charming Elodie is in your power.

COUNT. Can it be in truth!

MICH. Now, my lord, your orders: Shall I await you at Epinal, or must I conduct her instantly to Nantes?

COUNT. Neither—

MICH. How?

COUNT. Thou shalt direct thyself on Vesoul, and thou wilt await me at Joinville, where my meeting must take place with the King of France.

MICH. The King of France!

COUNT. Aye. 'Tis not to the Duke René, 'tis to Louis XI that I lead the troops that the Republic has permitted me to levy in Switzerland.

MICH. To Louis XI, that prince so inconstant in his politics!

COUNT. He has given me, this time, satisfactory guarantees. Greedy of dignities and honors, how canst thou have believed since nine years that thou art attached to me, that I would espouse in good faith the interests of the

Duke of Lorraine? What can a poor prince offer me, who is reduced to beg on every side props to preserve his states?

MICH. Has he not promised you the hand of his sister?

COUNT. Already possessor of immense wealth, 'tis to raise myself that I aspire; and the road on which I am will conduct me to the throne.

MICH. In that case, I pity the fate you reserve to the lovely orphan.

COUNT. Undeceive yourself, Michieli. Never that thought unworthy of a lofty mind could enter into my soul. In traversing this country to render myself at Berne, chance offered this young beauty to my view; she produced on me the liveliest impression; but I have not even imagined that she could ever become the object of any serious engagement.

MICH. Doubtless, because your desires have rarely experienced resistance; but, if some unforeseen obstacle should come to derange your dreams of happiness, you would then renounce her possession—

COUNT. No, Michieli. Perhaps then I might be weak enough to form ties—

MICH. I think I can see her at the end of the meadow.

COUNT. 'Tis she herself. I hasten to the Baron to prevent his having any suspicion. You will find me a confidential man. <Let me know> the result —let her not escape. Farewell. 'Tis when as I am a king I shall reward you. [*Exit right hand*]

MICH. It may be possible that he says the truth. Formed in the school of the Duke of Burgundy, who admitted him to his friendship, he has preserved the distinct character of his first master. Ambition devours him. All means to attain success seem to him legitimate. Hence his successes are seldom doubtful. Let us think to serve him well. [*He calls four soldiers, whom he places at the different issues, commanding them to conceal themselves. Elodie and Marceline traverse the stage from left to right, without, following the border of the lake. Soldiers present themselves abruptly to them and make them fly into the parlor, where they think to find shelter; but Michieli and his soldiers seize them. That the cries of Marceline may not be heard, they put a bandage on her mouth. Elodie escapes, flies towards the mountain, climbs the narrow, steep path which conducts to the old bridge. The ravishers pursue her and are near catching her. Clad in black armor, and his head covered with a helmet surmounted by black plumes, the Unknown rapidly descends the mountain and comes to place himself at the head of the bridge between Elodie and the soldiers. Each stroke of his steel strikes down one of the miscreants; then, with a vigorous arm, he tumbles him into the torrent. Elodie has fallen on her knees on the mountain, at the left, and thanks Heaven for this unexpected succor. Michieli, enraged at seeing his people perish, quits Marceline, scales the mountain, and arrives in [the] presence of*

*the Unknown, who disarms him, seizes him with the left hand, and holds
him down on the earth, while with the right he makes a sign to Elodie to
descend and to go and find Marceline. Elodie, trembling, obeys, without
losing sight of her liberator, for whom she seems penetrated with admiration.
When Elodie has descended, the Unknown forces Michieli to rise and to pass
to the right. He commands him to continue to ascend the mountain, so as to
make it obvious to the spectators that he wishes to draw from him light as
to what has passed. The soldiers, confounded and intimidated by the menacing gestures of the Solitary, remain immovable and leave to pass the orphan,
who rejoins her nurse, embraces her, and both put themselves on the route
for the priory]*

ACT II.

[SCENE:] *The stage represents the gardens of the priory, enclosed by an iron
rail fence, through which can be perceived in the background a chain of
mountains and far-distant glaciers. At the left a little Gothic chapel. From
the first to the second grooves at the right is a wall of enclosure forming a
narrowing angle. In that part facing the spectator is a little door. At the rise
of the curtain all the people of the Baron are occupied in embellishing that
part of the garden. They suspend garlands and festoons next to the rails; they
place vases of flowers on the terrace wall, etc. Marceline directs these prepa-
rations. Elodie enters thoughtfully; she walks at hazard, and without seeing
what passes around her.*

ELOD.   How to reconcile this courage, this extraordinary devotedness, with
his aversion for society? Why occupy one's self so much with those one hates
and only to do them good? All, in this mysterious being, astonishes me and
confounds my reason. I can neither comprehend him nor define him; and,
in the meantime, all my thoughts—

ELOI.   Young lady, are you pleased with our work?

ELOD.   [*Glancing all around*]   Yes, my friends, very well.

MAR.   Attend now. That great lord with all his knights thinks to dazzle us
by his tournaments, by his military sports. We must prove to him that in a
wild valley of Switzerland we know too how to receive genteelly one's
guests and to give 'em agreeable surprises.

ELOI.   All the handsomest young men of the neighborhood are apprised;
they'll all come in their gala dresses: it will be superb. There won't absolutely
be any but the most handsome. I shall be at the head of 'em—

ELOD.   And our youngest girls, <adorned> in their best, will they come
to dispute before these valiant knights the prize of grace?

ELOI. Yes, noble miss—

ELOD. Certainly they'll obtain it. Go, my friends. I thank you in advance for my uncle; he will be delighted with the promptitude and taste which you have shown in fulfilling his intentions. [*With a gesture she dismisses the country people, who depart by the right hand*]

ELOI. Pardon me, excuse me, our miss, if I dare to ask you one question. 'Tis from the attachment that I—

MAR. Silence and go. You see well that Miss Elodie isn't disposed to attend to your nonsense.

ELOI. Hold your tongue indeed! Nonsense! I suppose you think nobody here's a right to love our young mistress but you—

MAR. [*To Elodie, who is lost in thought*] How do you find yourself this morning?

ELOD. Alas! Do I know it myself!

MAR. Indeed, indeed, I declare to you, I am scarcely myself recovered from the fright.

ELOI. [*Advancing*] Is it then downright true what Mother Marceline has been telling me about your last night's adventure?

ELOD. Perfectly. [*To Marceline*] The advice I received was but too well founded.

ELOI. Those rascals are so venturesome—hardy—oh! if I had been there—

MAR. It's a sure point you wouldn't have done better than the Solitary.

ELOD. [*Much animated and emphatically*] Better! Say rather 'tis impossible to find united more bravery, energy, and above all disinterestedness.

ELOI. The fact is, that man can't be a man. 'Tis surely some devil or what they call a hobgoblin. Though for all that, I begin to get reconciled to him.

MAR. That's lucky. Once more I tell you, go and see if the Baron has need of your services.

ELOI. Alack, alack, Mother Marceline, don't fidget yourself. It may do you harm. [*Goes a little*]

MAR. [*To Elodie, who seems more and more buried in thought*] You vaunt of the disinterestedness of the Solitary. Undeceive yourself, my good mistress. 'Tis not without a personal interest, without an interest of the heart, that one devotes himself for a female—

ELOD. What! Can you think?

MAR. I do better: I don't doubt of it.

ELOD. To what end? Oh, no! Were it so, far from hiding himself from my looks, he would have sought to encounter them, to approach my uncle, to establish between us the relations of society. I experience, I avow it to thee, the liveliest desire of seeing him, of speaking to him, and that seems to me very natural, isn't it so, Marceline? I owe him so much gratitude!

MAR. That is not the only sentiment he would fain inspire in you. Perhaps, too, it is not the only one—

ELOI. [*In the back*] Here comes the Count de Palzo—

ELOD. Let us avoid him. Since yesterday he has endeavored many times to talk to me of the sudden impression that I have created in him. 'Tis thus he has said it to my uncle; but I am less disposed than ever to hear such avowals—

MAR. [*Tauntingly*] Above all from him, isn't it so? [*Enter the Count de Palzo [and] the Baron. A sign of the Baron stops Elodie. She wishes to retain Marceline, but the Baron dismisses her, as well as Eloi*]

COUNT. [*Aside*] Since other means have failed, I must try the more honorable. [*Aloud*] Lovely orphan, this morning I must quit this spot, and I, held in it by a power that till now I have braved—

ELOD. My uncle, the arrangements you have given to my charge require my presence. Permit—

COUNT. Yet one word, charming Elodie, and you will be forthwith free. If with the consent of the respectable relation who stands to you in place of a father, the friend of the Duke of Lorraine should fall at your feet and should offer to you the homage of a sincere heart, might he flatter himself with the hope of being favorably received?

ELOD. My lord—

COUNT. If you deign to listen to my vows, love, fortune, honors will environ your existence. Powerful by your riches, you will be able to satisfy the sole passion which to this moment can have occupied your fine soul, in bearing abundance and joy into the cottage of the poor: you will become, by your charms, the ornament of the Court of Lorraine, and the example of your virtues will lead back into it the virtues of your ancestors. In short, it may be that Heaven, calling me to the highest destinies, may prepare for you in the future a crown.

ELOD. Brought up in obscurity, I cannot believe myself called to the grandeurs of the earth, and the veil of the cloister would better suit my forehead than the diadem of sovereigns. I shall not quit the mountains of Helvetia. The last wishes of my mother make that my law. My uncle is not ignorant of it. Deign therefore to permit me not to accept the brilliant wedlock you propose to me. Gratitude is the only sentiment that the Count <de> Palzo can expect from me. [*She inclines her head and goes out. The Count and the Baron look after her with astonishment*]

COUNT. What pride!

Bar. I won't conceal it. My surprise is equal to yours.

Count. What! All that charms youth, all that seduces the heart of woman: the splendor of the best society, the vision of elevated rank, of an illustrious name, nothing to be able to touch in my favor an orphan elevated in a solitary valley—

Bar. Perhaps hereafter she may yield to new entreaties. Without wealth, with no stay but me, who will soon be wanting to her, it seems to me impossible that she resists seriously offers so brilliant.

Count. 'Tis for you, Baron, that it is proper to weigh these advantages and to make them valued. A father (and you stand in place of one to her), ought alone to regulate the fate of his children. Who more than him desires their happiness? Who better than he knows how to appreciate the diverse means which conduct them to it? Supreme judge in his own family, he ought long to reflect on his decrees; but, when he is well convinced of their equity, nothing can oppose their execution.

Bar. I do not think the answer of Elodie can be irrevocable. I go to essay upon her mind all the power that friendship and the respectable title that I have over her gives me. You doubt not of my efforts. They will arrive, I hope, to persuade her. Marceline! Eloi! [*Eloi appears*] Go tell my niece that I beg her to come to me.

Count. I confide to you my dearest interests. While you attack her reason and her heart, I go to occupy myself with that which may dazzle her eyes. The spectacle that we are about to offer is new to her. It will seduce her perhaps. [*Exit left hand. The Unknown, enveloped in his black mantle, as he was seen at the first appearance, shows himself outside of the garden, along the railing. He menaces the Count, who does not see him. When the Count has disappeared, Elodie arrives slowly by the right. The Unknown, placing himself always so as not to be seen, extends his hands towards her with a protective movement, then he disappears by the right*]

Elod. You have sent for me, my Uncle.

Bar. Yes, my child. Before the Count de Palzo I preserved silence. I left thee free to answer according to thy sentiments. Now I blame a determination too prompt to have been well weighed, and I owe it to thee to explain my motives—

Elod. My Uncle—

Bar. Hear me, dear Elodie. Certainly, if consolations could have descended into my soul, thy tender cares would have been enough to calm my regrets. It has not depended on thee to restore to me all at once a sister, a wife, an only and cherished daughter. Since thou hast not been able to succeed in removing from my thoughts the frightful remembrance of that separation, no one here below can operate that miracle. My existence, which would have been embellished, prolonged by those objects of the most tender affection, weakens itself without them. And I cannot conceal from thee, Elodie, though the avowal afflicts thee, I hasten with all my wishes the instant which should unite me in a better world to the souls I have lost.

ELOD. What a heart-rending thought! What a future do you offer to the sad Elodie!

BAR. Thou alone, my child, combatest this internal desire. I have never been able, without terror, to pause upon the idea that, in dying, I should leave thee without a stay. But at last I have a glimpse of a better future, and I embrace it greedily: A powerful protector offers to replace the old man ready to disappear. Accept him, my daughter. Reject not the noble spouse the Heavens seem to send thee. No inquietude then will come to trouble the peace of my bed of death.

ELOD. [*Apart*] I dare not avow to him what passes in my heart.

BAR. You do not answer me? Think well of it. The Count de Palzo unites all the conditions which ought to direct a woman in the choice of a husband. On this account, I ought not to repel his demand. His rank, his fortune, his age, his reputation, all shine in him with a splendor which I believe pure and without a stain. Alone in these deserts, thou hast only known the wild mountaineers, and thy heart has never yet been able to speak. Thy consent to this alliance would accomplish all my wishes. In the meantime, far be it from me the thought of constraining thy sentiments. Open to me thy soul. Elodie will be always mistress of herself.

ELOD. It is precisely, my Uncle, because the Count <de> Palzo seems called to high destinies, that I am not worthy of being his companion. Brought up in the midst of the mountains, I should find myself misplaced in the bosom of courts. Is it to me to be ambitious of royal dwellings, when it is in a palace that my father was assassinated? Remember the last words that my mother addressed to you: "Herstall," said she, "I commend to you my daughter. Never, if possible, let her quit that peaceful valley; never let her know the grandeurs of the earth and what they cost to those who possess them. Oh, my brother, let Elodie be brought up in all the simplicity of manners of the first age. Talk not to her of courts but as the shallows of the ocean, that none ought to approach but hardy navigators." I conjure you, my good Uncle, let us respect the last wish of my expiring mother—

BAR. What! Canst thou oppose me yet, when I shall tell thee that the Count has sworn to me on his honor that he was ready to quit for thee the Court of Lorraine and to despoil himself of the rank he occupies?

ELOD. For me, my Uncle! Such an engagement is indeed extraordinary! That sacrifice made by an ambitious—pardon me, but I can scarcely regard it as sincere.

BAR. What suspicions can you conceive?

ELOD. I cannot fix upon any; but your example and your conversation have raised in me a wise mistrust of men—

BAR. Perhaps I have pushed it too far.

ELOD. I have no right to think so.

BAR. I conceive that the event of yesterday—

ELOD. Had not ought to change my opinion—

BAR. Hence, thou persistest—

ELOD. You have commanded me to speak without feigning. Sooner than inhabit the Court and disobey the last wishes of my mother, I would rather consecrate myself in these mountains to the worship of the altar.

BAR. But, in fine, if the Count de Palzo, recognizing how praiseworthy your intentions are, should yield to this sacred desire; if, like you, he respects it; if he consent, in one word, to pass his life in this solitude, could you refuse yet to satisfy his desires and mine?

ELOD. Then, my Uncle, and if you make absolutely your happiness to depend on my condescension—

BAR. Well—and then—

ELOD. Spite of my aversion, I must yield. [*Aside*] But, merciful Providence, what will it cost! [*Enter Eloi, running*]

ELOI. Baron, our miss, come pray see. Oh! Isn't it beautiful! Isn't it superb! Oh, the beautiful soldiers that makes—

BAR. [*Aside*] I have already gained a half-victory. The entreaties of the Count must do the rest. [*During this aside speech Eloi is at the background, turned towards the left, kicking his heels together, at his ease. Elodie reflects. The Baron goes up the stage to see the procession and disappears. Marceline enters by the right and calls the child*]

MAR. Come, my little man, come and see the brave knights.

CHILD. [*Low to Marceline*] Is it now time to lead the beautiful miss to the little gate of the garden?

MAR. Not yet.

CHILD. Yet he told me it was immediately.

MAR. If he told you so, you must mind then. [*Military music is heard in the distance since the entrance of Eloi. The child comes to the right of Elodie and kisses her hand*]

ELOD. [*Recognizing him*] Ah, is that you, my pretty child?

CHILD. Yes, beautiful miss. Come with me.

ELOD. Where?

CHILD. Close by this door.

ELOD. What to do?

CHILD. I don't know; but he plainly told me—

ELOD. Who?

CHILD. That good gentleman who took me out of the lake.

ELOD. [*Troubled, to Marceline, who has approached and watches to prevent Elodie being surprised*] Hearest thou, Marceline?

MAR. Yes, noble miss.

ELOD. [*Somewhat startled*] What is his purpose? [*Going*]

MAR. I know not; but it cannot be dangerous. [*The child quits Elodie and opens the gate*]

CHILD. Nobody. [*Runs up leaping*]

MAR. See what he has written.

ELOD. [*Approaches and reads the following words traced in black on the external side of the door, which is entirely in view of the spectator:*] "Palzo deceives you and conspires against the Duke of Lorraine, who has promised him his sister. 'Tis he who sought to carry you off yesterday." The monster! [*At the cry of Elodie, Marceline shuts the gate*]

MAR. [*Low and quick to Elodie*] Don't betray yourself.

ELOD. What! How! The Count scarcely arrived and the Solitary apprised of his name, his engagements, his projects!

MAR. Have I not told you that he watches over your destinies? Beware of neglecting his advice! [*The military procession, headed by the Count de Palzo, advances and defiles before Elodie. It is as numerous as brilliant. The banners and the lances are lowered before the orphan*]

BAR. [*Low to the Count*] I have spoken to my niece, who already seems better disposed. Redouble your solicitations, and doubtless you will gain her consent.

COUNT. [*In the same manner*] Sweet hope—[*Tilts, games, military dance. Entrance of villagers, who dance to the sound of the instruments of the country. Warriors join them and animate the picture, which becomes general*]

COUNT. [*To his warriors*] Go, dispose everything for the departure. 'Tis probable that I shall not immediately follow you. My sojourn with the worthy Baron may be perhaps prolonged; but, in that case, I will send you my final orders. [*Exit the warriors and villagers. Elodie and Marceline also prepare to go in, but the Count retains Elodie. The Baron expresses to his niece the desire that she reject not the prayer of the Count. He leaves them alone*]

ELOD. What would the Count de Palzo with me?

COUNT. Charming orphan, your uncle induces me to hope—

ELOD. [*With cold dignity*] What, sir—

COUNT. That the lively expressions of my love may achieve to conquer a resistance which has already enfeebled the tenderness for that respectable relation.

ELOD. My uncle has deceived you, sir, or rather he has deceived himself. When moved by his entreaties I allowed him to glimpse, in the far distant future, at the possibility of our union, I knew not the engagements you had contracted at the Court of Lorraine; I knew not then that the august sister of René was destined to be your bride.

COUNT. [*Aside*] What have I heard?

ELOD. [*Same manner*] He recoils—

COUNT. [*With a studied indifference*] How a vague project of which the Court of Nantes has no knowledge, a hidden thought of the sovereign, scarcely disclosed to me whom it interests, can have been revealed to you in these remote solitudes!

ELOD. That is my secret.

COUNT. The Duke of Lorraine, it is true, deigned to propose to me the hand of his sister; but I am bound by no engagement. I can, without being wanting in honor, refuse the wedlock projected. What do I say? My duty even compels me this day to break it. I never more shall be able to make the Princess of Lorraine happy. Doubtless I shall lose the friendship of René; doubtless I shall draw on me his wrath, but love has totally changed my soul. Glory, fortune, dignities, you are no longer anything for me. Elodie is all. Yes, Elodie is the only woman to whom I can ever associate my fate.

ELOD. [*Ironically*] It is not perhaps with that noble view you attempted to cause her to be carried off yesterday?

COUNT. [*Aside*] I am betrayed. Michieli has spoken—

ELOD. [*Aside*] The Solitary has spoken the truth.

COUNT. This accusation—

ELOD. Is but too well founded. Count de Palzo, lay aside all dissembling. Why seek to deceive the simple and the good? What honor can you hope from a victory so easy? All your projects are known to me! All, you hear me! But I willingly promise you secrecy. Show yourself then as you are, and renounce frankly a union henceforth impossible. I swear by the revered names of the authors of my days, never shall Elodie become the wife of the Count de Palzo.

COUNT. That would be, then, a frightful fate for you?

ELOD. The most frightful! The orphan of St. Maur cannot forget from what noble blood she sprang. The husband that she will take must justify her choice by eminent qualities. He must, above all, merit her esteem; on these conditions you never can become her husband.

COUNT. [*Throwing off the mask*] Undeceive yourself, imprudent! In overwhelming me with the expressions of your hatred, in letting me see the contempt that I inspire you with, in showing yourself informed of my projects, you have yourself formed between us a tie which nothing but your death can sever.

ELOD. [*Terrified, aside*] What do I hear?

COUNT. [*Taking her by the hand*] In vain you flattered yourself to escape me. Mistress of my secrets, believe not that I permit you to divulge them, or to dispose of them for my destruction. Yes, I have quitted the cause of René to embrace that of Louis XI, because I find in it the means of satisfying my ardent ambition. I am wearied of being a subject and would reign in my turn; and the King of France has promised me a throne. Will it be then so unfortunate for you to be seated by my side?

ELOD. A legitimate diadem would not have dazzled my eyes; an usurped one makes me shudder. Never shall a chief of rebels be the husband of Elodie!

COUNT. What then is your hope in thus braving me? You think not, then, that I am absolute master in this place and that no human power can snatch you from my arms and withdraw you from my vengeance. Confidant in my designs, you ought to partake now my perils or my fortunes. We are inseparable. If you will not that I employ useless violence, swear before God to be mine, to follow me to the altar whenever I require.

ELOD. Sooner death!

COUNT. Dread lest I meet that cruel wish. [*Draws poignard*]

ELOD. <Wretch! Unfortunate!>

COUNT. [*Menacing and pursuing*] Silence! [*She flies towards the little chapel*] Do you promise?

ELOD. No—

COUNT. Swear, or this hand—

ELOD. Strike—[*She is fallen on one of the steps. He grasps her with one [hand] and with the other lifts his poignard*] Count. You wish it. Well then, die—[*A thicket placed behind the chapel and near Elodie opens. The Unknown passes, his head helmeted*]

UN. Hold!

COUNT. Who art thou?

UN. [*Lifting his visor*] Behold!

COUNT. [*Immovable, stupefied, drops his poignard*] Oh, Heaven!

UN. [*Coming out of the thicket*] Silence! I forbid you to pronounce my name. [*He raises Elodie*] Take courage—

ELOD. 'Tis him again.

UN. [*Advancing towards the right and thus making the Count recoil; draws his sword*] Wretch! Is it still necessary that I should shed blood?

ELOD. [*Stopping him*] Great Heavens! What would you do?

UN. Pardon the movement of indignation, which I could not control, and dissipate your alarms. The perfidious will be struck, but, thanks to you, not here. Tomorrow he will perish. But the sight of his death will not sully your eyes.

ELOD. Who then is this Unknown so terrible?

UN. [*To the Count, who covers his face with his hand and seems rooted*] Hence instantly from this spot! Hence! Alone, I order it. Henceforth thy soldiers, now undeceived, will not follow thee. Perhaps they will punish thee themselves for having believed them cowardly enough to sell themselves. The Baron de Herstall, instructed of thy felony, will conduct them to the Duke of Lorraine. As for thee, encircled by invisible watchers, whatever direction thou mayst take, never shalt thou be able to escape me! Tomorrow thy death will serve as an example to traitors. Hence!

ELOD. Whence comes this power almost supernatural? [*The Count, amazed, crushed by the irresistible ascendancy of the Unknown, goes out by the left. The Unknown goes after him with menaces*]

ELOD. [*With trembling voice*] What! You would quit me so soon?

UN. [*Stopping*] Angel of the monastery, detain me not. You lose yourself—

ELOD. I understand you not. Who can blame me for rendering you here the acknowledgments I owe you?

UN. [*Making all his efforts to rein the impetuous sentiment which animates him*] To blame you! On the contrary, you know not what danger—

ELOD. Near you, I dread no danger! Have you not been twice my liberator?

UN. What is that, when all my life is yours?

ELOD. How have I been able to merit an interest so lively?

UN. How? By all that which is made to inspire it. But in mercy, let me <no> longer hear that voice so powerful over all my being. Leave me to avoid you, to fly from you—forever!

ELOD. [*Livelily*] Forever!

UN. [*Returns*] Can you feel some regret for it?

ELOD. [*Ashamed of her first emotion, hesitates and replies timidly*] Gratitude.

UN. Intoxicating hope, that I had never conceived, thou snatchest from me the fatal avowal. [*He falls at the feet of Elodie*] Dear Elodie, learn then my secret. Yes, I love thee. Thou alone, as a beneficent star appeared amidst the shadows, art come to recall me to life! Now, here below, there is nothing more for me but Elodie! And judge to what a point I am wretched: that Elodie that I idolize never can be mine!

ELOD. Never?

UN. Adored woman! Let me fly thee; there is yet time. Save thyself! My delirium terrifies thee. Oh, seek not to comprehend the man of fatality. Content thyself with repelling him. Never let him approach thy dwelling.

ELOD. What can I answer? Alas! You have thrown into my heart a trouble it never knew before.

UN. Can it be true? Elodie, thou lovest me?

ELOD. To what end would that admission serve? Have you not said that Elodie never could be yours?

UN. Well! How to hope the reverse? Wandering, proscribed, unfortunate, what can I offer to my bride? A rock of exile, a name unknown, an existence unfortunate!

ELOD. What more than you then have I upon the earth?

UN. Have I heard aright? Divine Elodie! These words change my destiny. The thunderbolt has swept away from near my head! Thou lovest me! Heaven then has pardoned me. I can yet hope for happiness. Well, well, follow me. I will be thy guide, thy father, thy husband; I will be all for Elodie. I possess only a cabin in the midst of the rocks, but with thee, I shall be in it the happy <man> of nature. I shall have in my solitude no other treasures but thy love, no other enchantments but thy presence. Alone, in the midst of the mountains, far from human powers, our unknown happiness will not awaken envy. Alas, I have known grandeurs, and I have learnt to hate them; I have possessed riches, and I have rejected them; I have been cherished by glory, and I have cursed it. In this valley of miseries, to love is the only supreme wealth. Ah! To vivify the universe, what is then necessary to man cast among his kind? A heart which responds to his. There is no truly isolated but the insensible; there is no truly proscribed but he that is not loved. Elodie, consent to follow me!

ELOD. Whither would you conduct me?

UN. To Mount Savage. To love, to bliss.

ELOD. [*With terror*] Hold! I can only follow a husband. It can only be at the foot of the altar—

UN. There is one in the desert. Everywhere the Eternal receives the oaths of man! Everywhere are lighted the flambeaux of wedlock. A minister of the skies will unite our destinies. Come, Elodie, consent to follow me. The love with which thou hast inspired me has restored me to the first guides of my youth, the first sentiments of my life: honor, loyalty, virtue! [*With noble-ness*] Come, thou mayst confide in me!

ELOD. [*With a suppliant voice*]   None, I may not follow, till my uncle shall have given his consent to the union. He is my sole relation. 'Tis he who stands in place of the unfortunate father a cruel prince has snatched from me.

UN. [*Aside*]   St. Maur! Frightful remembrance! [*Aloud*] Pardon, Elodie, a moment of delirium. You, to love me? You, to follow me to the desert? To become my companion! What dared I hope? Am I deserving of such a sacrifice? Merit I so great a happiness? I? Oh, no! My mad wishes outrage Heaven and earth; so this dream of a moment succeeds a frightful waking. Farewell. I render myself justice. You are free. Return into the priory. As to me, I exile myself from this valley. You will see me no more.

ELOD.   I shall see you no more!

UN.   At least till a new danger comes to menace you. Elodie, if the succor of the Solitary can yet be useful to you, the fires lighted on the tower of the priory will inform him, and soon you will see him reappear. Adieu, I go to dig my tomb. [*Lost, beside himself, and fearing himself, he departs by the little gate*]

ELOD.   Unfortunate Elodie! [*She is about to fall on the steps of the little chapel, when Marceline runs in, followed by young girls, and sustains her. They carry her out fainting*]

ACT III.

[SCENE:] *The summit of Mount Savage. On all sides appear the tops of green trees and an immense extent of sky. A winding path cut in the rock is the only road for travellers. Its most elevated point is nearly in the middle of the stage, and its irregular declivity conducts to the right and left under the stage, in sight of the spectators. A little by-way, extremely abrupt, which communicates with the road, leads to the cabin of the Solitary, of which the entry is perceptible at the left extremity, on the summit of the mountain. This rough and wild site should be picturesque. It is moonlight. The Count de Palzo climbs painfully the road. He arrives by the right and sits down on a rock, in front of the scene.*

COUNT.   Fatigue overwhelms me. I shall pause here till day appears and leads me to those of my people whom I left behind. I have yielded in appearance, and for some hours only, to the ascendancy this extraordinary man exercises over me. Besides, it was difficult to preserve the presence of mind in an event so unforeseen, in the circumstance the most strange. I shall not delay to seize again the advantages of my position. Doubtless numerous agents are at his beck. I ought not to compromise success in struggling against unequal forces. But the rest of the troop cannot delay to rejoin me, and soon, I hope, I shall have made to return to their duty those of my soldiers whom gold or fear can have disposed to betray me. Someone spoke, I think. I hear a noise on this side. [*Rises and goes to listen at the left*] A march. [*He leans to the ground to hear better*] The steps are numerous and regular. 'Tis a troop. Let me not show myself at first. [*He holds himself aside, in the cleft of a rock, but without disappearing. Michieli appears by the left and scaling at the head of soldiers*]

MICH. By Heaven, the ascent is rough. I thought we never should get to the top but at last here we are.

COUNT. I recognize the voice of Michieli.

MICH. Someone named me. [*The troop halts in such a manner that there are some men entirely visible, and others the extremity of whose lances is only perceptible*]

COUNT. You are right.

MICH. 'Tis his lordship.

COUNT. Whence come you?

MICH. You see, I lead you the second column.

COUNT. Why didst thou not return to the priory?

MICH. Because somebody stronger than you and I wouldn't let me.

COUNT. You could at least send me some secret emissary.

MICH. Impossible, my lord. I have been for some hours in the power of a sort of devil, of whose name I am ignorant; of whom I have not even seen the face; who, to deliver the orphan, has slain and drowned half my men, has made me say whatever he liked, and has dismissed me with frightful menaces. Two leagues from this I met our brave fellows; then, finding myself reinforced, I set forward towards the priory in the hope of finding you in it and of telling you all which has passed since our separation.

COUNT. [*Aside*] No doubt! 'Tis he again! And I do not astonish myself that Michieli should have yielded to this terrible ascendant. All this is to such a degree extraordinary, that I think to be abused by my senses; but no, 'tis not an error, an illusion. I have distinctly recognized him. Be it as it may, I will not abandon a conquest of which I am now tenacious less by taste than pride. Elodie ought to be mine now, because I announced to her my desire. Nay, more, she knows my secrets. Now I return to the priory. If, as he has told me, the soldiers that I have left in it are unfaithful, I will combat them. [*Aloud and rejoining Michieli*] Come, Michieli, let us march.

MICH. May I venture to ask, my lord, where to?

COUNT. To bring my soldiers to their duty and seize Elodie. [*He departs by the right and descends the mountain at the head of his troops. The Unknown appears at the summit of the mountain, at the left. His entrance is at first rapid, then he stops and listens*]

UN. It seemed to me as if I heard the name of Elodie. I was deceived. Ah! This cherished name resounds ceaselessly to my ear and to my heart. 'Tis done. I shall see her no more. I have voluntarily banished myself from her presence; I ought to have done so; and that is, without doubt, the most cruel of the sacrifices I could impose upon myself. [*In speaking, he has descended*] Since I have inhabited this solitude, unknown, dead to the world, I have lived only to solace misfortune and to love Elodie. Love and repentance are the only virtues I have saved in my shipwreck. Yet I have reason to think the Eternal has not entirely turned from me his gaze, since my destiny interests the only person who attaches me to existence. But what do I say? That same interest, so flattering, so touching, is it not a continuance of the fatality which pursues me? Is it not a misfortune for those who prove it, since we cannot be each other's, since a solemn and voluntary vow has condemned me to nothingness? Who knows, besides, if this interest might not change to hate at the moment when Elodie should know my name and my errors? She must never know them—never—at least not till Heaven may have pardoned them. [*He sits down and falls overpowered by sad reflections. Soon he slumbers. His slumber appears much agitated. The mountain behind him is covered with clouds through which are distinguished successively the objects which agitate then so powerfully the imagination of the Solitary. A shade appears to come out of the earth. With one hand it points to the background and in the other bears a lamp. The furies agitate their serpents and torment the sufferer. They present him groaning shades; they unroll before his eyes the picture of war and the calamities which it draws in its train. The assassination of the Count de St. Maur is seen. Everywhere the angel of death wields her scythe. The shadows go to lose themselves under a monument named "The Ossuary of Morat" and composed of skulls and human bones. Seized with frightful convulsions, the Solitary repels these horrible images; his bosom is oppressed; he utters long groans; the perspiration rolls down his forehead; he lifts towards the sky his supplicating hands. At his prayer the picture changes color. Sweet chords are heard. All which bore the marks of sadness and of mourning vanishes. Old men, women, children, overwhelmed with the benefactions of the Solitary, and young wedded couples, happy through him, come to throw themselves on their knees, offer him thanksgivings, and seem to call on him the benediction of Heaven. In this suite of pictures is particularly seen the child saved*] *from the waves the night before, and who throws himself in the arms of his mother. The Solitary grows <calm>. All the groups united point out to him in the distance the figure of a young female who resembles Elodie. Suddenly armed men of a hideous aspect appear behind Elodie. She shrinks from them horror-struck. They pursue her. She flies, crying: "Solitary! Solitary! Elodie calls thee!" The Unknown, livelily struck with this vision, starts out from his sleep. All disappears. He springs up and cries]* Behold me! Behold me! *[He listens]* Can this dream be a warning sent by Heaven? Can my beloved be in peril? *[He mounts towards the summit and looks out towards the right]* What do I see! Fires lighted on the tower of the priory? 'Tis the signal of some new danger! *[Descends]* What cry resounds in the air and comes to wake the mountain echo?

ELOD. *[Calling from afar, without]* Solitary! Solitary!

UN. I do not deceive myself. 'Tis the voice of Elodie. She invokes my succor. Infamous Palzo! Let him tremble! Nothing will arrest the course of my vengeance.

ELOD. *[Without, at the back, but nearer]* Solitary, Elodie calls thee!

UN. Behold me! Behold me! *[He scales the summit and sustains Elodie who sinks exhausted into his arms]*

ELOD. *[Palpitating and scarcely able to articulate]* Spite of your forbidding, he is again at the priory.

UN. Palzo! The miscreant!

ELOD. I escaped by a secret door, and I have been happy enough not to fall in the hands of the soldiers who go through the valley. Believing nowhere to be able to find an asylum but near you, I have ascended the mountain and am here—

UN. *[Making her sit down on a rock at the right]* How much I thank you for having had this thought. Yes, dear Elodie, I will defend you. You are here safe from the pursuits of the monster. Woe to him if he should dare to penetrate to Mount Savage and offer himself to my view! This time, I swear it, he shall receive death. I will employ against him the means I have prepared to defend my retreat, in case they should attempt to penetrate to it in defiance of my prohibition. The quarters of the rock hurled by the thunderbolt, in rolling from the summit of the mountain, should crush in their fall the infamous Palzo and the accomplices of his crime. *[At these words he enters his cabin and brings out a lighted torch which he places behind a rock]*

ELOD. Oh, my worthy protector! Give me the means of acquitting my duty towards you!

UN. To acquit yourself—

Elod. To you do I not owe my honor and my life!

Un. In watching over Elodie, is it not to watch over my own preservation? Oh, you, of whom I bear in all places the remembrance and the image, have pity on a mad one that adores you, and do not be offended at the expressions of a love borne almost to delirium.

Elod. Have you not subjugated all my being?

Un. Alas! Thy hand, in pressing mine, has not effaced its stains! Thy sweet presence seems to purify the air that I breathe; but can thy look absolve me?

Elod. From what?

Un. I cannot make this fatal revelation to you! 'Tis in vain that to appease yon Heaven and my remorse, I am exiled on a steep rock, and that, alone for three years, reclined on the dry heather, I have lived on the waters of the torrent, on roots and wild fruits. I have not been able yet to appease the formidable voice of my conscience. All the benefactions I have shed around me cannot render peace to my distracted soul. Ah, I see it. All felicity is denied to me.

Elod. You judge yourself too severely, no doubt. The benefactor of this land cannot be a criminal.

Un. Dear Elodie! May thy heart justify me, and Heaven will pardon me. Love me, and I shall be saved.

Elod. [*Timidly*] Then be so.

Un. Is it then true?

Elod. Never has a falsehood sullied my thought nor my lips!

Un. What! You can deign?

Elod. Do you not love me?

Un. Think, my Elodie, that the unfortunate whose fate interests thee has no country, bears no title, is today without name, and has not even a pure heart to offer thee.

Elod. I never fled the unfortunate.

Un. In the meantime, if fortune and glory have for thee some charm, I can yet offer them to thee. Speak, dispose of all my future life.

Elod. I have always despised grandeurs.

Un. Thus, the cabin of the Solitary presents thee nothing terrific.

Elod. No.

Un. Thou swearest never to be anyone's but mine?

Elod. I swear—

Un. To become my bride—

Elod. Yes, if my uncle consents to it.

Un. Adored woman! What noise is this I hear? [*Enter Eloi, right hand, followed by villagers*]

Eloi. [*Before he is seen*] I am not mistaken. 'Tis she! Yes, 'tis our good miss. [*He throws himself at the feet of Elodie*] And 'tis still to the Solitary that we are indebted for her. Run to this side, all you perhaps will meet the Baron, and you'll tell him we've had the happiness of finding his beloved niece! I thank you, Mr. Invisible, in the name of all the country and above all for our excellent master. Won't he be happy to see his dear niece again? Everybody in the house thought she was lost. 'Twas a desolation general! Gazzooks, I was inspired when I took it into my head to come here!

Elod. Good Eloi!

Eloi. It strikes me, miss, you must be too much fatigued to return immediately to the priory. [*Low*] Stay with the wild man. I too, I'll go run after the Baron and send him to you. [*Turning towards the country people*] My comrades, are you mightily fatigued? Yes, a little, aren't you? Like me —but what of that? One hasn't every day such opportunities for showing one's <valor>, one's attachment to one's masters. When it offers, 'tis necessary to make the most of it. Let us get on the road again; let us beat all the little by-paths of the mountain and neighborhood, and perhaps we shall be lucky enough presently to rejoin our good master. [*To Elodie*] Till I see you again, our good miss—[*Conducted by Eloi, some country people direct their steps towards the left; others descend by the right; others at length clamber up the mountain and disappear by the little by-paths. At the moment when the country people are ready to disappear, a bustle is heard outside at the right*]

Elod. I do not deceive myself, it is my uncle's voice. [*All stop and look below. The Baron is heard without*]

Bar. Where is she? Where is she? [*All redescend. General movement. The Baron has climbed the mountain and appears*] Where is she?

Elod. In your arms, dear Uncle!

Bar. [*Pressing her to his heart*] My Elodie!

Un. [*Aside*] This hour will decide the fate of all my life. [*Lowers his visor*]

Bar. Well! What! Is it to you we are indebted for this new service? Without wishing to penetrate here the mystery which environs you and the honorable motive of so many wonderful deeds, which have brought down on you the benedictions of this valley, it <should be permitted>, without alarming your delicacy, to offer you the reward so far as my own family is concerned. Then acquaint me with the price you attach to it.

Un. A mighty one.

BAR. Whatever it may be, if it is in my power to give it to you, it will not be for nothing you have asked it.

UN. Speak, Elodie. [*To villagers*] Leave us, my friends. [*All descend right and left, expressing interest and curiosity*]

BAR. Since you know it, tell me what is the wish of the Solitary.

ELOD. That you should not be found adverse to my union.

BAR. With whom?

ELOD. With him whom all the land admires and dreads; of whom the existence is a problem, and of whom the power is a prodigy; whose name is on all lips, and whose benefactions in all recollections. With the man, in fine, of mystery and enchantments.

BAR. What do I hear? An unknown!

ELOD. He is brave, generous, long has loved me. I may not doubt it.

BAR. Without titles, without fortune—

ELOD. So far from this alliance being below me, it is perhaps the orphan of St. Maur who is herself unworthy of it.

BAR. What do I hear! Who told thee so?

ELOD. Himself.

BAR. You love him then?

ELOD. Would I consent to become his bride if I did not love him?

BAR. Alas! I know it too well. The prudent counsels of an old man and the cold words of reason can do nothing against the drawing away seduction of the heart. In the meantime, my daughter, wilt thou venture to yield thy fate to that mysterious being?

ELOD. He has unveiled to me his heart. I dread nothing in confiding to him my destiny. Before knowing him, I thought only about him. The marvellous recitals of the country had inflamed my imagination. In hearing each day recounted his traits of courage, his numberless benefactions, his heroic deeds, I represented him to my imagination at once as a protecting deity descended among men. Judge, my Uncle, when he disclosed himself to me, when I saw the noble expression of the features he hides from you, when his inconceivable courage has twice preserved my honor and my life; when, in fine, this superhuman being, falling at my feet, has made me hear the touching expressions of his love, judge if I could resist at once his heart and my own?

BAR. But, in short, who is he? Let him make himself known.

UN. [*Who, during the first part of this scene, has stood against a rock, his head propped on his hand, and in the attitude of profound meditation, advances between the Baron and Elodie, and then says in a solemn tone*] Baron de Herstall, in the name of honor, and you, dear Elodie, in the name of the tenderness you have deigned to accord to me, swear never to reveal the existence of a man who no longer desires to command among men, who has made a vow never to quit his retreat, and who only confides to you his name in presence of the Eternal.

BAR. and ELOD.   I swear! [*The Unknown lifts the visor of his helmet*]

BAR.   What do I see? The Duke of Burgundy!

ELOD.   The murderer of my father! [*She hides her face in her hands*]

UN.   Himself.

BAR.   Vile seducer! Infamous assassin! What! Thou breathest yet!

UN.   Yes, to suffer.

BAR.   What infernal power then has drawn thee from the tomb?

UN.   Since three years I have renounced human grandeurs. I have caused to circulate the report of my death, and I am exiled on this savage rock to punish myself and to appease Heaven. Baron de Herstall, pardon misfortune, repentance, or take this steel and revenge—

BAR.   I! To pardon the murderer of my brother! the assassin of my Irena! the executioner of all my family! Never!

ELOD. [*With a dying voice*]   Unfortunate me! I shall not survive it!

UN.   Inexorable man! Canst thou recognize the criminal of whom thou speakest in the unfortunate proscript who embraces thy knees?

BAR.   Retire, monster! Thou speakest of remorse, and thou meditatest new crimes! Dost thou not seek to seduce Elodie? How canst thou dare present her with thy hand yet disgusting with her father's blood? Barbarian! Between her and thee rises the tomb of Irena and the specter of St. Maur!

ELOD. [*More and more feeble*]   Already I feel a mortal coldness—

UN.   Spare me, spare Elodie herself—I implore thy pity. Hear—

BAR.   I hear the voice of thy victims. They cry to avenge us! Yes, yes, complaining names, I hear you. I will obey you. No pity for thee! May the maledictions of Heaven, joined with mine, follow thee to thy last hour. May the horrors of thy death equal the crimes of thy life; the world repel thee, the earth reject thee! Fly, bear far from this spot thy presence and thy remorse. 'Tis in the name of the Eternal that I pronounce the decree! A curse on the man of crime, on the murderer, the sacrilegious, the impious!

ELOD. [*Dying, turns towards Herstall and lifts towards him her supplicating hands*]   My father—

BAR. [*With a solemn and thundering voice*]   A curse, a curse—[*This terrible word is repeated by the echoes of the mountain; the wind hoarsely breathes; the bell of the Hermitage is agitated, and its dismal sound heard*] Behold my nuptial benediction!

ELOD.   Ah, I die! [*She falls*]

UN. [*Darts to the earth and strives to bring Elodie to herself*] Barbarian, 'tis thou who hast given her death! [*With a tone of wretchedness*] All succor is useless.

BAR. My Elodie!

UN. [*Distracted, and repelling the Baron with fury*] She is no longer thine, unpitying old man! If I was gone astray, I had at least love and ambition for my excuse; but thou, 'tis in cold blood thy hatred has plunged her into the coffin. Thou hast not chosen that living she should be my bride; now thou hast broken all the ties that united us, nothing now can separate me from her.

BAR. Thy bewildered rage—

UN. [*Completely distracted and drawing a poignard*] Approach not, or I add a crime more to all <that stain> my life. Come, my beloved! Come, my wife! Come! The tomb is about to unite us and close over us! [*Raises Elodie and holds her in his arms. To the Baron*] The rock in which I have dug it, this tomb <was less frozen than thy heart>. [*He bears Elodie to the summit of the mountain and places her on a stone at the entrance of his cabin. Herstall is rooted to earth*]

ELOI. [*Cries from afar and runs in with the villagers*] Behold the Count de Palzo!

UN. To dare to come hither. 'Tis Heaven that leads him. The traitor! His hour has struck.

ELOI. Baron, the mountain is surrounded by soldiers; but we'll all die before they shall get our good mistress.

UN. [*Who has redescended after having thrown his black mantle over the body of Elodie. His smile is frightful*] He is for my arm. [*To the Baron*] Away, old man. I would not touch thy life. Live to shed tears for my Elodie! Retire beneath these rocks. You there will be safe. [*The Baron, Eloi, and all the villagers enter a sort of cavern at the left. The Unknown remounts to the summit. The Count, Michieli, and soldiers scale all the sides at once. In an instant the mountain is covered with soldiers*]

COUNT. [*Before he appears*] Follow me, soldiers.

UN. 'Tis death thou callest on them as on thyself. Who permitted thee to violate this asylum?

COUNT. Love and vengeance. I came to seek for Elodie.

UN. Approach. I am going to restore her to thee and to avenge her. Behold—[*With one hand he lifts up the mantle and with the other, seizing the flambeaux, which he had placed behind a rock, he fires the mine. A terrible explosion takes place; the quarters of the rock, launched into the air, fall with a horrid crash. Palzo and Michieli are thrown down and crushed, as well as their suite. The Unknown is fallen dead by the side of his beloved. After the explosion the Baron and all those who were in the hollow come out. Herstall shows them the body of Elodie. All express their grief and their regrets*]

END

THE BOARDING SCHOOLS;
Or, LIFE AMONG THE LITTLE FOLKS

THE BOARDING SCHOOLS;
Or, LIFE AMONG THE LITTLE FOLKS

THE autograph manuscript of *The Boarding Schools; or, Life among the Little Folks* is in the Luquer collection.

The date of composition of this farce, which was probably never acted professionally, can only be conjectured. Its source, Maréchalle and Hubert's *Les Deux Pensions,* was performed for the first time at the Théâtre du Panorama Dramatique, April 16, 1822, and published the same year. Since Payne was generally in search of the current Paris hit, it seems likely that he made his adaptation soon after the appearance of the French comedy. (A. H. Quinn in *A History of the American Drama from the Beginning to the Civil War,* New York, 1923, p. 424, suggests that Payne may be the author of *The Boarding School* which according to G. C. D. Odell in *Annals of the New York Stage,* Vol. IV, p. 538, was performed at the Park, November 17, 1841; the names of the characters in the playbill, however, are not those of Payne's farce, but instead those of a play with this title by Bayle Bernard which opened in London at the Haymarket, September 1, 1841, and which is wholly unlike Payne's.)

Although Payne does not alter the series of pat coincidences with which the plot is developed, elsewhere he works with a good deal of freedom; for he changes the scene from Paris to London and portrays with English manners both the precocious children and the pompous grown-ups whom they outwit. The result is an enjoyable farce with a strongly topical flavor.

[CAST OF CHARACTERS

GUSTAVE

MR. PRETTYMAN, *Master of a boys' school*

JACKO, *Factotum of the Widow Wantmore*

CARTE-AND-TIERCE, *Fencing master*

PIROUETTE, *Dancing master*

SCHOOLBOYS

PAULINE

THE WIDOW WANTMORE, *Mistress of a girls' school*

PRUDENCE HORNBROOK, *Factotum of Mr. Prettyman*

CHARLOTTE

SCHOOLGIRLS

THE ACTION TAKES PLACE IN LONDON]

ACT I.

[SCENE:] *The stage, divided by a wall down the middle, through which there is a well half on one side and half on the other, represents at the right the garden of the boys' school, and at the left the garden of the girls' school. Each garden is backed by a wall with a rail gate opening on the country; over each of which gates there is a sign, on one side "Boarding School for Young Gentlemen," and on the other "Boarding School for Young Ladies." Near the well at the left stands a tree whose foliage rises over the wall. On each side, first wing, there is a bower. As the curtain rises, all the children are at play. The little girls are dancing, hands round, the little boys are playing.*

[JACK.] Now for my wife that expects to be, the lovely Prudence Hornbrook! Sweet Sunflower of my affections, that follows me with her broad face, whichever way I turn. These fine summer days have the same effect on men and women as they have on the birds. They make 'em think of coupling.

PRU. [*To the boys*] In short, young gentlemen, follow my example.

[JACK.] This is the hour mentioned in the letter she poked through that keyhole. The master's going out, then we can meet unknown, as true lovers ought, and coo in secret, as intended mates are in decency bound to do.

PRU. [*To the boys*] Go and take care to act openly and be above concealments.

JACK. Prudence has rare qualities. She has no notion of courting without something substantial along with it. She never listens to tender protestations but over a well covered table. Her stomach and her heart are in partnership. She loves good things and her love of me's a proof.

PRU. [*Seeing the boys eating something, snatches the cake and pockets it*] Beware, young gentlemen, of gormandizing. There's nothing so bad as giving way to one's appetite.

JACK. Accordingly, Miss Prudence Hornbrook and I feast on all possible occasions. This key she got made secretly. She most poetically terms it the key of her affections. By means of this conjuring little talisman, this first pledge of her love, when Mr. Prettyman goes out, I go in, and there we eat and sigh, sigh and eat, eat and sigh, and eat again! My Mistress Widow Wantmore's poor girls are all the better for it; for, as Prudence makes me supply the provisions (a heavy task), I'm obliged by so much to lighten the school larder; and that prevents the young gluttons from overloading their little stomachs and converts the irregularity of taking things without taking notice into a most important benefit to the rising generation. [*Enter Pauline jumping the rope*] Why, Miss Pauline, you do nothing all the play hours but dance. [*Apart*] She'll break her neck at last.

PAUL. That's for my health and by the doctor's orders.

JACK. Aye, aye. Thanks to the doctors of nowadays our little girls do what the little boys used to do in old times. They jump the rope like Madame Saqui, swim like fish, fence like Angelo, and ride a horseback like the folks at Astley's. Ah! If boys and girls go on so, 'twill be no very easy job to make out which is which.

PAUL. What would you have, sir? It's the education *à la mode.*

[JACK.] It may be *all à mode,* but it's not the mode of my time. The young folks of my time were brought up in another way.

[PAUL.] The young folks of your time are not the young folks of mine, sir.

[JACK.] So much the worse for both.

[PAUL.] Bless me, sir, have you never subscribed to Colburn's or Hookham's Circulating Libraries? Read the novels and they'll show you how necessary it is that a young lady should know all young gentlemen know. If a young lady knows how to ride, she can gallop from her persecutor; if she knows how to fence, she can defend her honor; and if she knows how to swim she can save her shipwrecked lover or perish with him. The story of Hero and Leander that we've been learning by heart would have been a thousand times more romantic if Hero had ever been taught to swim. I'd have you to know, sir, that there is nothing like the modern style of education to form young maids.

[JACK.] [*Aside*] To form maids—'twill rather put an end to the tribe and leave no maids to form.

GUS. [*To the boys*] Let's play Blind Man's Buff. [*Giving his handkerchief, and they tie it round his eyes*]

JACK. [*Aside*] But I'll go to dinner by way of staying my stomach till Miss Prue's treat. [*Striking his stomach*] There's room here for two meals. [*Aloud*] Young ladies, I wish you a good morning. [*Exit singing*] Dance away, my jolly dears, dance, dance, and be merry! [*The little girls begin to play*]

GUS. [*Seizing Prudence*] You're caught! You're caught!

PRU. [*Angrily*] What do you mean, sir! How dare you take such a liberty with me, sir! Mind what you're at—

Gus. [*Taking off the handkerchief*] Miss Prudence Hornbrook! [*To the others*] You rascals! Why did you let me go that way? [Why] didn't you call out, "Roast Beef"?

[Boys.] Ha! Ha! Ha! Roast Beef! Roast Beef! Miss Prudence must be blinded. Come, Miss Prudence!

<Gus.> Take off her spectacles. Then she'll be blind enough.

Pru. None of your impertinence, you little spoiled jackanapeses. Call me Roast Beef! Pray, sir, what do you mean by calling me Roast Beef! Take care how you treat me, sir, or I'll tell the Master and you shall be put to your tasks.

Gus. [*Aside*] I'd rather be at my tricks.

Pru. Can't you play quietly, and amuse yourselves without running after one another, and call out, without making a noise?

Gus. Impossible. That would be too dull for us to amuse ourselves <by>.

Pru. I'd have you know I—I—I'll be off instantly.

<Boys.> Ha! Ha! Ha! So much the better.

Pru. Yes, but before long you'll hear the study bell.

Gus. To tell no lies, I'd rather hear the dinner bell.

Pru. [*Aside, going*] I'll have my revenge. I'll go and put the clock a quarter of an hour forward and the little rascals shall hear the study bell when they little expect it. Roast Beef, indeed!

<Boys.> [*Conducting her*] Good-bye, good-bye, Miss Prudence.

Pru. Good-bye, little rogues. [*Exit*]

Gus. Well, I'm glad old Blowzybut's gone. Now, boys, what news do you think I've got to tell you?

<Boys.> What? What?

Gus. I went home, yesterday, to father; and I'll give you six months to guess what they're going to make of me.

1st <Boy.> 'Twould puzzle 'em to make much of you.

[Gus.] More than ever you'll make of yourself, I'll be bound. Guess.

1st <Boy.> A powder monkey.

Gus. Powder monkey!—Sir, a husband. [*All laugh*] Laugh if you like, but it's no joke.

1st <Boy.> Especially to your wife.

Gus. That's her affair. She may be of a different opinion. Now, I'll tell you how it happens. There's some bother between our family and another, and I'm to be married to settle it all comfortably. You shall all come to my wedding. You'll have time enough to get your new clothes made, and you shall all come. My wife belongs to the girls' school next door, and I must get to tell her the news. She'll be so pleased, she'll go wild with ecstasy; and she'll be right, boys, exceedingly right, for I'm a very good sort of a fellow, boys, that I am.

<1st Boy.> We've your own word for it, at any rate.

Gus. I've proofs: thanks to my father's presents to our master, hadn't I three medals at the last examination? But come, let's see how I shall contrive to get over the wall.

<1st Boy.> What! Into the girls' place—

Gus. Where else should my duty as a husband take me? Come, make a ladder for me. That's right. That's right. [*He prepares to scale the wall by mounting on the boys' shoulders. Enter Charlotte. All the little girls leave their play and run to her*]

Girls. Here's Charlotte. Here's Charlotte.

Char. Well, misses, and suppose it is Charlotte. Is it such a wonder to see Charlotte?

Girls. [*Getting round her*] Good morning, Charlotte, good morning! Oh, we're glad you're come, Charlotte, we're so glad you're come.

Char. Good morning, misses. [*Pushing them*] But, bless me, do keep off. Don't rumple me so, I shall look as if I came from the Lord knows where.

Paul. Well, Charley, tell us the news. Had you a merry day at home? Did you see Papa?

Char. Yes, I saw him. I was at your house with Mama. They talked of business, they said this and they said that. In short, I thought they'd never have done. They didn't mind me, for they look upon me as an infant even at my time of life; but I am sly and I didn't lose a word.

Paul. And what did you hear?

Char. All about your marriage!

Girls. Her marriage!

Paul. My marriage! Oh! Joy! Joy! And who's to be my husband?

Gus. [*On the wall*] I!

Paul. [*Astonished*] Gustave! [*He descends into the garden by the help of the trellis-work on the girls' side. The other boys begin their play again*]

Gus. I thought I should have something to teach you; but you're aforehand with me. It seems you know all—

Paul. Not the main point, though.

Gus. True; but now you *do* know it, an't you delighted?

Paul. Isn't it natural enough I should be?

Gus. Why, I think you're lucky. What a snug home we shall make of it!

Paul. We shall have nothing at all to do all day long, shall we?

Gus. Nothing to do? On the contrary, we shall have a great deal to do. We shall go to sights half the day; and to confectioners' shops to eat sugar plums and cakes and ice cream the other half. Then, when winter comes, of a morning, I shall sit by the grate in my white morning gown and red morocco slippers [*The girls who are playing in the background laugh*], with a dozen little monkeys round me, making at least as much racket as those young ladies. We shan't be able to hear our own voices, but that's nothing; it will be very charming, for they say there's nothing in the world to be compared with the pleasures of having a family.

PAUL.   And I shall have a nice satin gown and a beautiful head dress with great plumes of waving feathers; and you'll hear me call my servants— "Peter! Jack! Have my carriage ready at six o'clock." Because, you see, I mean to have a carriage. "I have a call to make before I go to the opera." But I shall only stop there long enough to see the audience and nod to the people of fashion in the boxes. At eight, I shall go to cards at the Baroness's; at nine, to the Marchioness's music party. I shall drive to the Ambassador's ball at one, then to the rout of the Bishop's Lady, which never breaks up till late on Sunday morning.

GUS.   Divine!

PAUL.   Delicious!

GUS.   Yes; but as this happiness is yet at some few years' distance, can't we contrive to meet often in the meantime?

PAUL.   As we are man and wife, there ought not to be any difficulty.

GUS.   There will be though, and a great deal.

PAUL.   That's very unjust—really, tyrannical.

GUS.   So it is. What should they be afraid of?

PAUL.   Not much, I should think.

GUS.   Mind me, now. There's a notion come into my head—it's rather wild—but [*in an imposing tone*] as a wife must obey her husband, I trust, madam, you will not throw any obstacles in the way of my wishes.

PAUL.   [*In the same tone*]   If they agree with mine, sir, you may count on my obedience.

GUS.   That's the way in all well regulated families. But mind what's to be done first. You must get me one of your gowns; I'll give you a suit of my clothes, and thus by changing about, we can manage to meet sometimes on your side, sometimes on mine, and always in spite of the master and ma'am.

PAUL.   Good; but how shall I get your clothes?

GUS.   As I shall yours, over the wall. In half an hour, let a little song be the signal, and I shall be on the spot.

PAUL.   And I too. Ah, Gustave, how pleasant our playtimes will be! [*They hear on each side the study bell. The boys and girls go off slowly giving signs of ill humor*]

Gus. This begins well; however, we must go in.

Paul. Make off quick.

Gus. But tell me first—

Paul. Adieu, adieu; don't forget the signal. [*She runs out*]

Gus. Come, she's off! I must make haste to do as much. Dear me! Dear me! How disagreeable this is! I think I like this side better than the other. [*He climbs the wall to return*] Heydey! The boys are gone—there's no getting down without breaking my neck. [*He remains astride the wall*] Here I am mounted, but my horse doesn't get me a bit forwarder—and, to crown all, here comes our master! I'm caught; and my next ride will be upon the stool of repentance. [*By means of the trellis-work he recedes on the side of the girls' school, not to be discovered by <Mr. Prettyman>. Enter <Mr. Prettyman> with a ladder and a basket of cherries. Gustave observing him*]

<Pret.> [*Thinking himself alone*] I was just in time with the cherries; had they been left any longer, there'd no longer have been any left.

Gus. [*Apart*] Master Prettyman's in the right. If it hadn't been holiday yesterday, and we all out, I'm afraid the cherry trees would have looked foolish this morning.

<Pret.> I can at least offer some to my charming neighbor, <Widow Wantmore>.

Gus. [*Aside*] Dear me! Dear me! If he should take it into his head to come this road with his offerings.

<Pret.> They are the emblem of the rosy lips and cheeks of the loveliest of widows. To her they go—the fruits of spring are the fit offerings of love. My heart pants for the happy moment of wedlock when our two establishments may be one.

Gus. [*Apart*] An excellent idea. Then my legs and arms will be safe, and I can see my wife without danger to my neck.

<Pret.> I trust at our appointed meeting presently behind Primrose Hill we shall be able to make both ends meet.

Gus. [*Apart*] Hallo! Another rendezvous. This is a day of business and there can't be any harm in taking after our teachers.

<Pret.> With this ladder, which I kept out of its place on purpose, let's see, if by chance, she may be in the garden.

Gus. [*Apart*] I don't wish the man any harm, but if he could only be taken blind now.

<Pret.> Now to mount and see if she be there.

Gus. [*Apart*] Bless us! If he isn't coming! I've half a mind to throw this handful of dust in his eyes.

<Pret.> Stay. First let me make sure there's no one looking.

Gus. [*Apart*] Oh, you needn't look for trouble.

<Pret.> Should I be seen, I don't know how I should get out of the scrape. [*Places his ladder and his basket near the wall and regards on all sides*]

Gus. [*Seeing the ladder*] Nor I. [*He descends by the ladder, while Mr. Prettyman looks out to see if anybody is coming—takes some cherries from the basket and escapes, exclaiming*] It's a bad rule that won't work both ways. Thank you, sir, very much obliged to you! Beelzebub is the schoolboy's friend. Victory! [*Exit*]

<Pret.> [*Alone*] Now there's nothing to be feared. I am alone and may sigh freely. He must be clever that can catch me tripping, for what I want in steadiness I make up in caution. If you'd planned a century, you couldn't have done it more effectually. [*He goes up the ladder softly to see if <Widow Wantmore> is in the garden, as Pauline enters on the other side with a little parcel*]

Paul. 'Tis time Gustave was at his post. Oh! How he frightened me! It's Mr. Prettyman's ugly moon face peeping over the wall. [*She hides in the little bower*] Is he too coming after clothes to turn himself into a girl? [*Enter <Widow Wantmore>*]

<Wid. W.> [*Thinking herself alone*] 'Tis near my dearest Prettyman's appointed hour. How my poor heart palpitates!

Paul. [*In the bower*] I see young fools are not the only fools. I hope she won't come here to cool herself in this bower; I don't want much to be caught by Mrs. Wantmore.

<Wid. W.> No obstacle, I think, can now prevent our marriage. I wish it may take place before the week is over. [*Mr. <Prettyman> listens and expresses his joy*]

Paul. <Widow Wantmore> is in a hurry.

<Wid. W.> Widowhood makes one sad and pouting.

Paul. She expects a husband will make her merry.

<Wid. W.> I think now I may go and fear nothing—all the girls are at their studies—

Paul. Present company always excepted—

<Wid. W.> Making the most of their time in youth—

Paul. While you make the most of yours in age.

<Wid. W.>I hasten to renew the memory of former bliss. But let me beware of being seen, lest somebody should suspect that there may be something at the bottom.

<Pret.> [*Leaning over*] Somebody don't suspect there's something at the top—

<Wid. W.> [*Surprised*] Bless me! How you disturbed my tender nerves. They have been so long in repose that these sudden jerks quite overpower them.

<Pret.> Joy of my heart! I have brought this basket of cherries, ripe as my affection and blooming as my hopes, as a tender pledge—[<*Apart, looking at the basket as she takes it*>] Hey! What! Why they're half gone—the birds have been to the feast without an invitation.

<Wid. W.> Oh, most accomplished of true lovers! None other can hope to reach the elevation to which you dare aspire. When you have mounted, the ladder must be drawn away.

<Pret.> [*Grasping the wall*] Lord bless me! I hope not, I—Stupid head that I have! Pray, forgive me. My nervousness had got the start of my imagination and I took your compliment too literally. Tell me, lovely top of the class of my affections, are you ready? Shall we adjourn instantly to Primrose Hill?

<Wid. W.> I am yours at discretion; and when I have given some few trifling orders, we meet to roam in Love's Elysium, beyond the Regent's Park.

<Pret.> Then swift I haste to hide the ladder—

<Wid. W.> Aye, avoid exciting suspicions. People are so censorious! There is no harm in these dovelike meetings, but there's great harm in their being known. We must be secret, love. The morals of the rising generation 'tis for us to keep.

<Pret.> Adieu, most lovely of the boarding school mistresses of the barrier of the virtues.

<Wid. W.> Fie! Fie! Funny man! You make me blush and feel so odd—

<Pret.> Loveliest of the New Road schoolmistresses, adieu! Adieu! Adieu!

<Wid. W.> Most amiable of the teachers of Middlesex! Farewell! But for one moment, farewell! Farewell! Farewell! [*Prettyman goes off with his ladder and Widow Wantmore with her basket of cherries*]

Paul. [*Alone*] They're gone at last! And the cherries too, unluckily; for, next to Gustave, they're what I like best. Now for the signal agreed on. Let's see. What shall I give to him? Yes, my song of the "Tomtit and the Owl." That exactly suits. The ugly owl is Mr. Prettyman; and the nice little tomtit is I. [*Sings*]

> Waiting her lover a tomtit sighed,
> When all of a sudden an owl she spy'd

And fluttered and hid in dismay.

Till the owl flew off; and she sang, "Don't fear,

For now, little tomtit, the coast is clear,

And that fright of an owl's gone away." [*Enter Gustave from the other side with two of his schoolfellows*]

GUS. [*To the boys, who seem afraid to approach*] Don't be afraid.

PAUL. [*After having listened*] I don't hear him. Oh! He's unfaithful. I'll go away this minute.

GUS. [*To the schoolfellows*] Nonsense! Should they catch us, we shall only get a few lashes.

PAUL. [*Continuing*] 'Twould be only what such conduct deserves. To forget his appointment! That's encouraging at any rate. I suppose that's a way with husbands, for Mama's always finding fault with Papa's falling short in his duty.

GUS. [*To the schoolfellows*] Hush! Hush! I hear her! I'm sure 'tis her voice!

PAUL. I'll try again and see if he'll answer. [[*Sings*]]

The tomtit listens, but hears no reply;

And though at the slight she could almost cry,

No reproaches her pangs betray;

And she only sings—"Why linger from me,

Since now, little tomtit, the coast is free,

And that fright of an owl's gone away?"

GUS. Pauline, here's your faithful tomtit; and he would sing too, dear wife, and tell his love in music, if he only knew how.

PAUL. Have you got my bundle? Here's yours.

GUS. [*Throwing the parcel over the wall*] Here's the breeches. Don them and wear them.

PAUL. [*The same*] Here's the petticoats. Catch!

GUS. You'll be astonished to find how I'll manage 'em.

PAUL. [*Aside*] These clothes will give me courage, and I shall be in the midst of the boys before he thinks. [*Singing heard behind the scenes*] Hush! There's somebody coming. [*Looks out*] I'll go and dress in the bower. [*She enters the bower*]

GUS. Now for my gown. I'll rig it on; and 'twill make me twice as full of tricks as ever.

<BOY.> That's a bold word.

GUS. And then my little coz will soon see what I can do. You shall be my lady's maid, if you're sly enough. [*He opens the parcel that Pauline threw over. Enter <Jacko>, in the girls' garden, with a great basket*]

JACK. Now the Widow Wantmore is gone, is my time to seek my lassie. I've got something here that will do her business.

GUS. [*Finding a little parcel in his robe*] Ha! Ha! Ha! A quarter of a pound of pins.

JACK. A dainty treat as ever a wench got.

GUS. [*To his comrades*] That's what one may call showing forethought.

JACK. I have lined my basket in great style. The weight shows that I can do things as they should be done.

GUS. [*To his comrades*] Come! Don't prick your mistress. Settle the scarf. There! Don't I look well? Now really one would scarcely find a pin's difference between me and Pauline—

JACK. [*Feeling his pockets*] What in the name of nonsense have I done with the key? 'Tisn't in this pocket; nor in this. Can I have lost it? Stay—I must run and see—I hope I haven't lost it. There's no getting in without the key. [*Goes out*]

GUS. [*Eying the way*] What a shame the boys shouldn't be all here to make a ladder for me again! Even on your shoulders, I shouldn't be tall enough to reach the top.

PAUL. [*Who, dressing in the bower, has heard Jacko*] So! So! Set a rogue to catch a rogue. I've found out two plots by means of mine; and in return for what you've stolen from the girls to treat old Prudence Hornbook with, you shall have a treat you don't expect. I'll teach you to filch from the girls' larder. Now I'm a boy, I'll play the devil. Let me look, first.

GUS. [*To his two schoolfellows*] Boys, I've got something in my head!

<Boy.> Is it possible!

[Gus.] This well you see goes through the wall. I'll get into the bucket, you'll let me down, and I'll get up in the other bucket. There's no other way of getting to my wife; but, mind you, no tricks. [*The boys let him down*]

PAUL. [*After a moment's thought*] The dress begins to produce its effect, and I'll save Miss <Prudence> an indigestion, by tossing all the things in this basket into the well. Gustave, I'm sure, couldn't do better himself. [*She empties Jacko's pannier into the well, while Gustave is in it*] Here comes Jacko—now to hide. [*Returns into the bower. Enter Jacko with the key*]

JACK. I was afraid 'twas lost. [*Trying to put it in*] It put me in such a tremble. Bless me, how odd! I can't do it. I—

PAUL. [*While he opens the gate*] I said I'd have a coach when I got my husband and now for my first ride. [*She gets into the basket. Jacko carries her into the boys' side. He is no sooner out, <than> Gustave comes out of the wall on the girls' side. The schoolfellows of Gustave are concealed behind the little gate when Jacko enters, and save themselves unperceived*]

JACK. [*On the boys' side*] It seems heavier than when I brought it—'troth, there's a good supply though. There's enough even in this little basket to amuse the whole school.

GUS. [*In the girls' school*] Dear me! Dear me! Which of the fair damsels was it that gave me this treat? Where's my wife? Really, there's a bunch coming on my forehead already. Bottles, cakes, pies! Though I got the touch, I couldn't get the taste, there's the mischief.

JACK. Here I am to wait for my beauty—

GUS. I got it over the head—

JACK. It's a long time since that happened to me for the first time.

GUS. The worst of all is that it went by my nose without my being able to catch it on the way.

JACK. I thought I heard somebody speak. Faith, 'tis a little girl escaped from study. Attention, friend Jacko, attention. [*He steals into the girls' side and shuts the little gate*] I was not deceived.

GUS. [*Thinking himself alone*] I'm lonesome here—*je m'ennuis*. Let's hunt for Pauline.

JACK. [*Taking Gustave for a little girl*] What is it you're doing there, miss?

GUS. [*Apart*] Aye, aye. It is not he I expected. [*Aloud and counterfeiting her voice*] I—am—doing—nothing.

JACK. That's the very thing I'm finding fault with. Can't you embroider, scallop, knit?

GUS. It would be fine fun to see me knitting.

JACK. It's play that has made you quit your work. Fie, miss, play! That it is that's so pernicious for young folks. Miss, remember, there's nothing so bad as play. [*Draws out his pocket handkerchief. A pack of cards drops out of his pocket*]

GUS. [*Laughing*] So it seems. Ha! Ha! Ha!

JACK. [*Embarrassed*] Well, what of that? If I do carry cards in my pocket, it's only because I want to keep them out of the way of such wild young things as you; not for my own use, I assure you, not for my own use.

GUS. [*Aside*] No, for the amusement of Miss Prudence Hornbook.

JACK. [<*Coughing*>] That if I had the same in my pocket, 'twasn't to play, but only to draw the cards [*Apart*] with Miss <Prudence>. [*Aloud*] Help me, pray, gather them up. [*They gather them, and when Jacko has them all, Gustave strikes them up out of his hands*]

PAUL. [*Coming out of the basket*] I think I may venture. [*Looks all around her*] Yes. Gustave! Gustave! Not here! Where shall I go then?

Where is he likely to be? I have it—in the orchard! I dare say he's in the orchard—[*She is going.* <*Prudence*> *meets and stops her.* <*Prudence*> *has a basket containing everything necessary for laying a table for two*]

<Pru.>   Aha! In the orchard indeed! So, sir, you're for going to rob the orchard, are you?

Paul. [*Aside*]   Unlucky. Hang it!

<Pru.>   Little rascal. 'Tis for that you quit study. This it is to have confidence in these young gentlemen.

Paul. [*Apart*]   Ah! If I was a girl.

<Pru.>   You'd better go and mind your Latin—

Paul.   That would be all Greek to me.

<Pru.>   Instead of quitting your studies to hunt after green fruit.

Paul.   If I like green fruit, what's that to you?

<Pru.>   What a shocking thing it is to love gormandizing. Imitate me. I think of nothing but my work—and my hands are always full of work. [*She draws her work from her sack. Biscuits drop out of it*]

Paul.   Ha! Ha! And your pockets of cake!

<Pru.>   Come, none of your rigs upon me, young gentleman. Here comes somebody that will cure your laughing. Here's the fencing master, Mr. Carte-and-Tierce.

Jack. [*To Gustave*]   So, so, you're for staying with your hands before you? Luckily, here's somebody that will prevent your legs from following so bad an example. Here comes Mr. Pirouette, the dancing master.

Gus.   So, now they're for making me dance? Luckily all the masters that come here are paid villainously and dance as badly as they are paid. So, now for it. They say one false step leads to another; and I'm in a fair way to prove it true. [*Enter* <*Pirouette*>. *In coming he salutes Gustave, whom he takes for a young girl and puts him in position for his lesson of dancing*]

<Pru.> [*To the fencing master*]   Mr. Carte-and-Tierce, pray, dispatch this lesson as quick as you can; you'll oblige me very much, and if you can give two thrusts at a time, you'll get through the faster.

Jack. [*To the master*]   I've a very particular affair to attend to, and if you could only contrive, make her dance double—

<Pru.> [*To Pauline, who doesn't wish to take her lesson*]   Mind your duty, I tell you, sir. On guard!

Jack. [*To Gustave*]   Come, miss, take your position. [*Gustave and* <*Pir-ouette*> *dance on one side, while Pauline and* <*Carte-and-Tierce*> *fence on the other. The fencing and the pas de deux are arranged on the air—*]

<Jack and Pru.> [[*Sing*]]

            No wry faces;
            Take your places.
            On guard! So!
            Point your toe!
            Come now! Show
            All your graces.

<Jack.> [[*Sings*]] To caper in tune take care!

<Pru.> [[*Sings*]] Of his long sword thrust beware!

<Jack.> [[*Sings*]] That's very well! She takes it with docility!

<Pru.> [[*Sings*]] That's very well! He does it with facility!

        [*To Pauline*] It is good, from the age most tender,
            To learn to defend
            One's honor, one's honor;
            'Tis I who announce it to you:
            Yes, honor; yes, honor!

<Jack.> [*Regarding Gustave dancing*] That one don't weigh an ounce.

<Pru.> [*Continuing* [*her song*]] To happiness ought to conduct you.

<Jack and Pru.> This lesson ought to suffice.

<Jack.> [*To the dancing master*] 'Tis enough; finish; twirl away; and part.

<Pru.> [[*Simultaneously; to the fencing master*]] 'Tis enough; finish; *pirouter*; and part. [*The masters go out each on his own side, and the children return to their classes*]

Jack. [*Opening the little gate*] Is the gentle Prudence Hornbook visible?

<Pru.> Always, to the eyes of love.

Jack. In this case, you are so for me. [*He enters*] You may see, by the basket there, that I've been here before.

<Pru.> Yes, Mr. Jacko.

Jack. Then, my dearest Prudence, it will be prudent for us to make the most of our time. This basket is my representative—

<Pru.> Ha! Ha! Ha! You're very facetious—because?—because?—

Jack. I see you take—aye, my baskets contain a proof of that—guess—go on. He! He! Guess now—

<Pru.> Because—it's—full of good things.

[Jack.] Ha! Ha! Ha! Your compliment quite over powers me. Let's set to work, my dear. We'll fill our bellies, while we're emptying our hearts: that's what they call killing two birds with one stone.

[Pru.] But an't you afraid?

[JACK.] Pshaw! The larder is well lined; and they'll never see what I've taken.

[PRU.] So I should fancy. [*They both arrange the cover while Pauline comes on*]

PAUL. [*Aside*] I'm sure that this is very tiresome. One would almost think 'twas done apurpose. I can't find Gustave, and I don't know how to get back into my school. [*Seeing the little door standing open*] This little gate is open! By what wonder! What do I see—Jacko and <Prudence>—

JACK. Oh! Miss Hornbook, my love begins to grow impatient. [*Trying to kiss her*]

[PRU.] You men are always so violent.

[JACK.] That's too much! Prudence!

PAUL. [*Apart*] Let's leave them and let us in—Their meeting will always have been good for me for something. [*She passes from the other side. Gustave at this moment arrives and stops <her>*]

GUS. [*To Pauline*] Wife! Dearest wife! Do I hold thee in my arms! [*Kisses her*]

<PRU.> [*To Jacko*] You must not—shall not take what Prudence forbids—[*Jacko kisses her*]

GUS. Hallo! There's an echo in these parts. [*Pauline makes a sign for him to be silent and shows him the gardener and the housekeeper*] Jacko and <Prudence>! Ha! Ha! I'll spoil your sport.

JACK. [*To <Prudence>*] Now, I can eat twice as much. [*He goes for his basket*]

PAUL. [*Low*] Stay. I've a notion how we can tease 'em. If they catch us, we shall never hear the last of it. We must be beforehand and turn the tables on 'em. Do you keep the reticule of Prudence, while I take possession of the hat of Jacko. Very well. That done, do you go and bring out all the girls while I fetch the boys.

GUS. But what to do? Hey?

PAUL. You shall see, when the time comes. Now, you two that are always telling tales to bring us poor scholars into scrapes, look to yourselves and get out of your own scrape as you can. [*Gustave enters on the side of the boys and Pauline on the girls*]

<PRU.> [*At table*] The table's ready, now, for the provisions.

JACK. And the provisions for the table. Now—[*Lifting the basket*] Powers of mischief! Has the devil been here? [*Apart*]

<PRU.> What ails you? Come, hand out the eatables. What have you got?

<JACK.> Nothing. There's the mischief.

<Pru.> Nothing, what does that mean?

<Jack.> I wish it meant nothing; but unluckily 'tis too true. And, really, ma'am, as the basket was so long here, when I was not here, and so full when it came here, it appears exceedingly odd that it should be as empty as I find it here. Very odd indeed!

<Pru.> Come, come, sir. I don't understand such sidelong insinuations. Pray, sir, dare you fancy that I ever dreamt of going near your trumpery basket.

<Jack.> Trumpery, indeed! Somebody more favored has no doubt been regaled with what you call my trumpery, which is ten times better than all your trumpery professions of love; and I'd have you to know, ma'am, once for all ma'am—I am in such a rage!

<Pru.> I am in such a fury! [A noise heard outside]

Jack. Bless my heart, what's that?

<Pru.> 'Tis Mr. Prettyman!

Jack. 'Tis Mrs. Wantmore!

[Pru.] Hide the basket.

[Jack.] Clear the table.

<Pru.> And clear your brow. Look as if nothing had happened, for the sake of appearances. [During the quarrel of Jacko and <Prudence>, Pauline and Gustave come in, one at the head of the girls and the other the boys. Having heard the noise, they both run off, the little boys in the girls' school, and the little girls in the boys' school. Jacko has shut the little door, and <Prudence> set to work, so that <Prettyman> and <Widow Wantmore>, in returning, <find> all in the most perfect tranquillity]

<Pret.> Miss Hornbook, has everything gone as it should do since I went out?

<Pru.> Yes, sir, everything [Aside] excepting my treat. [Aloud] Your pupils have studied as they generally do; I haven't let them a minute out of sight.

<Wid. W.> Well, Jacko, have my girls behaved well?

<Jack.> Aye, ma'am, they've been as well behaved as girls can be; I've never taken eyes off 'em.

<Wid. W.> Then they shall have half an hour's more recreation than usual. Call them. [Exit Jacko]

<Pret.> I must give the young gentlemen a proof of my satisfaction. Call 'em. [Exit <Prudence>. He knocks at the little gate] Neighbor!

<Wid. W.> Neighbor!

<Pret.> Thanks to Heaven, we are got back without anybody suspecting the least thing.

<Wid. W.>   All's gone on gloriously in my absence.

<Pret.>   My boys are coming. Silence!

<Wid. W.>   Hush! Here are my girls. [*During this scene, the children appear on the two sides and range in one line*]

<Pret.>   [*Turning*]   What do I see!

<Wid. W.>   [*The same*]   What does this mean!

<Pret.>   My boys are all little girls.

<Wid. W.>   My girls are all boys.

Jack. [*Astonished*]   Why, ma'am—I—

Paul. [*Low to Jacko*]   Silence, or I show your hat which I took while you were with Prudence Hornbook.

<Pru.>   [*Arriving*]   Oh, Heavens! What can have transformed—

Gus. [*Low to <Prudence>*]   Don't say a word, or I'll show your reticule which I took while you were making love to <Jacko>.

<Wid. W.>   And pray, sir, is this your discretion?

<Pret.>   Pray madam, is this your prudence?

Paul. [*Low to Jacko*]   Mention Mr. Prettyman's cherries to her—she'll be as gentle as a lamb.

Gus. [*Low to <Prudence>*]   Mention behind Primrose Hill. She and you'll get off in triumph.

Jack. [*To <Widow Wantmore>*]   I are guilty, 'tis true, but when I saw that basket of cherries that—

<Wid. W.>   [*Rapidly*]   Hush, and I'll increase your salary.

<Pru.>   [*To <Mr. Prettyman>*]   I know, sir, that I am greatly to blame, but, inspired by the example set behind Primrose Hill—

<Pret.>   [*Rapidly*]   Silence, and I'll double your wages. [*At the little gate*] Neighbor!

<Wid. W.>   Neighbor!

<Pret.>   There's been some mistake in the schools during our absence. The schools have been changed, and they must be changed back again. Aye! Very well! And now, young ladies and gentlemen, remember there's to be no scandal talked about Mr. Prettyman and Mrs. Wantmore, for they are about to be married, and you shall all come to the wedding. [*Jacko opens the little door. The girls go in on one side, and the boys on the other, to the tune of "Lou, lou, la, laissez les frapper"*]

Gus.   Faith, boarding schools forever, but if I had daughters, they should never go to them. [*Apart*] In the meantime, I will go see my wife when I like.

Jack. [*To Pauline*]   Little slyboots, you have got out of the scrape nicely, after all.

PAUL.   What would you have, my poor Jacko? Abuses slide into all things. But it must be allowed, if in our boarding schools nothing is learnt, at least we amuse ourselves, nicely. [*Apart*] I shall see Gustave as often as I like.

<PRU.>   When I think of their tricks, I cannot help doing justice to the progress which young folks make.

[PAUL.]   What a pleasant thing it would be if all our friends should take it into their heads to benefit by the advantage and come to our boarding schools.

[GUS.]   That might be too much to ask. One thing, however, we *may* venture to beg: that such as do come, may be indulgent and treat us as their children.

<ALL TOGETHER> [[*Sing*]]
>   Youth
>   Has too much address by half
>   And I confess
>   That in these times
>   One may say "There are no children."

PAUL. [[*Sings*]]   More than one master, in this abode,
>   Makes to himself each day a duty
>   To teach us, in less than an hour,
>   What it takes a year to know.
>   Nowadays a girl, I boast of it,
>   At ten years has the instruction
>   Which she had not formerly till thirty
>   And owes it to her boarding school.

[ALL TOGETHER [*Sing*]]   Youth, etc.

PAUL. [[*Sings*]]   If the public, our great masters,
>   Should abstain from certain flattering sounds
>   Our boarding schools might be perhaps
>   A school for our authors:
>   But what fortunate chance
>   If, charmed by our union,
>   It should desire all the year
>   To come to our boarding school.

PAUL [and] GUS. [[*Sing*]]
>   If youth
>   Has some address,
>   Do you, gentlemen, be indulgent.
>   Treat us as your children.

THE TWO SONS-IN-LAW

THE TWO SONS-IN-LAW

THE autograph manuscript of *The Two Sons-in-Law,* dated London, March 26, 1824, is in the Harvard collection.

How long Payne had been working on his unacted comedy *The Two Sons-in-Law* it is impossible to decide. Its source, Étienne's *Les Deux Gendres,* had long been available to him, as it had been performed first on August 11, 1810, at the Théâtre-Français, and published the same year. Étienne's comedy had become famous partly through the publicity gained during the controversy over its originality and partly through its literary merit. Although it is true that the central situation, which is much like the Lear theme, is an old one, yet as Étienne rightly informs his critics, he modernizes it. Interest in the much discussed play was so great that only a few nights after the opening, Napoleon ordered it to be performed before the court at St. Cloud; and gradually it became a repertory piece. The virtue of the play is the realistic treatment of setting and character, as the action takes place in the Paris of Étienne's day and develops with a convincing struggle between the ambitious sons-in-law and the disillusioned old man. The illusion of reality, however, in a domestic play seems somewhat limited by the use of the rhymed alexandrines.

Although Payne shows originality in the substitution of prose for verse, otherwise he follows the French closely and does not Anglicize setting and character. If he had done so he might have been able to arouse the interest of the Londoner of his day as Étienne did that of the contemporary Parisian.

CHARACTERS

Dupré, *a retired merchant*

Dervière, *a rich capitalist, Dupré's son-in-law*

Dalainville, *a man in office, Dupré's son-in-law*

Frémont, *an old ship broker, former partner of Dupré*

Charles, *godson of Dupré*

Comtois, *servant of Dupré*

Lafleur, *valet de chambre of Dalainville*

Champagne, *servant of Dervière*

Mme. Dalainville, *daughter of Dupré*

Amélie, *daughter of Dervière and granddaughter of Dupré*

THE ACTION TAKES PLACE IN PARIS DURING THE YEAR 1824

ACT I.

Scene: *Dalainville's* <*drawing-room. Enter Dupré, followed by Comtois.*>

Dup. Well, what is this mighty affair you were going to tell me about? Out with it.

Com. A moment's patience, master, and don't be angry with me.

Dup. Why should I be angry with you, hey?

Com. Let me ask you one question. Pray, sir, since I have been in your service, have you ever had any cause of complaint against me?

Dup. Complaint? No, not I. I always found you one of the most circumspect and faithful of servants and always spoke of you as such.

Com. I thank you, master, from my soul. Still, sir, much as I value you and your service, I must beg you would favor me by looking out for somebody to fill my place.

Dup. To fill your place?

Com. Yes, master, and that without delay.

Dup. And what has put that into your head, hey?

Com. My attachment to you, sir.

Dup. You take an odd way of showing it.

Com. Certainly, sir, you never gave me an opportunity to be dissatisfied. There is not a <more pleasant service anywhere> and it would have <been> my pride <to have remained with you and> to have ended my days beneath your roof with yourself at home under it; but, unluckily for both of us, sir, that is no longer the case; and out of the house I must go. I can't stand what I am obliged to see. Ah, sir, how unlike you are those two sons-in-law of yours, since they are become the possessors of your fortune! Try as I may, do the best I can to satisfy them, everything is done wrong, I'm lazy and ungain<ly>! If there's a blunder made, it's put upon my shoulders! The weakest party is always sure to be the oppressed one. I was the best fellow in the world while you had your wealth in your own hands; but now that you have nothing, I am good for nothing. The agreeable additions of "Blockhead! Knave! Blackguard!" are the most punctually paid of all my wages! In short, I am the scapegoat of the establishment. I have nobody to speak a kind word for me but you, master, and remonstrate as you may, who is respected when he is no longer feared? You have given them your lands, tenements, furniture, your house, everything except your virtues.

DUP. Come, come, I won't allow these <exaggerations.>

COM. Sir, things are come to such a <pass.> Treat the truth as you will, <sir, I will speak> loudly, too. It is by vile arts and pretended endearments alone that they have wheedled you out of everything. Attachment indeed! They love you as bears love the traveller. Embrace you to devour! Look at 'em: how civil, mild, and submissive they once were; and now what is their conduct towards you? First for the one we have just been staying with—that canting—

DUP. Dervière?

COM. Yes, sir, the greatest miser, to begin with—

DUP. You calumniate him, Comtois. Your prejudices prevent your seeing his good qualities. He's the greatest philanthropist of the day. There's not a charitable committee of which he is not a member; and scarcely a hospital over which he has not some direction. He's president of the Foundling and one of the managers of the Magdalen; and not a day passes but some <praise from his> admirable pen appears in <support of a charity> without showing his name at the head <of the news> paper subscription.

COM. True; but if he were obliged <to give anything> to the subscriptions but his name, I doubt <if you'd> ever see it there. Admirable friend to the necessitous! He lends his pen to their present miseries, but keeps his money for their future.

DUP. All the papers of this very day are filled with praises of his magnificence!

COM. These are the only proofs of it he ever pays for! He has invented cheap powders to supply the place of meat and drink, and, under the persuasion that charity begins at home, carries his philanthropic zeal so far as to make the first trial upon his own servants.

DUP. Hey?

COM. Would you believe it, sir? I was selected to begin the experiment. To show his benevolence, he half killed me, sir. If starvation be the consequence of your son-in-law's refinement, give me old fashioned brutality: let me live!

DUP. Well, well, if he is a little harsh at times, his daughter's kind-heartedness atones for her father's eccentricity.

COM. There, indeed, you have me, sir. The sweet, amiable young lady is another of the blessings he enjoys without deserving.

DUP. My darling, my beloved grandchild! Oh, it brings the tears into my eyes whenever I look upon her. Every turn, look, and accent so reminds me of her poor mother!

COM. Yet you see she is not allowed the slightest sway in the house.

Dup. She is too young, Comtois, too young.

Com. No, no. It is not her youth they fear; it is her good heart.

Dup. Have a little patience. You'll be more comfortable presently; according to my agreement you know I am to take turns with my sons-in-law, living first six months with one, then six months with the other. Today, you know <we changed our> abode. Dalainville's turn is <now come and our> business here is to give him <notice of it.>

Com. Ah, sir, we only jump out of the frying pan into the fire. This change of dwelling will be but a change of miseries. I can bear a master's superciliousness because fortune will turn men's heads and is some palliation for impertinence; but the airs and condescension of the lackeys is more than I can put up with. Because I have not their sumptuous livery, the whole troop are knit together in conspiracy against me. They won't let me eat at their table; and as they like carousing as much as they dislike labor, while they are enjoying themselves with a good fire and good wine, I get nothing but their work to do. I'm the last in bed and the first up; and when there's a party given, they post me in the street to look after the gentlemen's carriages. I'm obliged to obey the most disobedient of them. I'm the servant of all the servants. If it is hard to have such fellows for valets, it's ten times harder to have such servants for masters. In short, sir, I'm <so badly fed, badly> lodged, badly paid, and badly <clothed that> the only perquisite I receive is blows!

Dup. Why don't you complain to my daughter?

Com. I, sir! When you, so kind and doting a father complain to her to so little purpose! She's turned topsy-turvy with the world's turn. Show and dress have taken such possession of her heart that poor nature has been elbowed into a corner where she keeps close, like a debtor for six days, and is rapidly growing into such habits of seclusion, that presently she'll forget to show her face even on a seventh. Your daughter loves you, no doubt, but she loves the world too, and that's a dangerous rival. When you are announced, she's always either practising a step, or rehearsing some song to show off in at a party; for the fashion of the times is to teach children every<thing except respect> for their parents. She never <came> on your birthday; and <I do not know> whether it was illness preven<ted her from> singing "There's No Place like <Home," or a> splendid party in the neighborhood, a matter, of course, too important to suffer her to remember either her own home or the father to whom she was indebted for it. Oh, sir. I can't stand it, and I will go.

Dup. As you please, Comtois. I can't keep you against your will. I am not surprised that all should forsake me. Misfortune, like a pestilence, levels all attachments; and they who dare not let want of feeling appear as a pretext for deserting the sufferer vindicate themselves by the pretended dread of catching and spreading his disease.

Com. Never will I be one of that ungrateful <kind. They have for-sa>ken me to myself. I perceive <my own selfishness> and on my knees implore you to <believe my> intention and to let me <stay until> changed fortune show how <much I appreciate all> of the bounties you lavished on me <through> fifteen years of your splendor and prosperity. Yes, master, let them starve me or beat me to death, were my fate a thousand times harder, it should not take me from you. I beg your pardon, sir, for my impatience, but, to tell the plain truth, you were yourself the cause. That quietness of yours, sir, drove me mad. I could not bear to know you suffering and yet never hear you say a word about it. You always had such a comfortable look that it made me wretched; but now that you complain, I am quiet; and I shall be the happiest dog on earth, as long as you'll confess that you are miserable.

Dup. I'll speak for you, Comtois, I'll spe<ak for you.>

Com. All I want, sir, is that you yourself s<how> feeling and consideration.

Dup. My heart was so overcharged that <while> writing, the other day, to my old friend Frém<ont of> Bordeaux, my oldest friend, Comtois, and, would you think it? He has not even answered my letter.

Com. Think it, sir—I'd think anything after what I've seen. In misfortune there's no counting upon anybody. I've told you so a thousand times, sir.

Dup. But you must not confound the friends of old times with the friends of times like these. I'm sure of Frémont. His attachment was solid and I'm sure there's some mistake.

Com. When you were more fortunate all your friends were more sincere.

Dup. Go back to Dervière and get every thing ready for our removal.

Com. That's soon done, for the horse is only over the way; the two sons-in-law live face to face, to keep one another in countenance.

Dup. Go, go, here's Amélie coming—leave me alone.

Com. Done, sir. [Apart] I've spoken my mind and I am pleased with thee!—[Exit. Enter Amélie]

Amél. Grandpapa, is it true you are going to leave our house?

Dup. This very day, my dear. My six months are elapsed.

Amél. How rapidly they've flown! Those which are to follow will not glide so swiftly. You and I are to live apart.

Dup. But we shall meet daily.

Amél. Oh, Grandpapa, not so! My father has forbidden me!

Dup. Great Heaven! Forbidden you! And why? Wherefore? What reason?

Amél. He says he fears the effect which the air of this house may have upon me. He is apprehensive I may acquire a taste for expense from the magnificence which pervades it. Alas! The vain pleasures of display touch not my heart. I should have sought nothing here but you.

Dup. This interdiction seems certainly severe. But a child has no right to question a parent's orders, and you must submit, my dear, without a murmur.

Amél. I should be unworthy of you could I forget my duty.

Dup. But they shall never prevent my <seeing you.> Not a day shall pass, but I will go to you<r house.>

Amél. Oh, Grandpapa, remember, you have prom<ised.>

Dup. They shall take my life, ere they take yo<u away.>

Amél. But I have not yet told you all my <grieva>nces.

Dup. Well child, well, dearest.

Amél. Why, there's poor cousin Charles. Papa won't have him even speak to me; and the real reason why he denies me leave to come here is that he is afraid Charles may come.

Dup. I can't say I think your papa to blame in that.

Amél. No? Bless me! Charles always thought you his best friend.

Dup. I always shall be his friend and he knows it. He is the only son of a beloved sister. He has never known any parent but myself, and I take the dearest interest in him.

Amél. So do I, Grandpapa.

Dup. Too deep, I fear. Ah! That blush betrays you. My child, your secret is safe in my keeping, but Heaven grant I may have judged erroneously. Tell me the truth frankly. Do you love Charles?

<Amél. Alas! Hear> all and you may judge. From morn to <night I think only> of him. When he is gone, everything seems tedious; but oh! how happy I am the moment he appears! When he speaks I listen with entranced attention; all he says seems to me most sweet; and though I have no memory, whatever he utters I know instantly by heart. Does he give an opinion? It is mine at once. All I see brings back his image. Even by night he fills my dreams; and by day is ever on my lips. Is this love?

Dup. You must dismiss the object of it from your heart. Your inclination must give place to your interest. Charles is destitute of fortune.

Amél. But he has a most excellent situation. He is in one of the first banking houses in the kingdom; and you know how diligent and saving he is.

Dup. I know his worth full well; but, dear child, don't give way to delusive hopes—Charles can never expect to obtain your hand. If my eyes are true, here he comes. [*Enter Charles*]

Ch. Oh, sir, I am come to acquaint you with such a misfortune—

Dup. What misfortune?

Ch. Our banking house, the first in the kingdom, whose credit no one ever dared to call in question—

Dup. Aye, I guess the rest—it has stopped payment.

Ch. I am scarcely recovered from the strain of the sudden blow; never was there a calamity so unexpected. My situation and even the savings from my salary are both snatched from me at once. My master himself this morning disclosed to me the fatal truth. "You are witness," exclaimed he, "of my agony. After such a reverse I must of course become an exile. The world offers me no asylum, and henceforth I must live dependent on another's pity!" At these words he sprang into a splendid curricle, adding, in piteous accents which went to my very soul, "Banished to my wife, I go to bury myself on her estate!"

Amél. I see now upon what an unsure foundation I had built my hope!

Dup. Don't let your courage forsake you with your fortunes, Charles. None but he who can face adversity can be deemed truly independent. Such a man is wealthier in his poverty than the richest. Keep up your spirits. My son-in-law stands high in favor at court; and can readily get you into a better situation than you are now regretting.

Ch. He never seemed favorably inclined towards me; and I greatly fear—

Dup. Nay, nay, he must provide for his relations. Ha! here comes my daughter! [*Enter Madame Dalainville*]

Mme. Dal. Dearest father, how rejoiced I am to see you!

Dup. From this day, I take up my abode in your house.

Mme. Dal. This day! Is it possible! How the time flies! Really, it never once occurred to me; but pray don't think anything of it. In the brilliant round of pleasures I can scarcely find a moment's leisure to think. Every day some new concert, ball, party at the opera, rout—

Dup. Aye, aye, dashing, dancing, and stopping payment make up the current history of our great metropolis!

Mme. Dal. This very day we are to have a large party to dinner.

Dup. A large dinner party! From such an annoyance kind fate deliver me!

Mme. Dal. All our guests are people of the first consequence in the world. When you hear their names you'll own it—

DUP. I know them without knowing their names. Your dinner parties of the great are generally made up of the same material, and I'll venture to predict we shall have the usual coterie at yours: all the favorites of the day, the last new fashions in society, the guests who are coveted merely because they're difficult to be had; then the graver men of weight who are expected to pay their reckoning with their influence; then two or three foreign noblemen sparkling like meteors in the foggy atmosphere around them; then certain regular table jesters, ever floating on the surface of society and never in it, smelling a dinner a league off; others who live by every day inventing a new budget of scandal and sarcasms, which they retail to divert one great man at the expense of another; your true courtiers of public offices, and politicians of the stock exchange; men of lost character, greedy, and mercenary, who, agents by turns in business and pleasure, make the whole town despise them for their impertinence and gain a name by the mere force of public hatred. Now, tell me truly, is not this a pretty accurate catalogue of your intended party? Oh! What pleasure can I take in a feast to be shared between guests so high and creatures so low? Tell me rather of those festivals where friendship overflows, where we can talk and laugh with real jollity; where we are encircled by our friends and our relations, and where pleasure presides and makes all equal. But it seems these are days when everyone must dash, and family dinners are grown out of fashion.

MME. DAL. When there is a fashion, we only make ourselves ridiculous in resisting it.

DUP. Well, well, I'll not resist it, I; but I need not love it, for all that. But we must change the subject, for I've something to say that touches us nearer. Do you know the misfortune which has befallen poor Charles? His banker has stopped payment.

MME. DAL. Indeed! What a shame! But it's no more than might have been expected. He lived in the most unjustifiable extravagance. How can people thus impose upon the public?

DUP. When there is a fashion, we must not make ourselves ridiculous by resisting it. But the main point now is to repair the consequences to Charles. We must get him another situation. Your husband has the power—

MME. DAL. Leave that wholly to me. I have very little influence with him; but depend on my employing all my eloquence.

DUP. Are you doubtful of the result?

MME. DAL. Why, he always says it is necessary to be very circumspect in the exercise of his influence; for every failure to obtain what we are anxious for hurts our credit and gives malignant people grounds for reporting that we are out of favor. But here he comes. Dear father, let us unite; and do you begin by speaking to my husband first.

CH. My obligations will be everlasting.

AMÉL. And shall I speak too.

DUP. My dears, it is better you should both be away when he comes. [*To Amélie*] I shall come to take leave of you presently. And [*To Charles*], this evening, Charles, I trust I shall have good news for you. [*Exeunt Charles and Amélie. Enter Dalainville*]

DAL. Ah, madam, I am enchanted to see you. Is everything in readiness for the ball this evening? I trust none Paris ever saw can exceed it in splendor. Your wishes will be more than satisfied.

MME. DAL. Sir, my father!

DAL. Ah! Is it you? I beg your pardon, I do indeed.

MME. DAL. This is his day for coming to our house.

DAL. Indeed? This?

MME. DAL. It seems to put you out.

DAL. I think you'll have a very large party. But I am afraid I'm going to give you unwelcome news: Count St. Far has just sent an excuse; but to make up for it, you'll have another self, Madame de Plinval—

MME. DAL. Amazement! Can I receive *her* at my parties?

DAL. Of course you can.

MME. DAL. She has been greatly talked about.

DAL. But she is greatly in fashion, invited everywhere. Her person is loved though her conduct is blamed. Besides, it seems to suit her husband; and what right has the public to be more jealous than he?

MME. DAL. Has she a husband? Come, come, that's impossible; or if she has, it is an invisible husband. Nobody ever sees him.

DAL. No wonder. She has got a place for him in one of the neighboring counties.

DUP. [*Apart*] Enviable manners of the great! [*Aloud*] I have a word to say to you, sir. It is in behalf of my young friend Charles.

DAL. I am at your service.

MME. DAL. My father, one moment. You see we are upon important matters. [*To Dalainville*] And your friend Duparc?

DAL. Ah! Upon mature reflection, I thought it would be best not to ask him. He's a good man, a most honorable man, but he's a free talker, a little *frondeur* who takes a pride in assuming a character. Those who dine at my table ought to know how to hold their tongue.

MME. DAL. But he did you a most important service.

DAL. True, so he did. My heart will be ever grateful to him for it. I like to see him, too. Friendship makes it a duty. But I will invite him when I shall have nobody else.

DUP. Now have you leisure to hear me?

DAL. My dear sir, deign to excuse me. There is nothing, you know, my dear sir, nothing you can ask that I can refuse. I think you said you were interested about some young man? What friends has he?

DUP. His talents and his integrity—

DAL. But you don't name the friends who are to back his suit?

DUP. He has none but me. Ah, my son-in-law, in the name of goodness, try to get him into some moderate situation.

DAL. I have already stated that I can't very decently employ my credit upon so small a matter. But, I'll turn it over in my mind. Let him send me a memorial. [*Exit Dalainville*]

DUP. How!

MME. DAL. Don't push your request now, if you will let me advise you. Pray pardon him. We'll bring it about eventually. Charles shall have his place. I take it all upon myself. [*Exit Madame Dalainville*]

DUP. [*Alone*] Great Providence! Can there be such ingratitude! Now, selfish and unfeeling man, I know thee! Poor Charles! What is to become of him? But there's my other son-in-law, perhaps he—and lo! He comes! I have scarcely the heart to ask anything from him, but I will—[*Enter Dervière*]

DER. Ah, my dear father, I meet you in a happy moment. I am come to communicate my happiness to Dalainville. The project which from morning to night has exclusively occupied my mind at length is adopted.

DUP. I congratulate you on it.

DER. A brilliant triumph for me, you will admit. The minister has had it printed at his own expense.

DUP. And what do you hope from this fine project, son?

DER. The wretched will have no more tears to shed. It assures ease and repose to the aged, and offers honorable labor to the indigent. It stops the ravages of the elements and places the farmer under shelter from storms and all the calamities with which the irritated Heavens too often overwhelm afflicted human nature!

DUP. Exceedingly good. You will be able, in that case, to give a free scope to your benevolence.

DER. Speak. What shall I do? Are there sufferers? I am ready, if it be needful, to sacrifice myself for them.

Dup. I would interest you for a relative who is overwhelmed by calamity. My son, aid him. There was a time when I might myself have fulfilled so enviable a duty; but now, I am compelled to address myself to you.

Der. Alas! At this moment it is utterly out of my power. Ah! How such a denial afflicts my feeling heart! Why did you not speak to me for him yesterday? But today how is it possible I can do anything for him? All my years' savings have just been given to the sufferers by the fire in Constantinople.

Dup. Ah! You wander far indeed to seek for the unfortunate when there are plenty close to you who daily weary your eyes. Yes, son-in-law, however your pride may fire up at the truth, I must speak it and plainly too. This air of benevolence, and this brilliant varnish, deceive none but fools, believe me, none but fools. Of this fine ardor I am not the dupe. You wish everyone should talk about you; that's the mainspring of your actions. The world we live in teems with charlatans struggling to catch the eyes of all who pass. Are kindnesses conferred? There must be a newspaper editor got immediately to print a list of them in his paper. Charity once did its kindnesses in silence; nowadays it is become a trade in Paris. All is sunk down to calculation, and that factitious enthusiasm is but a new mask to cover avarice.

Der. Then be it your study to make people happy: the way to poison everything has been found already.

Dup. But where, if you please, are the happy you have made? I have never seen any excepting in the newspapers. Have you obliged parents or friends? Humanity breathes in all your writings. There you pity the fate of the Negroes of Africa, and yet you can't get a single servant to stay under the same roof with you.

Der. Excellent! Shoot all the arrows of your satire! These words will ne'er touch me. Are there any discontented? Let such speak unfearing.

Dup. There are some who are too high spirited to complain.

Der. If they will be obstinate in their silence, I really am no magician and cannot divine their thoughts.

Dup. Your wishes are accomplished. Such have spoken, son-in-law; but it does not appear that they have made themselves heard. Adieu. This day I quit your house. Never shall I forget the kindness of your reception, and you may count upon the gratitude with which I am penetrated by your benevolence. [*Exit Dupré*]

Der. [*Alone*] Great Heaven, what a dissatisfied, uncomfortable animal an old man is! What can have put him so into such bad humor this morning? He gets vexed and enraged at a nothing. But as good luck will have it, I am going to be quit of him. He's coming to fix himself here. My brother-in-law shall be instantly forewarned of the happiness which awaits him.

ACT II.

Scene: *The same as the former. Enter Amélie and Dervière.*

Der. Did I not forbid your returning hither? Am I to be obeyed or not, miss?

Amél. Nay, Papa, be not so severe. You will not be angry at my disobedience when you learn the cause. Grandpapa comes today to take up his abode beneath this roof. You know that he is never much attended to; and at this moment, when so many things interfere, will be less so than ever. I was anxious to see to his apartment with my own eyes, and to be sure of his having all his little comforts about him.

Der. Alas, 'tis all for nothing! Are you not aware, my dear, that they decline receiving your good grandpapa here.

Amél. How!

Der. A splendid gala is to be given. They wish to put him off upon me till tomorrow, under the pretense of his being annoyed at the bustle and the crowd. I'll not keep him an instant.

Amél. Why not?

Der. Not that it would not give me the greatest pleasure; I would he were with us always. Nothing could delight me more, but I am determined to humble the pride of your uncle. So! gratitude is grown a bother to him! He takes no interest in the old gentleman—nay, blushes at his city air. No wonder, in the age we live in the least dignities change men's hearts. Even if he would have had the civility to see me, but no, the gentleman was not at leisure and by his steward he has this very moment made his high commands known to me. [*Enter Comtois, with a little portmanteau on his back*] Ah, you here, Comtois? You are come to fix here, hey?

Com. Yes, we remove for six months, fortune be praised!

Der. Are you alone?

Com. I precede my master. You'll see him presently. If we have not been here ere now, no thanks to your people. Their memory, sir, is now and then excessively treacherous. They are the most extraordinary forgetters of dates! It was scarcely the twenty-third of last month, when they told me, "Pack up, the first is come."

Der. This chap never agrees with anybody. He's always disputing, always making some difficulty—

Com. I!

Der. A sluggard—

Com. Sir!

DER. A huge feeder—

COM. That would be hard indeed in your quarters.

DER. Silence, incorrigible knave! But I waste time in listening to thee, which should be devoted to suffering humanity. Let me hasten to my works against prevailing abuses and finish my report on the unnatural treatment of animals. [*Exit*]

AMÉL. [*Giving her purse to Comtois*] Here, Comtois, take this, take this—

COM. Miss!

AMÉL. Continue ever faithful to thy master. Be patient and you will not be forgotten. [*Exit Amélie*]

COM. Patient! Aye, I will make a virtue of necessity and be patient. It would be hard to exchange for the worse, and we shall see presently how the wind blows on this side of the way. [*Enter Lafleur*]

LAF. What are you about there, scapegrace?

COM. Promising commencement! The man seems even more amiable than the master.

LAF. You are on the trot from morning to night.

COM. If that annoys you, sir, I'll be seated.

LAF. No words. Take yourself off.

COM. If I do go, I must come back again. Does your vast reading ever extend so far as the almanac? If it did, you would be aware that this was the first of the month.

LAF. The first indeed! Don't tell me. At the most it is not more than the thirtieth.

COM. There are two almanacs in this house of an opposite description. The one is always too fast when we are going, and the other too slow when we are coming.

LAF. You can come back again tomorrow?

COM. Tomorrow?

LAF. Mr. Dervière must keep you one day longer. Today we give a grand dinner and ball. What would you do here? You'd only be uncomfortable. Your master's room is turned into a pantry.

COM. Oh! Let me occupy it, and you'll do me a service. Mr. Dervière is just gone from here, and he said <not> a word—

LAF. Do you doubt my word, then, blackguard? I'll teach you—

COM. To believe in the assurance of a gold-laced lackey? *That* I can without your teaching.

LAF. Come, come, vanish. I brook no delays.

Com. [*Apart*] Zounds! If there were no law against duelling, I should be greatly inclined to send my friend, Lord Flint's valet, to that fellow for an explanation.

Laf. There comes my gentleman. The door! The door! [*Exeunt. Enter Dalainville alone*]

Dal. This intelligence flutters me. The moment to put every spring in motion is arrived. An embassy to be filled and a place empty in the Cabinet! Who is likely to be named? There's the mystery. Have not I as much encouragement to enter the lists as any man? Aye, none can have fairer hopes. Who are my competitors? Dorval can never fill any but a subaltern place: his genius is confined; his wife governs him. Can Damis hope to be selected? How can a man of pleasure make a statesman? Ergaste has talents, but I fear him not: his bad character neutralizes his power. Truly I may cast my eyes on every side; I can see no one but myself. Where can they choose better? My rights are incontestable, my hope legitimate. The Court considers and the world esteems me. I have never struggled against opinion. My strict probity has long been proverbial. Scrupulous in my regard for the laws, ever upholding morality, I have always most punctiliously kept clear of provoking scandal. My triumph is most certain. But I have but one day before me. No time is to be lost. Let me appear at Court. It is essential that this very day I should show myself. It often happens that in order to be thought of it is necessary we should be seen. [*Enter Lafleur*]

Laf. Mr. Charles, sir—

Dal. Why did you not deny me? Importunate beggar! I must rid myself of him.

Ch. Ah, sir, my benefactor, forgive the impatience of my gratitude, which could not delay its thanks a moment for the kindness which Mr. Dupré has just assured me you deign to show me in my destitution—

Dal. Mr. Dupré has been premature, I fear. But it is his way.

Ch. But, sir, permit me—

Dal. I dare say he has even told me that I should grant you a place?

Ch. He did indeed.

Dal. There! I knew it. He is always committing me thus. Places, sir, are not so easily obtained. There are no passports to them but talents, integrity—

Ch. Sir!

Dal. Not that I mean to charge you with any lack of either. Oh, no! But you are not aware then that I have twenty applicants recommended by the highest patrons?

CH. By this you mean to say that my poor qualifications are not a sufficient recommendation. I confess I brought no other; but, if it must be, I hasten to seek patrons who may give them their due weight.

DAL. [*To a lackey*] My carriage. Announce me to your lady. I shall call on her before I go out. [*To Charles*] You are, I think I have been told, one of my wife's relations?

CH. I am; and there was a time when I believe she had none nearer.

DAL. My sword! [*To Charles*] No doubt you have a memorial. [*Charles gives it to him*] I take the greatest interest in it. [*Gives it to Lafleur*] Believe me, I do indeed. Still, I cannot promise you a situation; but, whenever I can be useful to you, my friend, count on me. [*Exit*]

CH. My blood boils—

LAF. [*Reading the memorial*] Aye, very well. You shall be taken care of—

CH. What?

LAF. Fear nothing. I mean to stand your friend.

CH. [*Snatching away the petition and tearing it*] I felt that the master meant me a slight, but could not have conceived that the valet would have dared to patronize me! If I was silent under the master's slight, I will not brook the valet's patronage!

LAF. What! The gentleman gets angry, and yet the gentleman petitions! I have seen people of great importance who have not been sorry to get my influence. I see you don't know the world yet. Our patronage is sometimes of more service than those who are made more fuss about.

CH. Let me starve sooner than thrive by such vile means.

LAF. Oh ho! Spirited and conscientious! Dear me! You'll never get up in the world. But here comes Mr. Dupré. Really, he's of the same kidney: always finding fault. You'll suit each other vastly. [*Enter Dupré and Comtois*]

COM. So, Lafleur!

LAF. How <now>?

COM. You would make laughing stocks of us, would you? You'd better take care how you amuse yourself at the expense of my master. We went to the other house, as you said, and we were the last persons expected. They don't know what the devil you mean by sending us.

LAF. Not know—

DUP. He tells the truth.

LAF. Astonishing, upon my honor!

COM. In short, they shut the door in my face; and here I come back again with all our baggage and more tired than ever of journeying!

LAF. Can you, sir, listen coolly to this knave?

Dup. [*To Lafleur*]   Out of my sight, you are a rascal!

Com.   Aye, out of our sight! [*Lafleur goes, threatening Comtois*]

Ch.   I fly to Dervière. He knows nothing of this indignity; I am sure he does not! He will be the first to punish his servants for it. Be certain he himself meant to be your guide and had said nothing to them. But if he should disappoint my just hope, Charles is still the possessor of a humble retreat, and you shall be master of all which he can still call his own. [*Exit Charles*]

Com.   Where shall we bend our steps now? We must admit, we are lodged. Did one ever see the like of this adventure? Between two homes, here we are in the street.

Dup.   To what an extremity do I find myself reduced! These are the fruits of my liberality to them! Ha! Frémont! [*Enter Frémont*]

Fré.   Aye, come all the way from Bordeaux expressly to give you a scolding.

Dup.   Come to my arms first and give me the scolding afterwards.

Fré.   Why, I have been hunting after you this hour, and haven't found out the place of your abode even yet. On this side of the way they tell me you live on the other. I fly thither, and they tell me you do not live there. In mercy, tell me what all this can mean?

Com.   Alas, my dear sir, let me inform you. We are cast out upon the wide world, without a home; for the truth must be confessed: we know not where we are to lay our heads this night.

Fré.   Great Heaven! Can this be the truth?

Dup.   I cannot hide it from you. You see before you the most unfortunate of fathers.

Fré.   Friend, your news afflicts me but does not surprise me. Too indulgent parents always make ungrateful children. If you will secure the gratitude of your offspring, always keep them dependent on you; and if you doubt it, zounds, come to my house and see mine. I'm more absolute than a king under my own roof. Everyone there obeys and reveres me. That don't prevent my being a good father; but my wealth is in my own hands; I preserve every farthing of it and shall know how, I'll be sworn, to enjoy it to the end. After thirty hard years' hard working to make myself independent, think you I would give up the fruits of my long toils in the decline of my life? The main point is to good rents, and with them defects are almost virtues. For instance, I know my temper. I'm irritable, abrupt, and even very passionate. Well, for all that I have the credit everywhere of being the fairest and best creature breathing. But, with my strong box empty, what should I then be? Why, a brute!

Com.   [*Apart*]   That now is what I call talking sensibly.

Dup. Aye, you are right. It is all too true!

Fré. Great Heaven! You have given up all your fortune, reserving nothing for yourself, absolutely nothing! Merciful powers! What blindness! What excess of weakness! See here the fruits of the imprudent tenderness of parents! He who does not feel the danger of such confidence soon becomes a stranger beneath his own roof! Can a more cruel torture be imagined! In the spot where one reigned master, to be forced to obey. Credit, wealth, liberty all gone at once, disinherited by his own children, and, to sum all up, the man thus despoiled surviving himself!

Dup. Time and misfortune have sufficiently convinced me, but condemn me not without a hearing. My sons-in-law, occupied with political interests, have long given themselves up to public affairs: the one filled an important post in the state without possessing the means of sustaining its splendor. Oh, said he to my daughter, had I but wealth enough, I would be the making of all the family. I should mount presently to the first rank in the nation. Alas! my dear friend, I would have given my heart's blood. Could I hesitate to give my wealth? The first days I was overwhelmed with caresses: both contended which should have me with them; and neither would give me up. Do what I could, they never could settle the point between them. Touched with this noble struggle of filial affection, I agreed with them, in order to show no partiality, that each one should keep me six months alternately. But, my friend, they soon ceased to dissemble.

Com. Ah! How happy it makes me to hear him complain.

Dup. Dalainville, at first so gentle, so complaisant, no longer regarded me but with a contemptuous air. Instead of occupying himself about the good he might achieve, he intrigues secretly and looks up to get into the ministry. Those whom he stands in need of are perfectly sure of being received, but his door is most punctiliously closed against his friends. Always offering aid, he never gives, patronizing all and obliging none, the other goes about weeping the calamities of others and agitates himself much in order to make himself talked about. His first object being to attract public attention, he has set up as a general redressor of wrongs: not from goodness, you may readily guess, but out of spite for being a mere cipher in the world. He would fain get a name; and is become benevolent in order to be something.

Fré. Two interesting portraits, as I live!

Com. I'll answer for the likenesses, sir, every turn and feature!

Fré. Are they most cordially hated?

Dup. Hated? No, no. So far from that, they are greatly esteemed; everybody thinks very highly of them. The one is thought benevolent and the other generous. They are never ill-conducted excepting at their own house.

A hidden error is nothing. The principal thing is never to give subjects for scandal. Alas! Not to have apparent vices is the sole virtue of many indeed nowadays.

Fré. Aye, this is the age of hypocrisy. But how have you the patience to remain with them? Come, come, take my advice and quit the rascals.

Dup. Under the circumstances there would be some difficulty in my doing that.

Fré. What difficulty? Take shelter under my roof at Bordeaux. We'll set off together—

Dup. Just Providence! This kindness—

Fré. I won't take a denial. When we dissolved partnership, we did not dissolve friendships. Well, now I call upon you to do me a favor: without ceremony come and live with me. You'll find a good fire, a good table, and what's more than all, happy and pleased faces and the pleasantest company in the world. Aye, quit your ungrateful kindred forever. You shall come and make one of a family of honest hearts.

Com. Oh, kind fate! What a man is this!

Dup. My friend, I thank you and most certainly I would—but here comes the man in office. [*Enter Dalainville*] My son-in-law, this gentleman is one of my oldest friends. May I beg leave to introduce him to you?

Fré. Yes, sir, I have the honor—

Dal. It is quite impossible. I have not, at this moment, a single place at my disposal. I have told you so already—

Dup. [*To Dalainville*] You misunderstand—

Fré. I really think he takes me for an office hunter. Who said anything about a place? Pshaw, I want no place!

Dal. Forgive me; did you but know how I am tortured by importunities—

Fré. Faith, these great men are greatly to be pitied: then they are never spoken to, I suppose, but when people stand in need of them?

Dup. I hope you will pardon my great audacity if I now importune you upon my own account.

Dal. How? Explain.

Dup. I am already very old. You see that at all ages we are ambitious. Do not be terrified at my humble petition: I demand a shelter to repose my head.

Dal. What do I hear? Can my brother-in-law have denied you one?

Dup. He has kept me six months. I have no cause to blame him.

Dal. I am shocked that he should have had the indecency. Be certain that nothing but a motive of the first importance could ever have prevailed on me for this one day to defer the moment which should restore you to our affection.

Dup.   I know the reason. You have company.

Dal.   True. You dislike the throng and I felt myself in duty bound to anticipate your wishes. You can instantly depart for my country house. I go to have everything made ready that you may be attended thither.

Dup.   My son-in-law!

Dal.   The greatest possible care will be taken of you. You will there enjoy the purest, gentlest pleasures. I know your inclinations, your taste for study; how happy you will be in your solitude! But pardon me, I quit you.

Dup.   But, sir, one moment.

Dal.   I must hasten to Court. Time presses; I am waited for. [*Exit Dalainville*]

Fré.   Well, do you renounce the sacred rights of a father? Damnation! 'Tis you that put me in a passion! So! You could stay with them after this. In that case, take my farewell!

Dup.   Dear friend, in Heaven's name.

Fré.   Your entreaties are fruitless. The blood boils in my veins. Every father is insulted in you, and public honor exacts that they should be avenged!

Dup.   'Tis well. I yield myself, dear friend, to your counsels. I am now ready to follow you to Bordeaux.

Fré.   No, your departure would be no punishment to them. It would only be obliging the ungrateful. You must have justice done you without delay; your voice must be heard in the midst of Paris. To all sentiments their hearts are closed, but one mode remains, they must be frightened.

Dup.   What! Is it on that you build your hope?

Fré.   Yes. Opinion governs the world. The fear it inspires is an all-powerful rein. It is, in some degree, the supplement of the laws. Your sons-in-law, till now, have only had the art of dissembling; they flatter the public; they have everything to fear from it. <Under> a brilliant mask they may do what they will to conceal themselves. If it be necessary, I shall know how to tear it off. Follow me; you shall instantly have an asylum.

Dup.   But are not resources necessary?

Fré.   There will be no want of them. My signature will produce in Paris furniture, houses, gold and friends. Lose no time; we must be under way.

Dup.   Comtois comes with us, does he not?

Fré.   Of course he does. For these bad relations have no more pity, and let yourself at last be guided by friendship.

ACT III.

[SCENE: *Same as the former*] *Enter Madame Dalainville and Dalainville.*

DAL. We must be silent, madam, on the subject, but most certainly I shall get into the Ministry.

MME. DAL. You a Minister!

DAL. It is no longer a secret at Court.

MME. DAL. How have you discovered it?

DAL. In the reception I met with there. Every eye fixed upon me seemed at once to declare it. I saw my enemies forced to smile on me. Everything already announces my greatness at hand. I am met everywhere with the most humble and fawning air; one might say that each divining my power strives to make his court to me before the other. Yes, all saluting me with the gentlest looks seem to say: Sir, I shall stand in need of you.

MME. DAL. In that case we must increase the magnificence of our establishment, add instantly to the numbers of our servants, twelve footmen, two coachmen, a running footman; behind my carriage I must have a chasseur. I would have presently the most beautiful equipages.

DAL. If this <goes> on you will stand in need of pages.

MME. DAL. There is another object of much greater importance, about which I must occupy myself instantly. I shall take a rather more showy livery. The one we have now is not brilliant enough. One is not perceived in the crowd. I would have my name known by my colors.

DAL. [*Apart*] I shall begin by creating a number of plans. We must make friends by spreading favors.

MME. DAL. We must have an estate.

DAL. [*Apart*] Aye, well—

MME. DAL. That's indispensable. Paris in the fine season is so gloomy that it terrifies one, but in the country there what pleasure one feels! A charm of paradise! All Paris is to be met there, and then solitude has a thousand attractions for me! One cannot make a step without one's heart melting! I idolize the calm seclusion of the woods! But don't forget we must have a private theater in our park? Nay, you do not answer me. Are you not enchanted?

DAL. We will see to all that when I shall be appointed. [*Enter a footman*]

FOOT. Sir, your brother-in-law. [*Exit*]

DAL. Come, I suppose he has heard something of the report.

MME. DAL. Oh! how mortally tiresome he is with his philanthropy! I leave you with him. [*Exit Madame Dalainville. Enter Dervière*]

DER. Ah, sir, permit me to offer you my congratulations. I see there is yet some respect paid to merit. You are then Minister!

DAL. My dear sir, what can have led you into that error? Far be it from me to aspire to such exalted honor. I feel myself incapable of sustaining the weight of it.

DER. A more honorable choice could not be made. I do not flatter you. Spite of our differences, no one could ever accuse me of not rendering every homage to your talents.

DAL. What! Can I be spoken of—

DER. Why, the fact is notorious. It is in everybody's mouth, and you yourself ought to feel persuaded it is intended.

DAL. This is the first I have heard of it.

DER. You then are the only one in Paris to whom it is unknown. Presently you will see that importunate crowd which attaches itself always to the car of fortune. I come, first of all, but guided by my heart; I demand here neither place nor favor. I come to speak to you of the indigent class; deign to protect it with your powerful hand; you will one day feel that this sacred object is worthy the attention of an enlightened minister.

DAL. If in truth I occupy that eminent place I will first serve suffering humanity: that is the noblest duty of the public man.

DER. Certainly it is. If I should ever have the least power—what do I say? Power could never seduce me, and I have badly expressed what I meant to say. Satisfied with my fate, I desire nothing. All my happiness consists in doing a little good.

DAL. Still this very day there was a conversation about the Financial Department, and your knowledge was greatly boasted of upon those subjects. It was even hinted for the good of the state that it would be advisable to charge you with this delicate responsibility. But of course with one word I silenced all.

DER. How so?

DAL. The reply was easily made: I said you would feel yourself flattered by the distinction, but you would decline any office whatsoever.

DER. You were greatly in the wrong.

DAL. How so?

DER. I repeat that I love to live unknown, that I cherish retreat; but when the public chooses to point me out, I know that it becomes my duty to resign myself to its choice. Every virtuous man owes himself to his country and 'tis with pleasure I should sacrifice myself.

DAL. Ha! Why did you not tell me so? Very well, I understand you.

DER. You have given the evil-disposed a handle against me. My vexation is but too well founded. Soon my refusal will be set down as a crime. Perhaps the place is already disposed of; that would be indeed annoying.

DAL. Rely on me. You will obtain the place.

DER. It will be most dear to me because I shall exercise it under your Ministry. In important cases should any doubts perplex me, suffer me to fly instantly to consult you. I shall often stand in need of your experience.

DAL. Yes, you may be always sure of my assistance. [*Apart*] I cannot endure this servile, flattering air.

DER. [*Apart*] I know not how to reconcile myself to this protecting tone. [*Aloud*] The public interest now brings us together. The time will come when we too shall be blest in company. [*Enter a valet*]

VAL. This letter has just been brought, sir.

DER. It is, I'll wager, the official intelligence. Oh, I was certain of it, I tell you. [*Dalainville reads*] Great Heaven! What a saddened look! Does it happen by any chance that you are not Minister?

DAL. I cannot recover.

DER. You seem in consternation.

DAL. See if I have not cause to be astonished.

DER. [*Reads*] "My son-in-law, your treatment has compelled me to withdraw from you forever. I had luckily put aside resources which restore my independence. Your conduct will presently be made public. Communicate this letter to your brother-in-law; it is meant for both."

DAL. Well! What say you to it?

DER. I cannot comprehend a word of it. This epistle I was far from expecting.

DAL. If you had kept him still! Had it been but for a single day!

DER. If you had received him! It was your turn.

DAL. What! To fly into a passion for such a trifle!

DER. The old man's temper now and then was very bad.

DAL. Now and then? It was always bad.

DER. At first I did not think so: since he has been under my roof I have noticed it; from morning to night he must always be grumbling.

DAL. Exactly as he is at my house. If I have company, in his perverse moods, he finds fault, contradicts, nay even openly censures men of influence. There is nothing he makes a scruple of saying. He has been twenty times on the brink of committing me. Soliciting, besides, for the whole human race, he never meets me without a petition in his hand.

DER. But between ourselves the affair is serious and may have very unpleasant consequences. All eyes now seem fixed on you. Your elevation has excited many jealousies. You must feel that this is a fine opening for them; tomorrow it will be the news of all Paris. I already see the public let loose upon you at the words "ungrateful son" and "deserted father." To the rising man it is <pitiless>; it makes it a principle always to find him in the wrong. The throng of demagogues will begin, I've no doubt, to say that a bad son must be a bad citizen.

DAL. They? What?

DER. Doubt not but you will be sacrificed. You are without reproach, and they calumniate you; but in the eyes of the public it would be almost as good to be a little more guilty and to appear innocent.

DAL. If *I* have reason to dread the injustice of the public, it may also exercise its malice on you. "Look," it will say, "at the beneficent creature, the stay of the unfortunate, the prop of the indigent; with his numberless benefactions he has filled the earth. He is humane to everybody excepting his father."

DER. Can they dare thus betray the truth?

DAL. Yes, you are right; it will be base; but as you very properly observed, it would be better that the thing should be more true and less probable.

DER. Hold! We lose time here in talking when a pressing danger calls on us for action. At heart he's a good-natured creature; a little complaisance, a few kind words will calm him, I'm persuaded. Don't you think so?

DAL. I'm sure of it.

DER. Let us unite our efforts. Let us admit, if it must come to that, that we are really to blame. For my part I will even <stoop> to supplication. There's no degradation in going upon one's knees to a father. No, nothing should be thought too hard, and in such a moment we should be deaf to everything but the voice of sentiment. [*Enter Lafleur and Champagne*]

CHAM. Ah, sir!

LAF. Just Heaven!

CHAM. Great Powers!

LAF. What a miracle!

CHAM. We have this moment seen—

DER. Whom?

DAL. What?

LAF. Your father in a carriage!

DER. Hey!

CHAM. We were both passing on our way, when suddenly, sir, at a door in the neighborhood we saw a brilliant equipage stop. Your father descends from it. Then, according to custom, I dart forward politely offering him my arm. Can you guess what he said? "Out of my sight, scoundrel!" I obeyed—

LAF. In my turn, I humbly advance, but had scarcely ended my bow, when I received (I am yet stunned with it), from a hand like a sledgehammer a tremendous box on the ear. A little more would have stretched me on the pavement. 'Twas from a countryman whose insolent audacity has outraged your whole house, sir, in my person. 'Tis for you, sir, now, to call him to account for it; and I hastened hither instantly to tell you the affair—

DER. [To Dalainville] Who is this stranger?

DAL. Oh, I suppose it is the man he brought here to introduce to me today, an old ship broker.

DER. No doubt, 'tis he. He has certainly been spiriting up the old man to this. But time presses. The tempest must be laid.

LAF. [To Champagne] They are settling low to themselves how I am to be avenged.

DER. Lafleur, hasten instantly to find this stranger.

LAF. Yes, sir. [To Champagne] Ah! I'll talk to him in a way—

DAL. Assure him of our highest respect. Lose not a moment, and take care to learn at what hour it may be convenient for him to allow us to wait on him—

LAF. Sir!

DAL. Obey or I dismiss you.

LAF. And pray must I thank him too?

DER. Of course you must. Your respect cannot be carried too far.

LAF. [To Champagne] Well! What do you think of that?

CHAM. Why, that they stand in need of him.

LAF. Sir, I am not the fittest person to deliver this message. I'm persuaded the man don't like my face. [To Champagne] 'Tis you must speak.

CHAM. I'd rather be excused. You can pass before. You risk no longer anything. [Exeunt]

DAL. There was no other way we could have suitably adopted.

DER. Yes; but I can't understand a syllable of their story. This splendid train—[Enter Madame Dalainville]

MME. DAL. Ah, sir, have I found you? The company are here this hour at least. We are going to put ourselves at table. How's this? What detains you?

DAL. A pretty moment to talk of pleasures and parties.

MME. DAL. You seem out of humor.

DAL. Not without cause. Your father, madam, has withdrawn himself from our house.

MME. DAL. Can it be! Great Heaven!

DAL. He is gone, I say—

MME. DAL. This abrupt secession both astonishes and afflicts me. Can I be the cause! No, no; still I am part of it. He has indeed a right to be dissatisfied. See to what a misfortune a denial exposes us. If he is gone, sir, you are the cause. I cannot conceal it.

DAL. What say you? Whom? I!

MME. DAL. He came to ask you to procure a situation for Charles. I joined my feeble voice to that of my father, and you were deaf to our prayer. If you do not take care, he will make a noise about it. You will pass everywhere for an ungrateful man—

DER. Sir, you must have a very unfeeling heart. What he asked was very easily achieved. Oh! Now I can readily understand his wrath.

DAL. How, sir, is it your place to—

DER. For the fault of one only, we are all punished—[*Enter Amélie*]

AMÉL. Ah, my father, ah, dear uncle, what is it I have just heard. Then there remains nothing for us but tears to shed. My grandpapa departed! Great Powers! What is become of him!

DER. Be calm, dear child.

AMÉL. This morning I have seen him. For the first time he was in wrath.

DER. Of what did he complain.

AMÉL. 'Twas of you, my father.

DER. How! Explain!

AMÉL. Yes. Nothing can be more true. He, as he told me, endeavored this morning to interest you in favor of a relation reduced to penury and obtained nothing from your benevolence. I saw clearly that this denial cut him to the heart. You can form no idea of the excess of his grief.

DAL. His wrath is, in truth, but too well founded. Answer: are you the victim of my errors?

AMÉL. Oh, be advised by me. Let us run and embrace his knees.

MME. DAL. You have been in fault. Why will you not own it? It is not yet too late.

DAL. Accuse not others; for the greatest faults, madam, have been committed by you. Were you not the hope and stay of a father? Who, then, but you was bound to watch over him? Overwhelmed by labor, was it my part, madam, to give him time which belongs to the public? Ah! Ought those tender and gentle cares due to a father to be ever fulfilled by any other than you? But the glare of greatness has dimmed your eyesight; and you dream of nothing but spectacles and parties; forgetting your friends and your poor relations, you seem incapable of living except with the great, and you would believe, no doubt, you imitated the vulgar if you could recall to mind that you have a father.

MME. DAL. Ah, cruel man, go on: tear my heart to pieces!

DER. You should speak more mildly to her.

MME. DAL. To this terrific charge must I reply? Oh, Heaven! You accuse me of too much love for the world! You dare to overwhelm me with an undeserved rage and to cast on me blame which belongs to you alone! To abandon my father! The word alone crushes me! Can I be believed capable of so black a deed? I, who so cherish him! I, who, this very day even recommended that the servants should watch over him.

DAL. [*To his wife*] Come, come, enough. Go in, my dear. 'Tis already too long to have left the company. If you are not there, who will do the honors?

MME. DAL. Great Heaven! At such a moment—

DAL. You are all in tears. Why, what will people think? Do you consider that, madam?

MME. DAL. What! With so cruel an arrow to pierce my heart, and still dare to talk to me of parties, fêtes, and pleasure!

DAL. Madam, sometimes it is necessary to know how to suffer. Come, come, go in, I tell you, and be without alarms. I will soon follow you. Dry then your tears. 'Tis most essential; I charge you dry them. Those who dine with me are not my friends.

MME. DAL. Great Powers! Must I impose upon myself this horrible constraint, when my father, perhaps—

AMÉL. Ah! Have no fear. I have seen more than once his wrath break forth; but he has never said a single word against you. You appear to suffer. Permit me, madam, not to quit you. [*Exeunt Amélie and Madame Dalainville*]

DER. The dear girl has the finest heart, the best disposition that ever was known. It is plain enough I have modelled her heart and disposition upon my own.

DAL. Lafleur does not return, and my impatience—his reply is of the greatest importance to us.

DER. Ha! I see the protégé of the old man coming this way. We have, between ourselves, rather neglected him. We must receive him kindly. [*Enter Charles*] My dear friend, Charles—

CH. Ah, sir, pardon—

DAL. I have something to say to you. The moment I got in, my friend, I hastened to read the petition you left with me. Why your titles are clear, your rights incontestable—

DER. Oh! You never can employ a person of more eminent qualifications.

CH. You have read it then, sir?

DAL. With the greatest attention—

DER. I can assure you he has. I myself was witness—

CH. Ah!

DAL. You are not formed for an obscure place. I destine you for an important post—

DER. Take my word for it, he will fill the highest post admirably. No merit exceeds his. I told my daughter so this very morning: that young man will be the honor of his family.

DAL. Under my protection from this day forward I take him.

DER. Of course. He's our nearest relation—

CH. So much goodness, gentlemen, confounds and overwhelms me. But to whom, if I may ask, am I to ascribe it? Mr. Dupré, no doubt—

DAL. Why, but—

CH. Yes, I see it; for he had promised to speak to you for me, and I fly to assure him of how sensible I am of it—

DER. Stop a moment. It cannot be: he is gone out—

DAL. And as he may not return till night, stop here, my friend; you can wait for him here. Pass into the drawing room—

CH. But, sir, I have this moment heard you have company, and not having been invited, I fear—

DAL. The neglectful wretches! What! To forget you—

CH. Ah! I do not presume—

DAL. They are eternally making such blunders. Why, your name stood at the head of the list.

DER. [*To Dalainville*] Here comes Lafleur. [*To Charles*] But I can guess how it happened: one's most particular friend is never expected to be so formal as to require a distinct invitation.

CH. Ah, gentlemen, be certain of my gratitude. It is at least equal to your attention. [*Exit Charles. Enter Lafleur*]

DER. Well, Lafleur, well—

LAF. Well, sir, this time we had better luck. Our ears escaped—

DER. I am enraptured—

DAL. Tell me, shall we see him?

LAF. Yes, here he comes himself. [*Enter Frémont*]

DER. Ha! What, sir—you here. This honor, this great condescension—

FRÉ. Yes, gentlemen, here I am, your most humble servant—

DAL. 'Twas our design to have called upon you, and we regret—

FRÉ. Say all you have to say without preamble, gentlemen, for I'm in a hurry.

DAL. Sir—

FRÉ. No ceremony. In two words, what is it you want of me? Above all, be brief.

DER. Just Powers! What a temper! You seem on very good terms with our father-in-law.

FRÉ. Yes. He's my old friend.

DER. Most distressing differences now divide the father from the children.

FRÉ. I know it.

DAL. He has long resided with us, and, without the slightest notice, has suddenly taken flight.

DER. He has done more: he wishes to stir up all Paris against his submissive, respectful sons—

FRÉ. Ungrateful man! And it is exactly that which is the source of your affliction?

DER. A more tender interest guides us now. Alas! None but his children can take proper care of him!

FRÉ. Undeceive yourselves, gentlemen; he no longer stands in need of them.

DAL. What do you say?

FRÉ. Without being in the bosom of opulence, he finds himself no longer dependent upon you. The good man has given up all his estates to you, but in so doing he preserved his pocketbook.

DER. How?

FRÉ. You seem surprised.

DAL. We were not aware—

FRÉ. Then I will inform you. Last year your father deposited in my hands in good hard money twenty thousand pounds—

DER. Twenty thousand pounds!

FRÉ. And I threw the funds into the way of profit as an honest man should. I owed my fortune to his old friendship. It was my duty to share the profits with him. We have, thanks to Heaven, been exceedingly fortunate. I have covered the ocean with my numerous privateers; and the gentlemen of England, spite of all their vessels, have, in less than six months, tripled our capital. At length I received a message from your father. Just at that moment I was about to come to Paris. I depart—it was time—when I arrived, I found my old friend turned into the street.

DAL. Do you believe it?

FRÉ. Heaven! Does it give you no shame?

DAL. You judge us, sir, very promptly.

FRÉ. He, who despoiled himself of all his estates for you! Horrible!

DAL. Nay, but, sir, hear us. Of a bad step we are perfectly incapable—

DER. We are innocent—

FRÉ. No. You are guilty.

DAL. Deign, but a moment, to hear us—

FRÉ. To what end? You would be still in the wrong, even if you should be in the right.

DAL. But, if you please, sir, what then is our crime?

FRÉ. Aye, crime, that is the word. That word alone can justly speak your manner of acting; and since you *can* hear me without blushing, in a few words, sirs, you shall be satisfied and hear how you have behaved to your father. Not an attention, not a kindness, not the slightest interest ever shown for him. He has no repose but when he was forgotten. Did he ever come trembling to entreat a favor? It seemed as though he had committed the excess of audacity. Did he dare express the most simple desire? All your people seemed to strive which should most eagerly disobey him—

DAL. Ah! 'Tis without my knowledge they have dared to neglect—

FRÉ. Servants never insult those who are respected by their masters.

DER. With regard to me, I see plainly, you are in error. But read my works and you will know my heart.

FRÉ. Oh, sir, your works make nobody live. The finest of your discourses are not worth an alms. And when an unfortunate stretches forth his hand to you, leave your writings and give him bread.

DAL. We want an aid. Deign to be one for us—

FRÉ. Ah! You may better choose some other. I serve you for an aid! You do not know me.

DAL. Pardon me, sir, you are frank and full of integrity. That air of truth, without ceremony, pleases and interests me. Yes, I love you, sir, even your very savageness. You never flatter the defects of another. But, I am convinced you have a good heart.

FRÉ. [*Aside*] He's trying to wheedle me over. Zounds! Stand firm!

DAL. To our divisions it is in your power to put an end. I shall no longer speak of all our differences. We have been in the wrong—more or less—but neither pride nor false shame shall stand in the way of my doing the best I can to repair them. Be the bearer to your friend of these words of peace. Place at his feet our wishes and our regrets. Ah! You will accept this noble ministry! You will reconcile the children and the father! To unite relations is so sweet a happiness! Refuse it not. The task is worthy of you—

FRÉ. You speak prodigiously well, sir, and I like of all things to hear you; but, once more, sir, I cannot be your advocate.

DER. Nay, then, I fly myself—

Fré. Don't hurry yourself. 'Twill be all time thrown away. What will he think of this sudden eagerness. Of course, he'll say that all your caresses have but one end in view: that of obtaining his newly discovered riches, and that, little satisfied with having had much gold, you return to him merely to get more.

Der. Can he suspect—

Dal. All I apprehend is that this report should get abroad to the world. Not that it could touch me. No, no, my name is quite sufficient to shelter me from any suspicion of the sort. But one always apprehends unpleasant consequences from a clamor, and without being alarmed, the honest man always avoids it.

Fré. Aye, I understand you: it might compromise you—

Der. Try to obtain your friend's secret—

Fré. You would fain force your father to silence. Complaint is now the only vengeance you have left in his power.

Der. Vengeance never takes possession of a delicate mind.

Fré. It should unpityingly pursue the ungrateful. Not only does it then become admissible, but it is almost a duty and authorized by Heaven! It has but too late made his wrath burst. In one word, he ought to have made you fall at his feet. Ah! I would I had been in his place. I would have forced you to come to me and ask pardon. Traversing all Paris with anguish on my brow, I would everywhere have made my cries echo. Aye, burning with the desire of avenging my outrage, I would have expressly thrown myself across your path; and when you should have, from the height of a brilliant car, cast on the people a lofty look, "See," I would have told them, "his splendor and my misery. This most powerful man, 'tis I who am his father!"

Der. We have addressed ourselves to the wrong person. I was afraid of it. This man has no sensibility. [*Enter Charles, running to Dalainville*]

Ch. I seek you, sir; hasten; time presses. I run to alarm the tenderness of your heart. Madame is extremely ill.

Dal. You make me shudder—

Ch. In Heaven's name, sir, to her side—

Dal. Just Powers!

Ch. Scarcely had she rejoined the company, when suddenly she fell into a swoon. Guess the horror of all present. Each regained his carriage and returned to his own house.

Dal. What will the world think! Ah! I fly to her. [*Enter Lafleur*]

Laf. The Secretary of State, sir, begs your immediate attendance. He expects you instantly at his hotel. It is, said his ambassador, for a pressing object.

DAL. The Minister! Great Heavens! Can he have heard the truth? My wife! [*To Charles*] Take care of her. Ho, there! Quick! My carriage!

LAF. 'Tis at the door.

DAL. [*To Dervière*] Sir, fly to her aid. I return on the instant.

DER. Count on me. I fly—[*Exeunt Dalainville, Dervière, Charles, and Lafleur*]

FRÉ. [*Alone*] How! For a Minister, to quit one's wife! This is ambition! Infamous! But now without delay to rejoin my friend. He has need of being encouraged in his firm purpose. Ah, gentlemen, I know at length your rule of morals. You fear a noise. You dread the scandal of your misdoings. Well, then, 'tis I who will proclaim your exploits. All Paris shall against you make one universal cry!

ACT IV.

SCENE: *The residence of Dupré. Comtois discovered, alone, sitting in an armchair.*

COM. Ah! This is something like. Bless my stars! How comfortable I am here! Good cheer, good bed, nothing wanting. Yesterday my nourishment was very scant, my apartment in the sky parlor, and my lodging "on the cold ground." I was obliged to pass day and night waiting upon others. Today, I am waited on. I command in my turn. In a great armchair I repose most comfortably. A little gold has produced this metamorphosis. Now anybody else, I'm sure, would take airs upon themselves and grow impudent upon such a revolution. But not I: I'm no prouder than I was. Yes, I'm superior to such weaknesses; and had I all the riches of Peru to myself entirely, I shouldn't be a bit the prouder or vainer for it. What I was yesterday I shall be tomorrow. Forgetting the past, without ill humor, without rancor, I shall know how to enjoy my luck mildly. No vanity, never the least superciliousness. In one word I shall always be a good fellow. [*Enter Dupré*]

DUP. So, Comtois! At last, then, I have a moment to breathe in. Really, I can't reply to all the congratulations and attentions I find. The worst treatment suddenly changed to the kindest. I escape from the ungrateful to find flatterers.

COM. And so do I, sir, exactly my case.

DUP. How so?

COM. Yes, that's easily accounted for. When you were maltreated, I was cuffed. Now you are flattered, I am caressed. Ah, sir! That's the old way. When the master holds a court, the valet holds his.

Dup. Frémont does not return. I am very anxious to know from him the effect which my departure has produced.

Com. Your sons-in-law must have cut a sorry figure. It seems to me as if I could see 'em! Ha, ha!

Dup. Comtois, my heart is closed forever against these ungrateful wretches. I will never see them more.

Com. Don't say so, sir. I know you better. The moment you see their consternation you will pardon them. Do you think you are tear proof? No, no, sir, not you.

Dup. Never will they have power to subdue my wrath. A wall of brass is reared between us. Yet it is cruel to quit Amélie—

Com. Ah, sir, I know it must be. She's your mistress—

Dup. Dear child! She alone has charmed away my griefs. Ah! may I soon press her to my heart. Go, seek her, Comtois.

Com. I fly, dear master. [*Madame Dalainville and Charles appear in the background*]

Ch. [*To Madame Dalainville*] Approach—

Mme. Dal. I tremble to appear before him.

Ch. Wherefore? Fear nothing.

Dup. [*To Comtois*] Say I expect her here.

Com. Yes, sir. [*Exit Comtois*]

Dup. Deserted by cruel relations, at least she remains to me, and, far from my family, I shall always have my daughter to console me.

Mme. Dal. [*Approaching*] What have I heard? Great Heaven!

Dup. How, madam, you here!

Mme. Dal. Yes, my father, I come to embrace your knees. You do not then forget your cherished daughter! Ah! I heard all.

Dup. I spoke of Amélie. She seems today to shun my presence. She never shunned me when I was wretched.

Mme. Dal. Agonizing reproach! Scarcely can I breathe!

Dup. [*To Charles*] My friend, fortune has deigned to smile on me. You will no longer stand in need of succor or employ. From this day forward you shall take up your abode in my house. I will not offer you the dazzling magnificence of opulence; but, enjoying here a modest competency, you will not have to fatigue the pity of the great, and you will live peacefully in the bosom of friendship.

Ch. Ah! My fate henceforth will be worthy of envy, and you may be sure—

Dup. Someone comes. 'Tis Amélie. Yes, 'tis she. [*Enter Comtois and Amélie*]

Com.   Yes, sir, here she is. I met her coming.

Dup. [*Embracing her*]   Ah! What charms this moment has for me! Dear child!

Amél.   Just Heaven! Do I see tears?

Dup.   Yes, but no longer tears of grief. Those I now shed are full of sweetness. Behold at my side the daughter who is dear to me! She has never blushed to own her unfortunate father. She always anticipated his slightest wishes. To love, to console him were ever her pleasures.

Mme. Dal.   Great Heaven! How I suffer!

Amél.   We all felt alike. All who were about you ever loved you equally.

Dup. [*Taking the hand of Charles and of Amélie*]   Of my love be also convinced.

Amél. [*Taking the hand of Madame Dalainville*]   It shall be a struggle between us three which shall cherish you the most. [*To Madame Dalainville*] Shall it not?

Mme. Dal.   Oh! Yes—yes—yes—! Darling niece, how my heart is touched by your delicacy. What! My father—is it indeed so—have I afflicted you? Hear me ere you condemn. To yourself your daughter now appeals. Alas! I was inconsiderate, but not criminal. The pernicious temptations of grandeur, I admit, vanity, pride dazzled my eyes, but never have their temptations stifled in my bosom the voice of nature.

Amél.   Embrace her quickly; she is worthy of you. Does it not seem as if you saw my mother at your feet?

Dup.   Your mother! It is done. One word disarms me. My dear children—
[*Clasps Amélie and Madame Dalainville to his bosom. Enter Frémont*]

Fré.   Hey dey. What's here? Tears! [*Low to Dupré*] A word with you.

Amél. [*Aside*]   Oh, what a stern look—

Dup.   Let me beg you will all pass into this apartment. I will follow you thither presently.

Mme. Dal.   Oh! best of fathers! [*Exeunt Charles, Madame Dalainville, Amélie, and Comtois*]

Fré.   I come to inform you of the state of your affairs.

Dup.   My sons-in-law.

Fré.   All goes on admirably. I have seen them both. Your departure has worked wonders. They don't know what to be at. They are annihilated. 'Tis a thunderbolt.

Dup.   Oh, Heavens! Has repentance touched their hearts?

Fré.   As yet they are only moved by their fears. Their popularity is endangered and that public opinion to escape them and being corrected they are aware it must fall heavily on their misdeeds. So here we are at the worst of the tempest. 'Tis here, Dupré, you must stand firm. They are about to set their friends on you. They themselves even, I'll wager, with the most submissive air, will come to you and protest their delicacy, talk of respect and tenderness. You know them well—fine talkers! And, for aught I know, perhaps they'll even shed tears, for there is no effort which will be impossible to them. And the ambitious have such sensitive hearts! But don't let yourself be taken in by their fine phrases. Let reason come to your succor. You have been outraged; show decision. Today, be a judge; tomorrow, you may be a father.

Dup. My friend, rely on me. It is a hard task and trying, but I shall have courage and you shall be satisfied. [*Enter Comtois*]

Fré. Well, what now, Comtois?

Com. Mr. Dalainville, sir.

Fré. There! Didn't I tell you so. He's a clever man!

Com. Must I admit him?

Dup. Demand why without my leave he ventures to my house? And tell him, if he dares again infringe my order which forbids him, I will find a way to punish his impertinence.

Fré. I could not have done it better myself. Excellent! Perfect! [*To Comtois*] You must not forget the compliment, my friend.

Com. It shall be repeated word for word.

Fré. Ah ha! We've got you in the toils, gentlemen hypocrites! You are not at the end. Come, my dear friend, let me hence. You will apprise us when he shall be gone. [*They enter a side room. Enter Dalainville, greatly agitated*]

Dal. Ah, Comtois, good Comtois, let me see my father-in-law.

Com. Sir, how shall I have the courage to tell him? Ah, dear me! Dear me! I may try and try but—know, sir.

Dal. What say you?

Com. [*Apart*] I can't for the soul of me. I am really gentler hearted than I could have conceived. [*Aloud*] It is not possible.

Dal. How! You refuse me? But, by the way, I had forgotten to ask, have my servants apologized to you?

Com. Oh, yes, sir. They were so humble I really thought they were going on their knees.

Dal. My father-in-law.

Com. Is gone out.

Dal. Comtois, you are deceiving me.

Com. Sir.

Dal. Go tell him—Be certain 'tis of the greatest importance I should speak with him.

Com. I dare not, sir. I fear to trouble him. He is outing with his clerk. His door is forbidden to be opened.

Dal. You drive me to despair.

Com. When you lock your door, do you allow yourself to be interrupted?

Dal. I am in the most imminent danger, Comtois, if I do not see him. Go, I supplicate.

Com. Well, if it must be, it must. [*Dalainville tries to force a purse into his hand*] Oh, sir, you humble me too much. [*Exit Comtois*]

Dal. [*Alone*] How painful a part, oh, Heaven, am I reduced to act! This shocking business has already made a noise. It is spoken of at Court. If things go on thus, by night all Paris will know it. 'Twill be the town talk. There's not a moment to be lost. The step is delicate, but I cannot get myself out of the scrape but by a bold stroke. Shall I see the reward of my services snatched from me and fifteen years of sacrifices gone in one day? At what a moment too! When a signal honor was about to environ me with glory and splendor, and must I fall at the end of my career? No, hope sustains me. Let me speak to my father-in-law. There is no effort which ought to cost me too dear. When we know how to flatter old men we have our point gained with them. Let me invoke in turns his goodness, his justice. My glory is the goal. He must be softened. [*Enter Dervière*]

Dal. My brother, I am enchanted to see you here. Tell me, pray tell me, is my wife better?

Der. Much. What news? What hopes?

Dal. None. Things are as bad as they can be.

Der. Patience. Time will bring them round.

Dal. I am in despair. The Minister knows all. "It is reported," said he to me, with a severe look, "that you have been treating your father-in-law extremely ill. That notwithstanding you owe all your wealth to his generosity, you have conducted yourself in the most disgraceful way towards him, and that your cruel and insulting conduct has forced him to quit the mansion."

Der. Heavens! Can it be!

Dal. "But," adds he, "I cannot think the truth has been told me. In short, I am too well convinced how the calumny often tarnishes the purest virtue, and how a public man, surrounded by the jealous, is thrown more open than any other to its lash. So I wished to have an understanding with you upon so grave a point. Calumny, you know, spreads rapidly. Then justify yourself the first moment you can. You were about to obtain the most brilliant distinction."

Der. Great Powers!

Dal. "You are aware there is a place about to be vacated in the Ministry; that place was to have been yours."

Der. Oh, cursed father-in-law!

Dal. "But hope not to rise to a level with us while such a suspicion darkens o'er your head. Public opinion is everything. It would be inexcusable to recompense those who are branded by that. Without the esteem of others, no good can be done. A magistrate must be a good citizen!" Then I denied everything, as you may imagine. I made great complaints even of so black a plot.

Der. You have done well.

Dal. The Minister appeared satisfied. "You will gain," said he, "a complete triumph. Presently your innocence will appear in full glory. The outrage was public; the acquittal must be so too. I can fortunately serve you in that. This very evening all the Court and the city will be at my house. My proposal no doubt will make you happy. Appear there yourself with your father-in-law."

Der. And what did you answer?

Dal. Why, of course, I promised and I am come hither to seek for him.

Der. How? Will he consent?

Dal. I fear—

Der. And I hope. He can't refuse to come; he must be a very bad father, if he does.

Dal. Unite with me to subdue him. A common interest should impel us to make common cause.

Der. Aye—but—

Dal. On the one's fate depends the others; my place escaping me, you cannot have yours.

Der. I know the old man; we shall be able to gain him over. I too would accompany him to the Minister's.

Dal. You—to what end?

Der. My successes have alarmed the malignant. I too would silence them, like you. Just now I happened to be reading my report upon foundlings. With one voice the whole auditory did me justice, but a colleague maliciously remarked, "No doubt there are plenty of barbarous parents in the world, who remorselessly forsake their children, but are there not, also, guilty children deserting their venerable parents? Do not these also require their case considered? You may, upon this point, make a new report."

Dal. 'Tis plain all's known.

Der. I felt the apostrophe, but I conducted myself like a true philosopher. I made no answer.

DAL.   Great Powers! Time presses; let us go in. We are lost if we deliberate. [*They are going into Dupré's room, as Dupré appears*]

DUP.   What would you with me? I have nothing to say to you. I have already apprised you of my intentions. I will not suffer myself to be braved here. I am no longer in your house. I will be obeyed.

DAL.   Great Heavens, what have I heard! Overwhelming contempt?

DER.   Oh, deign to us a favorable look! Your wrath fills our hearts with affliction!

DUP.   Spare me, in mercy, an explanation. It is, at this moment, altogether useless. I scarcely begin to feel tranquil. Expose me not to new torments; you know, gentlemen, I need repose.

DAL.   Oh, great Heaven! Are our misdeeds not to be repaired?

DER.   At least let us avow how guilty we feel ourselves.

DAL.   Deny not at least to hear me for a moment.

DER.   I only wish to speak to you of my repentance.

DUP.   There is nothing in the step you have taken to surprise me. I know the reason which brings you both hither. It is not repentance.

DER.   What is it then?

DUP.   The fear of passing for ungrateful. Forbear to use of the language of virtue. You have never had anything but the cloak of the wise. It falls and you tremble to appear in your nakedness, but it was indeed time you should be known.

DAL.   We are, on every point, ready to satisfy you.

DER.   Henceforward all our care shall be to please you. Return with us—you will see—

DUP.   Return! You have insulted; you never shall degrade me. You must have strong reliance on my weakness.

DER.   Not so, I know the tenderness of your nature.

DUP.   When I found it necessary to carry things to this extremity, think you, ungrateful men, it cost me little? But you had worn out my courage. What do I say? My departure is your own wish. By dint of contempt you repelled me. It is in short, you, <he>, who drove me away.

DAL.   Ah! Am I no longer the husband of your daughter?

DUP.   I owe a great example to fathers.

DER.   Oh Heaven! Who will take care of you when your old age comes on?

DUP.   Be sure, I shall not apply to you. My situation is not so bad as you may believe. I can do myself justice with what remains. I can have friends enough, should such be my desire. [*Eyeing Dalainville*] Those who will receive me will have no cause to blush.

DAL. Is it to me, just Powers, you speak thus? What? I? I blush for you! What guilty madness could have ever compelled me to such business? Oh, then, I should indeed be ashamed to complain of your contempt. But there remains a way to put me to the proof of my respect for you. I offer you a public testimony. This very day the Minister gives a large party and all Paris this evening is to go to his house. If you will permit I will conduct you thither.

DER. I trust you have nothing today against it?

DAL. Ah! How exquisite would be such a moment for my feelings! I should be truly proud to appear there with you.

DUP. That would be most useful to you then?

DER. Most truly so, but it is already late. We should be on the way.

DUP. Ah! So you are to be of the party too?

DER. 'Tis for the sake of being with you.

DUP. I see but one objection to the fulfillment of your wishes, gentlemen. 'Tis that I have no notion of making myself a show of. Have you flattered yourself that I would be for a moment the servile instrument of your ambition? I know you have need of my presence to force the world and myself to silence, for that is your purpose. Can you deny it? You don't catch me; the snare's too evident.

DAL. Well then, know all; I have no wish to hide anything. This step is altogether necessary to me. Come with me to the Minister's or be certain that by your refusal I am dishonored.

DER. Yield to his wishes; be merciful. That is the noblest vengeance.

DAL. My fate is in your hands. If you remain, I am lost. Deign but one step and honor is restored to me. What do I say? This moment will meet my every wish; it will enable me this day to obtain a brilliant place. I am a Minister! What an exulting moment for you! My father! Admit that it will be delightful to you to see me encircled with dignities and honors. You will see all Paris following your footsteps. Think of the good you can do—do you feel its value? I promise instantly to oblige your friends. They all shall have places!

DER. I, I shall have the Secretary of the Treasury—finances. I shall have it in my power to content all your acquaintances.

DAL. In Heaven's name speak.

DUP. I fear not. I should be sorry to see the ungrateful honored. You would only be named through an injustice. I will not, sir, be its accomplice. Adieu.

DAL. What! Gone!

DER. In mercy, hear!

Dup. Hence!

Dal. Must he embrace your knees?

Der. Yield to the repentance with which my soul is filled. [*They both fall at his feet*]

Dup. 'Tis not remorse; 'tis pride which supplicates.

Dal. What! Am I not sufficiently humbled?

Der. Let yourself be softened.

Dup. [*Going*] You make me pity you! [*Exit Dupré*]

Dal. Great God! Can insult be carried to this pitch! I suffocate, I feel it, with fury and with rage!

Der. And, for my part, I cannot deny but I'm almost ashamed of myself. To be thus treated! Horrible!

Dal. Can hatred and vengeance be carried this far?

Der. Ah! His heart has never known benevolence.

Dal. Were there any way to do without him?

Der. Someone might be found on reflection.

Dal. Public opinion may waver for a moment, but we shall get it into our interests eventually. Our names are most advantageously known.

Der. We have always had our virtue spoken of.

Dal. We have friends; I trust they'll act.

Der. Oh yes, besides everybody knows what a father-in-law is.

Dal. Let us hence without delay.

Der. Never more to return.

Dal. I swear it.

Der. And I!

Dal. Lose not courage and we shall still have it in our power to face the storm!

ACT V.

Scene: *As in last act, on the following morning.*

Com. You here, sir, and so early! Astonishing!

Der. Most important business brings me. Where is your master.

Com. In bed. Not a soul is up yet.

Der. And his friend from Bordeaux?

Com. He's not come yet.

Der. What is he doing?

Com. What doing? Why sleeping in his lodging, I suppose, as every honest man is.

Der. I am most anxious to see him.

COM. But he is not here.

DER. How, not here? Then his lodgings are elsewhere?

COM. Yes, sir, thank Heaven. We are very much attached to him, but though he is one of our own, master don't like to lodge any more in the house with others. [*Knocking*] Another knock! Are people mad to disturb folks at this time of the morning? Whoever saw the like!

DER. If it should be my brother-in-law! It's as likely he might be return-ing here without having apprised me.

COM. Oh, no! He never comes out so early.

DER. If it should happen to be him, you must not say a word of my being here.

COM. Why this mystery?

DER. I have good reasons for not showing myself. In the name of Heaven, Comtois, don't let him come in.

COM. To drive him away, sir, I will do my best. [*Exit Comtois*]

DER. [*Alone*] To the most cruel affronts this man is insensible! Can he have forgotten his yesterday's oath. My father-in-law nevertheless has treated him without pity. At least for returning I may be excusable, for he never said anything too disagreeable to me. Ah! Why is it that Dalainville must appear with me! Had I been alone, I might have obtained everything I want. [*Com-tois runs in*]

COM. You were right; it is your brother.

DER. There's perjury!

COM. Ah, good Heaven, what's to be done? I could not succeed in put-ting him out of doors. He is come, sir, spite of all my efforts, but pass if you please, into the next room. I'll get him off.

DER. Very well, but if he will not be got off?

COM. If he will not, I'll give him his dismissal in a twinkling.

DER. He will not see me, and I shall hear him. [*Exit Dervière, into the cabinet. Enter Dalainville*]

DAL. Well, Comtois?

COM. Sir, it cannot be—master cannot be seen this morning.

DAL. But I must see him. Nothing shall prevent me.

COM. But, sir, I tell you—

DAL. I will wait till evening. I will fasten upon his traces like his shadow. To get me out of the house you must tear me hence. He may curse me, he may detest me, I will not complain, but hear me he must. Everything is going wrong with me since he left. Perhaps my Ministry is already given—mine I may call it, for it belonged to me. I shall be lucky, indeed, if I can even keep my situation. Yesterday evening, however, I got off with a plausible excuse about my father-in-law. Yes, but now nothing must be neglected to make him appear. I have promised this very day to call on the Minister with him. Can he resist my supplication?

COM. [*Apart*] How agitated he is! His fever torments him.

DAL. To determine him what means can be employed? I am ready, if necessary, to make every sacrifice. [*Enter Frémont*]

COM. Oh, sir, make haste; 'tis Heaven itself guides you hither!

DAL. [*Sitting down*] Now for a moment's breath. I can scarcely stand.

COM. Our sons-in-law are come, one after the other. They were at the door before daybreak.

FRÉ. Well! What say they?

COM. Ah, sir, they sigh and groan! Did you but hear them! Truly they melt me. The proud Dalainville is there in a state of stupefaction. The benevolent Dervière is in the cabinet.

FRÉ. How?

COM. He fears the presence of his brother-in-law. I fancy there is not the most thorough understanding between them.

FRÉ. Leave us. [*Apart*] Behold them then disunited.

COM. [*Going*] They must be forgiven. They have suffered enough. [*Exit Comtois. During the following dialogue, Dervière from time to time half opens the cabinet and listens attentively. Frémont shows by his action that he sees him*]

DAL. [*Rising*] Comtois—ha! You, sir!

FRÉ. Aye, truly, I myself.

DAL. How happy I am to find you here. Deign to have the goodness to hear me but for a moment.

FRÉ. Why I have already spoken to you with the utmost frankness.

DAL. Excuse me, sir, if I am importunate; but my fortune, my fate is in your hands. On you alone depends my restoration to honor. Ah! Refuse not to become my benefactor!

FRÉ. I can have nothing to do in any such affair! I tell you again, apply to your father-in-law.

DAL. He shuts his doors against me.

FRÉ. You saw him yesterday. I predicted to you: he received you ill—

DAL. Today I must make another effort. With your aid it must prove decisive. Yesterday I am persuaded my brother-in-law did me injury. I should have settled the matter offhand but for him. In short, his presence was fatal to me.

FRÉ. How so?

DAL. Between ourselves, your friend detests him. 'Tis an eccentric man, a downright original, and my father was excessively ill-treated at his house. And wherefore should I be the victim of his faults? At the bottom of his heart my father-in-law esteems me. I admit indeed I have not shown him the most delicate attentions, but it was only because I could not. I am often carried away by the whirlpool of business, from which even my own interest cannot protect me. I must admit, I may have given false impressions of myself, for when I am busy, my ways are not even polite.

FRÉ. You are very often busy?

DAL. Overwhelmingly so. I can assure you, I am not guilty. Come, fly, speak to your friend in my favor.

FRÉ. Ah! What he has given up to you, he has taken much to heart. His great annoyance is having allowed himself to be made your dupe. That one thought absorbs all.

DAL. Hey? Why, what has he ever given me?

FRÉ. Oh! Only two hundred thousand crowns, that's all!

DAL. Would to Heaven I had never accepted them! What are they in comparison with political situation, the loss of my place and of public esteem? If he would have only gone with me yesterday to the Minister, I would have restored them to all with the heartiest satisfaction.

FRÉ. Maybe, but it is too late now.

DAL. Not at all. It can be done yet. Let him come to the Minister with me this morning; there, speak strongly in my favor, boast of my love, my attachment. In short, let him appear in public with me from this day forth, and give me open marks of affection, and instantly everything he has given me shall be restored. What better can I propose?

FRÉ. Certainly you are in the right. But he won't: it is too late.

DAL. I'm sure if that won't satisfy him, I am at a loss to guess what will. Only consider: every sou shall be reimbursed. Can one act more disinterestedly, sir?

FRÉ. Oh, most certainly that is speaking like an honest man; but, in fact, you will be the gainer, even in restoring the sum. You'll never be able to gain the point, however. He don't want now—he'll refuse every sou—

DAL. Nevertheless, I shall still, even if he won't take it, possess merit in his eyes of being anxious to give it up. What do you think? Come, don't you agree with me?

FRÉ. Why, stop—

DAL. Well?

FRÉ. Let me think. No, I won't charge myself with the business, that's settled. But I'll give you an excellent idea, for you have won me over; that I declare to you frankly, by this greatness of soul, this noble devotedness. I know I have some sway over your father-in-law, but certainly not enough to change his fixed purpose. To effect that his heart must be touched, and who can attempt that so well as his daughter? He always loved her dearly, and to send her to him would be like going yourself. Let her, in your name, offer what you propose, and all your old offenses may be excused—

DAL.   Admirable! I hasten to concert with her—

FRÉ.   And I, on my side, to prove my zeal, will go and talk to Dupré about you; endeavor to call up gentler sentiments in his bosom; speak of your virtues, of your disposition. It will be very easy, too, to throw everything upon your good brother-in-law's shoulders, for he, you know, won't give up a farthing. [*Here Dervière opens the door and listens*]

DAL.   Oh, not he indeed! Such a notion never would come into his head. His heart is dry and cold. Interest alone can touch it.

FRÉ.   The name of benevolence is ever on his lips.

DAL.   Downright charlatanism, and long known as such. Never did a poor man get a sou from him. By a hypocritical zeal he makes himself popular; and 'tis only, in a word, a color he has taken. This man, who could be taken for being utterly destitute of the slightest ambitious inclination, never had but one view: that of getting power—

FRÉ.   Why, he always seemed utterly insensible to worldly honors.

DAL.   He is suffocating with ambition—

FRÉ.   Oh, Heavens! Is it possible? Why, what an impostor!

DAL.   Nay! Whatever he may be, you cannot think I would call him by so harsh a name, much as he may deserve it.

FRÉ.   Oh, that's right. Like a charitable relation defend him; but then, you know, the vengeance must light on some head. There must be a victim. Well, let him be the victim. Everything must be settled this day—

DAL.   Right. I fly to my own house. Never shall I forget your extreme indulgence.

FRÉ.   Nay, nay, you deceive yourself. This is always the way I act when there is question of obliging my friends. Till we meet again, adieu. Don't forget to give madame her lesson—[*Bows and goes out. Frémont going on the opposite side. Dervière running out of the cabinet*]

DER.   [*Alone*]   Oh, what an infamous plot! Truly 'tis a horror for which there is no name! Dare he prate of ambition, who, covered with honors, is still desirous of them? Who is devoured by the thirst for power and greatness. He the basest and the most aspiring of men, capable of flattering even the valet of a great man, who, when occasion suits can turn vice to profit, accepts by calculation, and restores through avarice! But to unmask his plot

I must be beforehand with him. I'll give up all myself, expressly to punish him. To my father-in-law instantly I'll send my daughter. 'Tis she he cherishes the most of all the family. [*Enter Amélie*]

AMÉL. My father here! Just Heavens!

DER. And here she comes. Ah, I am enchanted to find you here—

AMÉL. May my fault be forgotten by you. With my good grandpapa I have no quarrel. Ah! don't be angry. Don't be vexed. My father, I came hither to supplicate him for you—

DER. The time is precious. I must make the best use of it. [*Sits down to a table*] Now instantly to make a written promise to restore all I have received. My child, without delay, you will go and present him this note from me. Cursed father-in-law!

AMÉL. Oh, Heaven! how angry he is! The letter he writes seems to displease him. By this fatal note does he intend to spoil all? Ah! I hope he does not intend to make me the bearer!

DER. [*Rising and holding the promise*]   There's no denying the vengeance is most hard. But he will not accept. Oh, no, certainly he will not. Nevertheless I am happy to have heard all. I don't think I should have given up but for that. [*To Amélie*] Come, take this writing. Bear it instantly to my father-in-law—

AMÉL. Alas! Are you not afraid of making him more angry?

DER. How?

AMÉL. In Heaven's name, father, trust me. Don't send it till tomorrow—

DER. What say you? Inexplicable! Will you do as I bid?

AMÉL. Ah! Behold him here. Speak to him yourself, father. That will be much better! [*Enter Dupré and Charles*]

DUP. How, sir, do I still find you here?

DER. I am with my daughter, and I come to promise-you—but read that paper.

AMÉL. I dare not give it.

DUP. Let us see what it is.

AMÉL. Believe not a word he says in it. It is not, believe me, it is not from his heart it springs—

DER. Ah, the cursed child! Will you hold your tongue?

AMÉL. When you wrote it you were in anger—

DUP. What do I see! Is it possible? Oh, Heaven! You here declare—
[*Enter Comtois, preceding Madame Dalainville*]

COM. There he is. Yes, madam, courage. Hasten—

MME. DAL. [*With emotion*]   Oh, my father, one moment listen to your daughter. Happiness may once more dawn upon my family. I come at this moment, in the name of my husband, to restore to you all the wealth he has received from you. To put it all at your feet I flew. Here is the legal instrument by which he makes full restitution. Oh! refuse not, and deign to accomplish our wishes in restoring to us your love.

DER. [*Apart*] They are a day after the fair. My promise has been in first.

DUP. I cannot recover yet from my surprise. Is it an illusion? What! Dalainville too!

AMÉL. I cannot comprehend a syllable of all this.

DUP. Dear Frémont, you here! [*Enter Frémont, followed by Dalainville, whom he leaves at the back of the stage*]

FRÉ. You seem in great joy, friend. What news?

DUP. If I am joyful, I have cause. I am at last restored to the possession of my property.

FRÉ. Can it be?

DUP. Yes, truly, and if you doubt it, see this double promise of my sons-in-law.

FRÉ. And yet you dared doubt their tenderness! [*To Dalainville*] Approach, my good friend. Come and receive the recompense you have merited.

DAL. I have only done my duty!

FRÉ. Gods! What a magnanimous competition of love and gratitude!

DAL. My brother-in-law has given up all. What am I to think of it?

FRÉ. One might almost fancy there was an understanding between them; yet there is not the remotest accord.

DUP. The restitution has so much the greater merit. The struggle was which of the two should bring his in first. But I would in my turn show my generosity. It is not my fortune which can render me happy. I regard that, alas! with perfect indifference. But since you restore it, my children, I keep it in my own hands and henceforward I alone must direct how it shall be employed. I did dwell beneath your roofs; henceforward you shall reside under mine.

DER. [*Apart*] I was far from expecting such a conclusion!

COM. [*Apart*] Oh, good Heaven! I trembled lest he should give it all up again!

AMÉL. We are now all happy.

COM. Oh! how pleased I am!

DAL. You have no longer, I hope, any resentment?

DUP. To Charles, remember, you owe a place.

CH. Ah, sir!

DAL. Well, what would you have me do? Come to the Minister—

Dup.   So be it. I consent. But I can't answer for your being still in time. I will give Charles a dowry. [*To Dervière*] And you, I presume [*Pointing to Amélie*], will do something in his favor.

Der.   Yes; I understand you, but—

Dup.   No conditi<ons or I will> not accept the restitution.

Fré.   Oh! Do not make such a threat. You'll terrify him.

Dup.   [*To Frémont*]   Friend, I render you my thanks. To your generous concern I owe my liberty. Take back this money you have lent me; for I must begin by paying my debts. Look, my friend, how many you have made happy!

Der.   Ha! Tricked!

Fré.   Ah! I'll answer for it. Truly I never turned my money to more profitable account.

Dup.   My sons-in-law, I owe you a salutary counsel. To the peace of your days I <believe it necessary.> You have children, deserve <their love; if> you would screen yours<elf from too much suffering> through them, <never show complais>ance towa<rds them. And never renounce your independence.>

CURTAIN

MAZEPPA;

Or, THE WILD HORSE OF TARTARY

MAZEPPA;
Or, THE WILD HORSE OF TARTARY

THE manuscript of *Mazeppa; or, The Wild Horse of Tartary*, in Payne's own hand, is in the Harvard collection.

Mazeppa, an equestrian melodrama, which was probably never performed, was written in 1825, when its source, Léopold and Cuvelier's *Mazeppa; ou, Le Cheval Tartare*, was produced at the Franconis' Cirque Olympique, and published in Paris. Payne's manuscript is dated November 12 of that year, but the play was practically complete by October 2; for at that time Irving, returning it with revisions, advised Payne to send it to Price. Failing to interest Price, Payne offered it, apparently without success, to Fawcett, January 7, 1826.

With the publication of Byron's *Mazeppa* in 1819, the legend became extremely popular; but the relationships among the important versions are not always clear. Byron's narrative, generally thought to have been inspired by Voltaire's sketchy account in *Charles XII*, itself inspired, according to the contemporary review in *The Drama*, the anonymous *Mazeppa; or, The Wild Horse of the Ukraine*, which was acted early in November 1823, at the Royal Coburg, but which has not been preserved in either manuscript or printed form. Léopold and Cuvelier acknowledge their indebtedness to Byron; but they introduce important changes, for their heroine at the opening is unmarried, and their hero, a Tartar Prince, eventually marries her. Payne, except for slight alterations, translates the French play closely. Milner's version, called, like Payne's, *Mazeppa; or, The Wild Horse of Tartary*, was performed April 4, 1831, at the Royal Adelphi, and later was revived in both England and America, and published several times; although Milner states that Byron is his source, he apparently makes a free adaptation of the French play, altering the names of some of the minor characters. (A. H. Quinn in *A History of the American Drama from the Beginning to the Civil War*, New York, 1923, p. 442, suggests that Payne may have been the author of the play with this title acted at the Bowery, July 22, 1833; but the names of the characters in the bill are those of Milner's version.) Interest in the legend died slowly, for later versions appeared sporadically.

It seems impossible to account for Payne's failure to find a producer, for the play has all the qualities necessary to satisfy the demand for elaborate romantic spectacle.

CHARACTERS

ABDER KHAN, *sovereign chief of a horde of Tartars*

MAZEPPA, *his grandson, reared in Poland under the name of Casimir*

THE CASTELLAN OF LAURINSKI, *a Polish lord*

PREMISLAS, *Count Palatine*

THAMAR, *chief of a Tartar tribe*

RUDZOLOFF, *head officer of the castle of Laurinski*

OZEB, *Tartar warrior of the suite of Abder Khan*

ZELOS, *an aged Tartar*

DROLINSKO, *head of the huntsmen*

KOSKAR, *a young Tartar shepherd*

ANOTHER TARTAR SHEPHERD

POLISH LORDS, SQUIRES, PAGES, SERVANTS,
SHEPHERDS, SOLDIERS

OLINSKA, *daughter of the Castellan, loved by Mazeppa*

AGATHA, *nurse of Olinska*

KORELLA, *a Tartar female, revered among them as a prophetess*

LADIES, SHEPHERDESSES, ETC.

SCENE: *first and third acts in Poland on the banks of the Dnieper.
Second act in the midst of the deserts of Independent Tartary.*

ACT I.

SCENE 1: *A terrace, or open gallery, giving a view to the back of the stage, which is crossed at the boundary of the terrace by a balustrade high enough to lean upon, beyond which appears a circular enclosure forming an area, a riding ring, for jousts and tournaments, with seats ranged amphitheatrically around its remote edge.*

At the rising of the curtain, Rudzoloff, Drolinsko, with several servants of the castle, are discovered upon the terrace, looking on at what passes in the riding ring, where several esquires and huntsmen are seen preparing for the exercises.

DRO. [*To Rudzoloff*] What an odd freak of the castellan! To think of having the untamable horse tamed during this grand display of feats of arms and horsemanship! He'll frighten everybody off the ground and we shall have no sport.

RUD. As his highness destines this wild Tartar courser for the head of his four-legged establishment, he has set apart a day of festivity as the fittest to begin the stranger's education for the intended dignity.

DRO. With all due deference, his highness is a fool for his pains. What hope is there of the quadruped's ever bearing bit or bridle, when even the want of food won't make him docile? They are obliged to throw it at him as they would to a tiger. He must be the most incorrigible of independents, who will not even become submissive at the call of his stomach.

RUD. All stomachs are not so eloquent as yours.

DRO. I tell thee, godfather, there is no hope of man or beast after they become insensible to the allied powers of hunger and food. Let the castellan waste no more time and labor, but take my advice and send this devil upon all fours back to his native Tartary. He's the most patriotic of horses, for whenever he fancies he sees a chance of escaping, he always makes toward his native country.

RUD. When he once gets accustomed to our more civilized habits, he will forget Tartary and love Poland.

DRO. What! Would you have a brute more rational than a man? There never yet was a native of that country, whether wearing one pair of legs or two, that came to any good by being in a better. The young Tartar, for example, who was picked up, according to your account, half dead near the fountain of St. Casimir in the valley of the forest more than eighteen years since, after our great battle with the Tartars—

RUD. Well. Is he not a proof against your assertion? Do you think the Countess would have made so much of the poor orphan after he was brought to the castle and restored to life, if he had not deserved it? Do you think she would have herself given him the name of Casimir, in remembrance of the place where he was found, and had him brought up amongst her pages, had she not seen in him indications of those great qualities which have since rendered him the envy of all the men and the idol of all the women?

DRO. Not *all* the men! For my part, I would, of the two, prefer his brother barbarian, the wild horse. Casimir indeed! A fellow who never talks but with his sword and orders one about as if a foundling had a right to set himself over people of known pedigree like you and I. Let the Countess beware. She may find, too late perhaps, that she has indeed caught a Tartar! [*Enter Casimir, unperceived, who, overhearing Drolinsko, slaps him on the shoulder*]

CAS. Ha! What says the slave?

DRO. [*Aside and affrighted*] By all that's terrible, the Tartar has caught me!

CAS. No muttering. You spoke of me.

DRO. Of you, did I? Well, if I did, I'm sure you would have been pleased, delighted, if you'd heard all; that is, if the praises of such a poor devil as I could be of any value to a gentleman of your dignity; for I'm sure I, among the rest, am most forward to acknowledge *what* you are, however much we may all, as well as you yourself, be puzzled to understand *who* you are.

CAS. Insolent knave! Another word like that! [*Seizing him*]

DRO. Let me go, pray let me go, and I'll never speak another word of any sort.

CAS. [*Flinging him off*] You are not worth my anger.

DRO. I thank you for estimating me so justly.

RUD. How now, Drolinsko! What means your absurd innuendo? Can he be accounted as unknown who is the favorite esquire of my lord, and the favored protégé of his noble daughter, the beautiful Olinska!

CAS. [*Moved*] Olinska! [*At this word all his anger vanishes; he lifts his eyes to Heaven, puts his hand upon his heart, and sighs*]

RUD. And happy indeed we all are at your good fortune in being so; and it would make us now still happier if we did not know that your duty to them must presently take you far from us.

CAS. [*With disquietude*] How? What mean you?

Rud. Why, you know as my Lady Olinska is going to be married to the Count Palatine Premislas, one of the richest and most powerful noblemen of Poland—

Cas. [*Troubled*] It *is* then true!

Dro. True. Yes, that it is; and it is equally true that the husband of Lady Olinska, at her recommendation, is likely to take you as her first esquire; and then, you know—

Cas. [*In a violent rage and seizing him by the collar*] Wretch! Who *dared* make that assertion? Speak! Who dared insult me thus?

Dro. [*Screaming*] Help! Help! Are you mad? Is one's health never safe within reach of your throttlers? Help! Help, I say!

Cas. Away! Away! [*Dashes Drolinsko from him to the ground, then rushes out, leaving all present in astonishment*]

Rud. [*Following Casimir with his eyes*] The man's possessed! How strange that ever at the mention of Olinska—

Dro. [*Getting up*] Godfather! That man will come to no good! Oh, that they would set him upon his brother, the Tartarean horse, for a gallop to Tartar*y* or Tartar*us,* as either or both may best approve, but as far as possible from my throat! And you, too, who stood calmly by to see me slaughtered!

Rud. Oh! I am too sensible of your prudence to be afraid of your ever coming to any damage beyond a drubbing, which, once in a <while>, is not only harmless but healthful: circulates the blood and saves doctor's bills and should be encouraged rather than prevented. But, hark! The hour for the exercises of our young esquires! [*Flourish of trumpets*] That trumpet speaks the approach of my lord, with the beautiful Olinska and the neighboring noblemen. Away! We must see that all is ready for their reception. [*Goes up the stage. Enter the Castellan, Olinska, Polish lords and ladies, esquires, pages, hunters, and vassals. The trumpets continue to sound. The seats in the circus become filled with vassals, who run from all sides to see the exercises. The competitors are set in array. Casimir is amongst them. The Castellan advances with Olinska and lords and ladies. The esquires, who are about to contend, salute them, as they pass, in the military style. The Castellan's company are placed on elevated seats to the right and left*]

Cast. [*Still standing near the balustrade*] My friends, display before us your address and courage. These noble sports are the image of war. Learn by them to defend your prince and country. My daughter will crown the conqueror. [*Movements of Olinska and Casimir*] Let the signal be given for them to begin. [*The Castellan sits down by Olinska. Rudzoloff makes a sign. The trumpets sound. The games begin. Different exercises of the manège, fencing, and horsemanship. Amongst the esquires and pages who *engage in them Casimir is distinguishable as the most skilful, whether on horse or foot; and Drolinsko, on the contrary, is remarkable for his awkwardness. Repulsed, he quits the riding ring, especially as he perceives the wild Tartarean horse, which is led curvetting into the middle of the circus. Drolinsko makes his escape and comes to place himself near the balustrade as a mere spectator. Several esquires are dismounted in striving to master the Tartarean horse. As they endeavor to remount, the horse escapes furiously. All the esquires, frightened and discouraged, leave him. Casimir alone, who appears unintimidated, runs after him. Sight of them is lost for a minute; everyone's eyes follow him with restless curiosity. Olinska, especially, is trembling, but quickly recovers on beholding Casimir quietly reappear on the Tartarean courser, whom he has mastered, and who appears docile under his hands. Casimir is proclaimed first victor in the games and comes with those who distinguished themselves to bow before balcony, where the Castellan and his daughter are placed. The latter with difficulty hides her lively emotion which is shared by Casimir*]

CAST.   Casimir, it is with pleasure I behold you victor! I have already remarked your courage and address and have distinguished you from the crowd of my servants. Merit always thus my favor, and new rewards will be the result.

CAS. [*Aside*]   Ah! There's but one reward in which my heart can set a value! [*Casimir, fearful of being remarked, hastens to kneel at the feet of Olinska, who, not daring to look at him lest she betray herself, presents him a scarf and a sword as the recompense of his victory, having previously distributed crowns to the other victors. After the distribution of prizes the Castellan comes forward with his daughter. The noblemen and ladies, Casimir and his companions, remain at the bottom ranged in order*]

CAST.   Let this day be given up to sports and pleasures. I depart presently to visit the Count Palatine Premislas. [*To Olinska*] My daughter, I shall soon return, I trust, with tidings which may make you happy. [*Inquietude of Olinska. Jealous movement of Casimir. The Castellan kisses his daughter's forehead and, mounting a horse which Rudzoloff leads him from the back of the stage, departs accompanied by the lords. Olinska retires slowly on the opposite side, appearing to meditate some project; and Casimir, scarcely able to contain himself, is compelled to follow his companions*]

SCENE 2: *A magnificent apartment of the castle, with an immense curtain spreading across the back. Enter Olinska, slowly, sad and musing.*

OLIN. [*Alone*]   Will she ne'er come? Be still, poor heart! Oh, like the imprisoned bird, beat, beat thyself to rest! [*Dame Agatha enters, whom,*

Olinska perceiving, runs to her] Dear nurse! My impatience for your coming—

AG. And yet I made the best of my way and came faster than I have trudged this many a day. Heigho! Really, I'm quite done up! But you are looking very unwell. You should be in bed, my dear—

OLIN. Nay, nurse, to the point—

AG. Aye, aye—well, well—to the point, then. What is this unforeseen misfortune? And in what manner can I be serviceable to you? Speak, speak, my dear Olinska. Tell your old Agatha.

OLIN. Oh, I am deeply to be pitied.

AG. Pitied? You! When there's nothing talked of at the castle but your approaching nuptials with a young nobleman so rich and—

OLIN. Those nuptials never can take place—

AG. Never! If, however, the Castellan, your father—he is imperative, absolute—

OLIN. Sooner let me die!

AG. [*Terrified*] Oh, blessed St. Dominic! Die? You shall never die! But speak—explain! You are silent; you cast down your eyes—

OLIN. Do not ask me.

AG. Oh, I shudder at the doubt which comes across my mind. Have I divined the secret of the impediment?

OLIN. What deem you the impediment?

AG. Love!

OLIN. Nurse—

AG. And for some object which is not worthy—

OLIN. [*With vivacity*] Casimir not worthy!

AG. Casimir! It is then true? This orphan without name, without country! And you, the heiress of a noble castellan of Poland—

OLIN. I will be sworn, were his rank known, he would be found at least my equal. The richness of the vestments wherein he was wrapped when found, the chain of gold which held a star glittering with diamonds, those letters graven in Arabic on his right arm, and whose assemblage forms the strange word *Mazeppa,* all indicate a birth above the common, which his valor and noble sentiments confirm.

AG. We always wish to believe what we desire; but all those proofs will not suffice for the Castellan, who has ever regarded Casimir as one of his servants.

OLIN. Have you forgotten, nurse, that in my infancy he saved my life?

AG. Your father rewarded him for that act; and in return for his benefits, Casimir has dared to raise his thoughts to the daughter of his master.

OLIN. Ah! Do not accuse him! Carried away, both, by feelings irresistible, our mutual vows—

AG. Such vows are void.

OLIN. They are recorded in the skies.

AG. Without the consent of your father, what right had you to utter them?

OLIN. One not to be disputed.

AG. How?

OLIN. Public report had spread abroad the dreadful story of my father's death in the last contest against the Turks. I was believed an orphan, without protection. I was surrounded by ambitious neighbors, ready to snatch from me my inheritance. 'Twas then I found in him you deem unworthy of me, a friend to share my sorrows, a warrior to defend me at the hazard of his life. After the generous devotedness of Casimir, who could have considered it a crime in me to think of uniting my destiny with his? Such was my intention. My father's return, snatched from the hands of the infidels by the Palatine Premislas, prevented its fulfillment. Yesterday, yielding to the prayers of Casimir, I went to make an avowal of our love to my father; but judge of my astonishment, my agony, when he anticipated me by announcing that he had solemnly engaged my hand to the Count Palatine, his liberator. Now that you know my cruel situation, judge me, condemn me if you can, but at least pity the unhappy Olinska!

AG. I condemn you! Ah, my dear young lady, my bosom can harbor no sentiments towards you but the tenderest, nor entertain any wish except to do you service. But how can you brave the will of the Castellan? How will you ever dare to refuse the coronet of a countess which, according to the form of proposing marriage among persons of his rank, he is about to offer? How set a father's authority openly at defiance?

OLIN. Oh, that is beyond my courage! I dare not decline the offered coronet—

AG. And its acceptance is a marriage promise!

OLIN. Its rejection would prevent my purpose of escaping from the castle this very night to the holy monastery of which the Countess Eliska, my aunt, is sovereign abbess.

AG. Would you renounce the world?

OLIN. Yes, if my father, insensible to my tears, should command me to renounce my love—

AG. A project so bold—

OLIN. Is the only means of protection from a hateful marriage; and it is you, you who fostered my infancy, that must conduct me to my mother's sister—

Ag. I! And does Casimir know of this?

Olin. As yet he does not even know of the intended marriage which makes this necessary. I fear the temerity of his character, the excess of his love. 'Tis only from my sacred asylum that I purpose to apprise him—[*A noise is heard of hurried footsteps*] Ha! Someone approaches! 'Tis he! 'Tis Casimir! Great Heaven, how agitated! [*Casimir advances suddenly from the back entrance. He stops, with a vexed air, on seeing that Olinska is not alone. With difficulty he constrains himself*]

Cas. Noble lady—

Olin. Speak without reserve, Casimir. My second mother here knows all.

Cas. Before her, then, pronounce my fate.

Olin. Your fate!

Cas. Yes, on you, and on this moment, depend the destinies of my life.

Olin. What mean you?

Cas. Listen, Olinska. There remains for us but one resource: We must fly. The deserts of Tartary where I first drew breath, and from which we are separated only by a river and a few days' journey, offer us an assured retreat. Ah, long since, breaking the fetters of a shameful subjection, I would have returned into the midst of my brethren. I would have sought to discover what blood flows in my veins, whence the impetuous stream whose high pulsations speak that it must take its source from no unworthy fountain. To thee I sacrificed the desire for independence; to remain near thee I submitted to the disgrace of servitude. I was beloved, and a smile of Olinska made me forget I was a slave. But now, when the bonds which unite us are to be torn asunder, have I not the right to require of Olinska who has chosen me for her husband that she should seek with me in my own country that happiness which is denied to us in hers?

Olin. Oh, Heavens! What dost thou ask? I seek an asylum amongst barbarians, the enemies, the devastators of Poland? Never! Never!

Cas. Thou refusest, then, to follow me?

Olin. I will not place an insurmountable barrier between us and forgiveness.

Cas. Olinska, wouldst thou regret thy titles of honor?

Olin. Canst thou think thus of Olinska?

Cas. [*With a gleam of jealousy*] The coronet of a countess possesses tempting charms! I have nothing to offer thee but a heart burning with love and jealousy!

Olin. Casimir!

Cas. [*With increased agitation*] But let this hated rival tremble—

Olin. Casimir! I supplicate thee, listen to me—learn—

CAS. Dread to reduce me to despair! I care not for life; I am ready to sacrifice my life, but I will not perish alone! [*He is at the height of frenzy. Olinska in her grief has flung herself upon a seat. Agatha, who was at the end of the stage, to watch for the safety of the two lovers, returns quickly towards them to induce them to separate. Casimir resists. He wishes a positive answer*]

AG. Your father comes. Ah, for both your sakes, hide from him your tears. Casimir, away! [*The central curtains are suddenly withdrawn, and the Castellan and his suite, including Rudzoloff and Drolinsko, appear. The Castellan appears surprised at the embarrassment caused by his presence and starts on seeing Casimir*]

CAST. [*With severity*] Casimir! What do you here, Casimir!

CAS. [*Confused*] My lord Castellan—[*Agatha, fearing he may betray himself, hastens between him and the Castellan*]

AG. My lord, Casimir is only come—[*Hesitating*] to—to—to—to request my influence with the destined bride of the Count Premislas to obtain for him the place of first esquire with her intended husband—[*The Castellan regards by turns Agatha and the two lovers, who remain thunderstruck, with downcast eyes*]

DRO. [*Aside to Rudzoloff*] Indeed! It was that, then, which took him so suddenly away from his comrades. The Tartar seems to know which side his bread is buttered.

RUD. [*To the Castellan*] This young man's coming hither, my lord, is an act of insubordination which—

CAST. 'Twould be your duty to punish, but I am willing to excuse. I call to mind his conduct during my absence. His courage and fidelity deserve a signal recompense. I name him officer of men at arms, whom I am sending to Warsaw to be incorporated in the royal guard. He will depart tomorrow at daybreak—

CAS. My lord, permit me—

CAST. Rudzoloff, I charge you to see this order executed.

RUD. Enough, my lord. [*Exit*]

DRO. [*Aside*] Bless the fates, we shall get rid of him at last!

CAST. My daughter, I have just left the Count Premislas, who has formally demanded your hand.

CAS. [*Aside*] Just Providence!

CAST. The king himself approves this marriage. My daughter, it is thou who will acquit my debt of gratitude. What happiness for thy father!

OLIN. [*Aside to Agatha*] Support me, oh, support me!

CAST. The Count Premislas wished to come even on the instant and present to thee his homage; but an ancient custom does not permit a Palatine of Poland to offer his vows in person till after a solemn ceremony. The Countess's coronet must be presented to the intended and she return her ring in exchange. From that moment she is his affianced bride. The envoy of the Count this very day will come on the important mission.

OLIN. [*Troubled*] What, my father! This very day?

CAST. Even so. Prepare for his reception. My daughter, obedience should be easy, when honors and fortune are its reward. [*Enter Rudzoloff*]

RUD. My lord, an envoy from the Count Palatine Premislas requests the honor of being presented.

CAST. Let him be conducted hither and received with all the honors due to his noble master. [*Low to his daughter*] Olinska, be mindful of your duty. [*Olinska sighs and casts down her eyes in token of submission. Rudzoloff has given his orders. All assemble. Casimir is in his place. Enter the envoy, esquires, pages, soldiers, etc. The train is displayed at the back and on the sides of the stage. In the midst of the pages and esquires who compose it is the envoy of the Palatine. He offers, with great ceremony, rich presents to Olinska. He takes out of a superb casket, borne by two pages, a countess's coronet sparkling with diamonds, and presents it on his knees to the daughter of the Castellan, who directs on her a severe and scrutinizing look. Casimir, with his eyes fixed on his beloved, is in hopes that she is about to refuse the brilliant gift offered to her, in order to take away all hope from his rival. What is his astonishment on seeing her accept it after a moment's hesitation. The Castellan, satisfied, approaches Olinska with kindness and directs the coronet to be placed upon her head. She receives it with a feigned submission. All the followers of the Palatine bow before her whom they already regard as their mistress. During this time Olinska has sought the eyes of Casimir to assure him by a glance; but he cannot perceive it, being plunged in somber reflections. He believes her false and meditates his vengeance apart. The Castellan orders his daughter to give the envoy of her future lord the ring which should be exchanged for the diadem. This is a new test for Olinska. Impelled by the looks of her father, who, seeing her hesitate, has resumed his severe air, she takes the ring from her finger, and, heaving a profound sigh, she advances towards the envoy to present it to him. As soon as she has extended her hand to give it, the envoy, instead of receiving it, makes a sign, the numerous group that surrounds him opens, and Premislas himself appears, receives the ring, and throws himself at Olinska's feet*]

OLIN. [*Motionless with surprise*] What do I see?

CAST. The Count Premislas!

Cas. [*Aside*] Down, rebel nature, down!

Prem. [*Rising and holding Olinska's ring*] Pardon me, beautiful Olinska, for not awaiting the sentence which was to decide my fate. Had my homage been refused, I should have quitted the castle without intruding upon your view; but, on seeing you accept the diadem, I hastened to receive myself this precious pledge of happiness.

Cast. This eagerness, my dear Count, is a proof of love which cannot but be flattering to my daughter.

Prem. To deserve her smiles shall be the study of my life. [*He takes the hand of Olinska and kisses it. Casimir makes a movement in his jealous fury to spring upon his happy rival. A thought stops him. He has conceived a surer way of revenging himself*]

Cas. [*Aside*] This very night! Vengeance! Death! [*He rushes out, without being perceived by anyone but Olinska, who shudders at beholding his rage. Premislas, who still retains the hand of Olinska, perceives her agitation. The day begins to close*]

Prem. Fair Olinska, why this agitation? Your hand trembles in mine—

Olin. Pardon me, my lord, but your sudden arrival, these unlooked-for honors—I need a moment's calm. [*To the Castellan*] Permit me, father— [*Going*]

Cast. How, daughter! So soon departing?

Olin. Suffer me, my father—I am overcome—a moment's repose will— oh, suffer me to withdraw hence with my nurse—

Cast. Daughter, the Count Premislas—

Prem. The least desires of Olinska are commands for me; but I hope tomorrow to be more happy.

Olin. Yes, my lord, tomorrow you shall know that Olinska is not unworthy of your esteem.

Cast. Deign to follow me, Count. Everything is prepared to receive you with the honors due to him, who, becoming my son, will presently have a right to command where now he is guest. [*A general sortie. All the suite retire, following the Castellan and Premislas. The latter offers his hand to Olinska, who cannot decline it. The curtain is let fall, and the scene changes*]

Scene 3: *A Gothic apartment. In the flat, three glazed doors, which open on a picturesque country seen through an iron rail fence. At the horizon a craggy mountain terminating at the left extremity with a foaming torrent. On changing the scene, it is complete night. Servants bring in lights which are placed on a table. To the right, the darkness only appears from the exterior through the glazed doors. Enter Rudzoloff and several esquires.*

RUD. Come, gentlemen officers of the Count Palatine. Upon me, in my capacity of <major-domo>, devolves the honor of doing the honors of the house. [*Pointing to a door at the left*] Here is the apartment of your master. You see, my friends, that nothing has been omitted for his service. [*He is interrupted by the crash of falling armor*] What noise is this? It comes from the armory. [*The stifled cries of Drolinsko are heard, who, in a voice changed by fear, seems to call for help*] That simpleton Drolinsko's voice! He's always running his head into some silly scrape! Has he quarrelled with the armory and got a box on the ear from some old gauntlet? [*They all go up the stage. Drolinsko staggers on, half dead with fear, and holding in his hand a flambeau, violently agitated from his trembling*]

DRO. Bless my soul! Oh, dear! Oh, dear!

RUD. What is the matter?

DRO. What is the matter? I have just seen—

RUD. Whom?

DRO. The devil, godfather, as plainly as I see you.

ALL. [*Laughing*] The devil!

RUD. Are you mad?

DRO. It was enough to make me so. Listen. I am going to relate what will make you shake in your shoes.

RUD. Some new fooleries, I wager. Come, go on—go on. [*All assemble around Drolinsko with curiosity*]

DRO. I was coming to rejoin you as you directed—

RUD. [*Impatiently*] Be brief—

DRO. In order to arrive sooner, I took my way through the armory, where all the ancestors of our Castellan stand in their steel, visors down, lances in rest, as if still living they were going to make a charge upon the Turks—

RUD. And then—

DRO. I walked along, quietly, thinking—what was I thinking of? I think I wasn't thinking of anything. On a sudden, I heard a noise. I was close to the great-grandfather of my lord who has been dead more than a hundred years—you know who I mean, godfather—he with so terrible a frown, who always holds his arm uplifted with a drawn saber, he with the awful black helmet—

RUD. Will you never be done?

DRO. I am just done. Suddenly the great arm falls on my shoulder; I raised my eyes, with a little fright, I own; and I saw, I saw the great-grandfather of my lord without his head—[*All burst into shouts of laughter*] Yes, laugh—laugh. I should have liked to see you there, gentlemen. I started—I turned round, when, lo! I perceived, as plainly as I see you, I did indeed!

That very head—with its helmet shaded with black plumes, gliding softly away upon another body, covered with a great ghostlike mantle. It moved without a sound, majestically, thus and thus—to the bottom of the armory, through all the coats of mail, whose clinkings, ah! I shiver still at the very recollection! [*Whilst he is speaking, Casimir is seen to pass at the back of the stage, covered with a mantle, a helmet with black plumes on his head. He raises his visor for a moment*]

CAS. [*Aside*] Could he have recognized me? [*He listens*]

DRO. By'r Lady, but I could no longer hold it out, and I fled, thinking all the specters of my lord's ancestors were at my heels.

RUD. I don't know which is the most ridiculous, the fool who tells such tales, or we who listen to them.

DRO. It is impossible, godfather, not to—

RUD. Enough, enough of this. Give Casimir notice that his detachment is to depart before the drawbridge is raised for the night. He will quarter his men in the village, in order to set out at an early hour without disturbing the castle. Such is the will of his lordship.

DRO. So much the better. His room was always more agreeable to me than his company. [*Casimir goes out as Premislas and pages enter. The Count advances, preceded by two pages with lighted flambeaux. All the servants of the Palatine range themselves respectfully about their master. Rudzoloff points out to him his apartment where everything is prepared for his reception. Premislas looks that way and testifies his satisfaction to Rudzoloff, who bows low and goes out, making a sign to Drolinsko to follow him. Premislas, while some of the servants enter his apartment, sits down near the table. His esquires take off his sword and spurs. His pages remove his mantle, which is placed on the back of the chair, and his cap, which they set on the table near his sword*]

PREM. You may retire. I dispense with all service from you for this evening. [*All go out. Premislas, alone*] I shall be presently united to Olinska. Called, too, by my sovereign, to one of the first offices at court, love and fortune unite to crown my wishes! [*He reflects. His countenance assumes a more serious character*] Still, the extraordinary emotion of Olinska haunts me—her disturbed looks—her eyes moistened with tears! [*A pause*] What would be her hand without her heart? Perhaps some knight more blessed than I—[*He rises*] but, no! Olinska was brought up in retirement. Her heart will be thoroughly her husband's. [*This idea restores calm and satisfaction, which are pictured in his countenance. He takes a light and prepares to enter into the chamber. In going up the stage, he faces Casimir, who has come on during the soliloquy. Casimir is entirely enveloped in his mantle, and his head covered by a helmet with black plumes, the visor drawn. At sight of him Premislas makes a movement of surprise, approaches the table upon which his sword is placed, and seizes it to oppose the mischief which he apprehends from his mysterious visitor*] Who art thou?

CAS. Thine enemy!

PREM. How entered you this castle?

CAS. What matters that to thee?

PREM. What is thy will?

CAS. Thy death!

PREM. Wouldst thou be my murderer?

CAS. No. I would fight thee fairly.

PREM. [*Proudly*] Thy name?

CAS. Thou shalt know that when thou art conquered.

PREM. This arrogance—

CAS. Befits a jealous and offended man.

PREM. What! Can you be—

CAS. Thy rival!

PREM. [*Doubtfully*] Beloved?

CAS. Till yesterday I believed so.

PREM. [*With pride*] But today thou findest that the beautiful Olinska accords to me the preference?

CAS. Not to thee, but to thy honors and thy titles.

PREM. Ha! Darest thou insult me—

CAS. I have told thee but the truth. My sword shall do the rest.

PREM. Rash intruder! Thinkest thou a Palatine will measure swords with an unknown, doubtless unworthy of that honor?

CAS. My blows will teach thee whether I be worthy.

PREM. Hence! Or my servants shall chastise thy boldness. [*Seizes a hand bell from the table*]

CAS. One word, one gesture, and I stretch thee at my feet—dead! [*Presenting a pistol*]

PREM. Coward! If our arms were equal—

CAS. [*Throwing aside his pistol*] They are so. [*Opens his mantle*] Behold! My bosom is unarmed! I wear this helmet for concealment, not protection. Aim at my heart. It has now no defense but courage and this good sword! [*Pushed to the point, Premislas is forced to place himself upon his guard. A lively and bloody combat commences between them. Victory is not long uncertain. Premislas, pierced in the left shoulder, falls at the feet of Casimir*]

PREM. I yield!

CAS. [*Resuming his mantle*] I am revenged! [*A great tumult without. The three doors at the bottom are flung open with a crash, and a crowd of servants are seen with flambeaux. Drolinsko is in advance and leads them*]

DRO. I tell you the unknown who took the armor is in that gallery. [*Perceiving Casimir*] Look! Lo! Behold him! There! There! There he is! [*The servants rush into the hall, but stop upon seeing the Count extended and making vain efforts to raise himself. Two servants run towards him, while the others endeavor to master Casimir, who, disengaging himself from those who press too closely on him, by presenting his pistols at them and profiting by the general tumult, escapes by leaping through a window. Premislas is raised and placed in an armchair. He recovers his senses a little. He recognizes his servants. Enter the Castellan, Rudzoloff, and suite*]

CAST. [*Hurrying in*] Great Heaven! The Palatine assassinated!

PREM. [*Faintly*] A rival! Vengeance—

CAST. You shall obtain it, and whoever the murderer may prove, it shall be terrible! [*Two discharges of pistols are heard. Enter Drolinsko, followed by vassals*]

DRO. [*Running in first*] We've got him! He is taken! He is taken! [*Casimir is brought in, still wrapped in his mantle and his visor down. He appears calm in the midst of the trouble that reigns around him. About the same time Olinska and Agatha, followed by her women, enter at the opposite side*]

PREM. [*Rising to point out Casimir*] Yes! That is the assassin.

CAST. Remove the mantle that conceals the wretch! [*Before anyone has time to execute this order, Casimir flings his mantle and helmet on the ground*]

ALL. Casimir!

CAST. My suspicions were, then, true!

SERVANTS OF PREM. [*Ready to spring on him, exclaim*] Let him die!

CAST. [*In the height of fury*] Hold! Reserve him for the punishment inflicted upon rebel slaves! Bring out the fiery, untamed horse! Tie this vile Tartar on his back, and turn him loose to scour their native deserts! There let the murderer be borne through sands and rocks and wilds, till hunger, thirst, and scorching suns and frequent bruise and restless motion kill him piecemeal! [*This cruel sentence is executed. Casimir, firm and tranquil, seems to brave it. He is dragged off the stage by the servants of Premislas and the Castellan's soldiers. Olinska, who remained a moment motionless with horror, seeing her lover depart, wishes to fly towards him. She is prevented. She throws herself upon her knees at the feet of her father*]

OLIN. Oh, my father! Pardon for him who saved your daughter's life!

CAST. Unworthy girl! Darest thou plead for him who has dishonored thy hospitality? All powers on earth combined were powerless o'er my vengeance! [*He repels her with harshness and goes to Premislas, who seems to regain a little strength. Olinska, wild with grief, escapes from the arms of Agatha, traverses the stage, and endeavors to get away. On every side the passage is closed against her. She stops at the bottom of the stage and recoils with horror from the spectacle that presents itself to her view. The entire end of the stage has become suddenly illuminated by a great number of flambeaux, borne by the servants. Beyond the iron railing is seen Casimir, fastened to the wild horse, who, violently excited, darts across the stage with the rapidity of lightning. Casimir bids a last adieu to his beloved by calling on her name with heart-rending cries and disappears for a moment. Olinska, anew, is desirious of running to Casimir. She is restrained, and at that moment the courser reappears on the mountain, dashes down the torrent, and disappears in the midst of the waves of the abyss. Olinska gives a piercing shriek and falls into a swoon*]

ACT II.

SCENE 1: *In front, the interior of a grotto or cavern, open at the back, through which appears a wild and rugged prospect of the desert plains, or steppes of Tartary, crossed by an extensive lake. In the grotto, righthand, is the entrance of another cavern which seems to descend deep into the mountain. This entrance is closed with a barrier of unhewn wood. At the side, a natural bank covered with moss and detached. Several groups of horses are discovered grazing at large in the steppes beyond the lake. Ozeb and Zelos appear at the back, come round the borders of the lake, and enter mysteriously into the grotto.*

OZEB. This, then, is the mysterious dwelling of the Tartar prophetess?

ZEL. It is. But the part which my inspired mistress makes her habitation is a deep cave, cut in this side of the rock.

OZEB. Is she now in that cave?

ZEL. No. Korella passes her nights upon the summit of the rocks, whence the view stretches o'er the immense deserts of Tartary, even to the misty mountains, at whose feet rolls the Dnieper, which parts us from Poland.

OZEB. What does she there?

ZEL. 'Tis said that, warned by a celestial revelation, she awaits the return of him who is to reign over us, of Mazeppa, grandson of the ruling Khan, last of his line and rightful heir to the throne of Tartary.

OZEB. Alas! Mazeppa perished when an infant, in the invasion of the Polish frontier.

ZEL. The prophetess believes that he escaped from death but dwells in slavery.

OZEB. Knows she that the King is come and that he encamped, this very night, not far hence?

ZEL. She cannot help but know it. Her vision, it is said, embraces the past, the present, and the future. [*Sorrowful and mysterious sounds are heard*] Hark! 'Tis she! Look, stranger! How rapt in thought and gloomy is her mien!

OZEB. [*Looking*] Her eyes are fixed on Heaven. Deep meditations seem to absorb her mind.

ZEL. Such is ever her air in moments of inspiration. If you would now consult her—

OZEB. [*Absorbed*] No, no—not now. Tomorrow we may meet, perhaps this very day—but—[*Apart*] Now to apprise the Khan of all I have just learned. [*He departs at the back, on one side, as Korella advances from the other without perceiving him*]

KOR. Omens of woe! On Poland the stormcloud driven by the hurricane —[*She stops*] My brain is burning! [*Supports herself against a rock*] Scarce will my strength sustain me—

ZEL. [*Approaching*] Nay, good mistress, cheerly—be composed—

KOR. [*Recovering*] Ha! Thou here, my trusty Zelos?

ZEL. You seem o'erpowered. A little rest—

KOR. Right. You are right. I do indeed want rest. Oh, this night's wild and wondrous visions! Warnings from the skies—[*Pastoral music heard*]

ZEL. Our friends approach, the shepherds of the desert.

KOR. Is their repast in readiness?

ZEL. Everything is prepared. [*Pointing to a jutting rock on which are baskets and vases*]

KOR. 'Tis well. Let them seek shelter here. Oh! Should the thunderbolts fall on them! But, no! Their humility is their safety. 'Tis the proud oak which tempts the storm and not the lowly shrub. [*Pauses*] Now to my secret chamber. If any come to claim my aid or counsel, seek me on the instant. Let none turn hence unanswered. [*Exit Korella. The rustic strains draw nearer as Korella enters the cave, whose barrier closes after her. Zelos ushers in the shepherds. He directs before them free naked horses, who go to seek the others, where all remain together grazing. Enter Koskar and shepherds and shepherdesses*]

Kos. Here we are at last, Father Zelos. Bless my weary legs! The heat makes it seem as if one were wading through flames! This journeying in the desert is a marvellous quickener of the appetite for liquids, hey, father?

Zel. Korella has anticipated your wants. Look! Here's milk and cakes of maize. [*All dart upon the vases and cakes*]

Kos. Truest of prophetesses! Bless her inspirations! [*The shepherds are grouped with the females on divers sides. They eat and drink gaily*]

Zel. [*Clapping Koskar on the shoulder as he is drinking*] Hollo, friend! Your thirst seems to be running a race with your hunger.

Kos. Yes, but thanks to your inspired mistress, they're both getting near the goal.

Zel. In that case, my good lad, take your rustic reed [*Pointing to a pipe hanging at his girdle*], and accompany this old shepherd [*Turning to a Tartar*], who will give us the song of the Volpas. There's nothing like music after meals. It helps digestion.

Kos. What! That song of the wild genius of the desert? The very thought of it gives me an indigestion.

Zel. Pshaw! Children's tales! You can't believe what they say of the Volpas? I thought you had more sense.

Kos. Believe? I don't believe, but I know it. It never appears but as a forerunner of wonderful events. The very mention of the terrible Volpas turns all the milk I've been drinking! The ravager! The destroyer! Come, come— no more of the Volpas! [*The pastoral groups form. Koskar mounts a hillock and plays upon his Pandean pipe. The old shepherd below sings, accompanying himself upon an instrument formed of several sticks, upon which he strikes with a rod of iron. Upon each return of the burthen, all the men and women figure a heavy dance, almost without stirring from their places, with extravagant movements of their heads and arms, terminating every time in grotesque and varied groups*]

Across the wilds of Tartary there whirls a demon form;
His voice is not of this world and mingles with the storm!
Through blasts of forked lightning his snorting courser dashes,
And death and terror as his guides, smile grimly mid the flashes!

Let the lovely shepherd maid
Most of all his sight evade!
Haste! Haste! To your tents hasten back!
A pursuer is on your track!
Fly! Fly!
'Tis the Volpas that's coming! The Volpas is nigh!

[The last couplets are repeated in a dancing chorus as above mentioned, with signs of terror]

His black and fiery courser's mane stands bristled by the blast,
And from his feet the dust in air is up in whirlwinds cast.
His wide and smoky nostrils dart before him fires of wrath,
And nothing that's of mortal born can live upon his path!

> Let the lovely shepherd maid
> Most of all his sight evade!
> Haste! Haste! To your tents hasten back!
> A pursuer is on your track!
> Fly! Fly!
> 'Tis the Volpas that's coming! The Volpas is nigh!
> *[Chorus and dance]*

Oh, when that horse and rider come, the astonished earth and ocean
Shake and shrink back with terror at the mystical commotion!
Nature, as if she writhed her last, heaves with the horrid pang,
And trumpets shriek i' th' troubled air their war-denouncing clang!

[Trumpets suddenly interrupt the singer. Koskar stands silent and shuddering. All the shepherds and shepherdesses press close to each other. Old Zelos goes up the stage]

ZEL. These warlike sounds announce the coming of brave Thamar, first chief of Abder Khan.

Kos. *[Affecting courage]* Didn't I tell you so? Didn't I say there was nothing to be afraid of? As it's Thamar, you know, it can't be the Volpas. *[Low]* Though, between ourselves one's almost as bad as the other.

ZEL. *[Low]* Silence! Should Thamar hear—[*Makes an expressive gesture, on which Koskar recoils and slinks back to his companions. Thamar, with a suite of Tartar warriors, appears, and all bow submissively]*

THAM. Shepherds of the desert, form in procession and depart for the great encampment. Abder Khan, our prince, has directed the tributary Tartars o'er whom he reigns to assemble before the royal tent. *[Koskar sounds a trumpet. The sounds are echoed from afar, and being heard by the docile steeds grazing in the distance, several of them come forward with no direction but the signal. Tartars spring upon their naked backs and disappear, crossing each other at various sides. The movement is repeated on the greensward beyond the lake. Groups of riders appear, recede, and are presently lost to view in the forest. All the shepherds are now gone off. Thamar addresses Zelos]* Acquaint Korella that I would consult her in private.

ZEL. *You* consult the prophetess? You, who till now have scorned her words as idle—

THAM. I ask not for thy counsel. Be silent and obey.

ZEL. You shall be obeyed. [*Aside*] What would he with Korella? I distrust this Thamar! [*Thamar makes a gesture of impatience which interrupts the old man, who, urged by the warriors, enters the cave*]

THAM. [*To his train*] I would win this woman to our purposes. Not that my reason stoops to a belief in superhuman powers, but she has a resistless influence over the superstitious multitude. All Tartary consider her as Heaven descended. Gold will tempt her to aid me to attain the sacred scimitar, emblem of sovereign rule, which, once within my grasp, my strength and courage will find means to keep there. [*All make a movement expressive of concurrence and devotedness. Zelos appears at the entrance of the cave. Terrified at the menacing air of the warriors, he pauses. Korella follows him. He points her out to Thamar, who gives a sign for the warriors to retire. Zelos disappears with them. Thamar, alone with Korella, addresses her*] Korella, Thamar stands before thee.

KOR. [*Without looking at him*] What would he of the prophetess of the desert?

THAM. Her judgment.

KOR. [*Pointing upward*] On the future?

THAM. [*Disdainfully*] The future is hidden with a veil which human weakness may not draw aside.

KOR. He who thinks thus needs not the counsels of the divines. Farewell.

THAM. Hold. [*She turns. On seeing him, she gazes with astonishment*]

KOR. [*After a long pause*] That voice doth shake me to the inmost soul. The protecting genius of Tartary inspires me!

THAM. [*With marked earnestness*] Engrave, then, my words upon thy mind, that it may return an oracle suited to our tribes.

KOR. Speak. I hear thee.

THAM. Thou knowest the Tartars need a warrior at their head. Thou knowest, too, that in battle I am ever foremost.

KOR. And would be on the throne, is it not so?

THAM. Dost deem me undeserving to be there?

KOR. [*Her eyes upraised*] He who reads hearts, he only, can know that.

THAM. 'Tis he has planted in my heart the thirst for power. Hear me, Korella. The aged Abder Khan, cherishing the idle hope of recovering his lost grandson, Mazeppa, has, till now, refused to designate a successor. At length, urged by the pressure of years and the prayers of his subjects, he has consented and will name one tomorrow.

KOR.   I know he does intend it.

THAM.   But, ere he choose, he would consult, disguised, with thee; thee, whom his subjects deem the oracle of fate.

KOR.   I await his coming.

THAM.   'Tis well. Summon up thy arts and spells then. Tell the Prince that the genius of the desert, the awful Volpas, whose very name strikes terror through the empire, will presently appear among us and point out, in some signal manner, the warrior destined to the sovereign power.

KOR.   And this warrior will be—

THAM.   Thamar!

KOR.   Thou! How knowest thou the genius of the desert will appear?

THAM.   My plan is prearranged. Success is certain. Pronounce thy oracle. Trust to me for its fulfilment.

KOR.   Is it, then, by impious stratagem that Thamar hopes to reach the throne?

THAM.   Dost thou presume to judge? Korella, beware! If thou betrayest the secret, this very night, inevitable destruction—

KOR.   [*With a glance of disdain*]   And should I serve thy ambition?

THAM.   Thy glory and thy fortune are achieved.

KOR.   [*Absorbed*]   A tide of thoughts are rushing through my brain. This strange proposal, the visions of this night, a force resistless impels my tongue. Thamar, thou shalt be satisfied!

THAM.   Thou makst me then indeed a worshiper! [*A bustle heard from without*] Abder Khan advances with the ancients of our tribes, disguised in lowly garb, and seeks to try thy powers. Thou mayest identify the monarch by his white girdle, the only sign which marks him from the rest.

KOR.   He has thrown off that girdle. The gods will guide me. [*Thamar, surprised, goes up the stage to rejoin the warriors who reappear on one side, while the procession of old men advances on the other. Korella remains, alone, in front, plunged in deep thought. Abder Khan, Ozeb, with the royal suite of Tartars and old men, are clad uniformly, with no distinguishing mark. They advance slowly and salute Korella with respect. At the back, on the opposite side, are standing Thamar and his warriors*]

OZEB.   Korella, the wretched shepherds come to thee for succor. A mortal plague now desolates the plain. Thy prayers alone can soothe the wrath of Heaven.

KOR.   My aid is ne'er withheld from those who seek it with sincerity. But beware of trifling with Heaven. There is an eye that sees through all deceit.

OZEB.   Korella!

Kor. In vain wouldst thou attempt to hide the truth from me. Fate unveils all things to Korella's vision. [*All the old men approach and gaze on her, astonished. Thamar, in the distance, scrutinizes her with a sort of uneasiness*] The woes of which you speak are fabled. Higher interests fill your minds, and one among you would propound a question big with the fate of Tartary.

Ozeb. One among us? [*Receives an affirmative sign from Abder Khan*] Well, then, I'll not dissemble longer. In me behold the sovereign of this land. [*Korella makes a gesture*] Aye, in me know Abder Khan! What have I to hope for? What to fear?

Kor. In vain you seek to lead me into error. [*Gently putting him aside*] Ozeb, away! 'Tis for thy master to disclose his will. [*Going directly to him*] Hail, Abder Khan!

Abd. Korella!

Kor. Prince! Thinkest thou to hide thee from the eyes of him, my great inspirer? [*Kneeling*] Khan of the Tartars, what wouldst thou of thy slave?

Abd. Arise and answer! At the appointed hour for naming my successor, omens of dire import fill me with dismay.

Kor. [*With gradually increasing emphasis*] I know the omens. This very night thou sawest in vision the heir of the great throne of Tartary, he who was left upon the battle plain in Poland.

Abd. [*With emotion*] 'Tis true. I saw the young, the unfortunate Mazeppa. I stretched my arms to clasp him. Alas! 'Twas but a dream! [*Thamar, who has approached the suite of the Prince, makes signs to Korella, who goes on without heeding him*]

Kor. And as thy arms were stretched to strain him to thy bosom, a tiger darted on the long lost Prince. [*Thamar expresses fury*]

Abd. Enough. I feel thy inspiration. Tell me, thou favored of the stars, tell me, shall I once more, in truth, behold Mazeppa? Does he, in truth, still live? Be thy doom good or bad, pronounce it. Speak! Who is the future monarch Heaven decrees for Tartary? [*The day declines*]

Tham. [*Low to Korella*] Remember! My bounty or my vengeance! [*Distant thunder; lightnings*]

Kor. [*In a continued tone of inspiration*] The spirit of the desert is thy protector! Soon, soon will his will be manifest! Aye, from this lake, amid the flash of thunderbolts; 'tis he, 'tis he himself reveals thy destined heir! [*Rapid and repeated flashes of lightning and loud claps of thunder, amid the deepening darkness. General astonishment*]

Tham. [*Apart, exultingly, to Korella*] Thy word is kept. I am satisfied! [*Aside*] Now, then, for the fulfilment of the oracle! [*The storm drives nearer. The thunders become more terrific. Alarm and horror pervade all the groups, while hope calls smiles upon the lips of the aged Khan and those of Thamar, though from opposite causes. The prophetess appears oppressed. The vision of her mind seems planted on an object imperceptible to all but her. The lightnings, discovering her pale and agitated countenance, attract the looks of the Prince and all his attendants towards hers. She gives a sudden shriek of terror. A loud clap of thunder seems to answer to the shriek. She reels against a rock, exclaiming]*

Kor. He comes! He comes! *[The darkness deepens and the storm grows wilder. Koskar, shepherds, women, and children rush in, terrified]*

Kos. The Volpas! The Volpas!

All. The Volpas!

Kos. *[In a voice almost inaudible from consternation]* I saw him in a hurricane of dust. He flies hither from the mountains bordering on Poland. He rides a wild horse which scours the desert like a tempest. He comes! He comes! *[General shriek of horror. The storm is at its height. Beyond the lake appears the horse to which Casimir is bound. He crosses the steps in a furious gallop. The shepherds, the women, and the children prostrate themselves in groups. Casimir seems to make his last efforts to tear asunder his bonds and cries with stifled shrieks]*

Cas. Set me free! Oh, release me! Set me free! *[For a moment he disappears with the horse. All the characters are grouped on the edge of the lake. Thamar, alone, at the front, knows not how to explain the strange sight. Thamar is disturbed, agitated, irresolute. He consults with his confidants apart, and threatens Korella with his gestures; but she seems overwhelmed and to have lost all perception. Various Tartar groups flow back upon the stage. The thunder redoubles; terror is at its climax. The wild horse reappears, but nearer, upon a rock, forming a little platform which overhangs the lake. In struggling, Casimir has freed his head and one of his arms. He shrieks again]*

Cas. In mercy, set me free! Release me! Set me free! *[At this moment, with the rapidity of thought, a thunderbolt bursts and falls near the rock upon a fir tree, which breaks and falls. On the very instant the wild horse plunges with his rider into the lake, and both disappear. A barque is at the edge of the lake. Two Tartars, the most daring of the throng, spring into it. During these various movements, amid the confusion and terror which reign on all sides, Thamar, overpowered with uneasiness, is desirous of questioning Korella upon this strange event, for which he is utterly unable to account. He approaches her with threats. She preserves a gloomy silence, points to Heaven, and opposes a cold disdain to the menaces of Thamar, who, by the presence of Abder Khan, is kept in check. The tempest gradually subsides. A rainbow appears in the distance through the trees and the returning light discloses Casimir, whom the fall had loosened from the wild horse, struggling with the waves. He swims towards the barque, which receives him; but no sooner has he entered it than he swoons. The barque is brought to the edge of the lake. The Tartars, variously grouped, regard the stranger whom they bear to the front in a lifeless state and place him on the bank of moss. Thamar and his conspirators remain in mingled astonishment and rage. The aged Prince, his mind struck with the prediction he has heard, approaches Casimir with emotion and concern]*

ABD. Poor sufferer! Those torn habiliments and that death-white brow! *[Raising up his head]* Korella! Hasten to his succor. If it be possible, restore him back to life.

THAM. *[Apart]* By what miracle! I had yet given no order. Can Korella have conceived a project similar to mine? And can she be the favorer of some rival? *[Korella eagerly obeys the mandate of Abder Khan. All her attentions are lavished on Casimir. The Tartars group themselves in divers picturesque postures around the wounded. The aged Khan himself attempts to stop the flow of blood. Suddenly he is struck motionless with surprise, in discovering around the neck of the young stranger the chain of gold and star of precious gems. He scrutinizes the latter, opens it; his emotion increases with his astonishment. He falls upon his knees, uncovers the breast of the wounded, looks at his bosom, then at his right arm, and utters a cry of joy]*

ABD. Great Heaven! That chain, that star, that royal emblem stamped above his heart! Mazeppa's name engraven! Friends! Our prayers are answered! Korella's prophecy's fulfilled! Chieftains of the tribes, Tartars, approach! Behold and recognize Mazeppa, your prince! My son and rightful heir! *[Points to the indubitable signs by which he recognizes his grandson. All express the most lively joy, which forms a strong contrast with the ill-dissembled fury of Thamar and his conspirators]*

KOR. Prince, give not way to a deceitful joy. The slumber of the youth is deep and fearful. The moment when his eyes unclose decides his life or death.

ABD. Protecting genius of Tartary, hast thou then but given me back my son, again to snatch him from my arms? Look down with pity on a prostrate people! *[Kneels. All the Tartars follow his example and lift their arms to Heaven. Alone at the back, Thamar seems to meditate some guilty deed and threatens while the rest supplicate. Abder Khan rises]* Be everything made ready for my son's removal to the royal tent. Inspired Korella, forsake him not! Give him your superhuman aid! *[To his suite]* Be the prophetess obeyed implicitly. [*Korella makes a sign to Zelos and others of the attendants. They follow her into the cavern*] Gallant Thamar, proclaim the joyful tidings of my son's return. Assemble the grand council of the chiefs to hear my sovereign will.

THAM. [*Smothering his rage*]   Enough, my liege.

ABD.   Guard the exterior of the royal tent. Let the most trusty warriors, chosen by your care, be called to watch the safety of my son.

THAM.   Your orders shall be obeyed. [*He bows, affecting entire submission to the aged Khan, who turns toward his son, expressing the most affectionate solicitude. Korella appears with a vase and cofferet. She is followed by Zelos and Tartars, bearing a litter covered with skins of wild beasts. Mazeppa is placed on the litter carefully. Korella applies to him a phial, which she takes from her bosom, which seems in some degree to revive him. He places his hand on his heart, lifts his head, and immediately drops it again upon the bosom of Abder Khan, murmuring the name of Olinska. On the side opposite Korella has caught the hand of the young Prince and gazes on him with returning hope. The characters group around the litter as the Tartars raise it up, and the procession moves. It disappears in the distance, after winding round the lake. Thamar is left upon the stage with his warriors, all wrapped in gloomy silence, and ranged around their discontented chief, who thus addresses them*]

THAM.   My gallant partners, the golden prize is slipping from my grasp. To you I turn for aid. [*All the Tartars press more closely round Thamar, with ferocious eagerness*] Speak. Shall the sovereign sway be juggled from your chief to be transferred into the hands of strangers? The perfidious Korella has proved a traitress to her plighted promise! Her treason must be paid for by her blood! As for the youth, led hither by chance or by contrivance, be he, or be he not the rightful heir of Abder Khan, his death is sealed! [*With savage exultation*] His guard to me has been entrusted. The moment is propitious and must not be lost. Even this very night—[*The Tartars, all with their hands upon their dagger hilts, make a gesture of assent*] Enough. Away! [*They depart on the side opposite to the exit of the procession*]

SCENE 2: *The tent of Abder Khan. Right hand, at the back, an alcove hung with bear skins and surrounded with fasces of arms and standards. At its side, a stand sustaining a cofferet, and on which are ranged the arms of the Khan. Koskar and slaves, directed by Zelos, are settling the things in the tent. It is night, and they place a lighted candelabra near the stand. The procession accompanying Mazeppa enters the tent in silence. Mazeppa is still supported on the litter by Abder Khan and Korella. He is placed gently in the alcove. All recede respectfully. The aged Khan and Korella alone remain at the young man's side. Korella endeavors to encourage the Khan, whose anxiety concerning his grandson is become intense.*

Kor. Subdue your fears, King! A little more repose will be enough to bring him to himself. We shall then learn the miracle by which the guardian angels of the land have restored him to his longing kingdom. Then, Prince, you may yourself announce to him his royal lineage and welcome him to his high destiny.

Abd. You answer for his life, then? Oh, Korella! How can I evince my gratitude?

Kor. I have fulfilled the mission given me by Heaven; my heart requires no further recompense! But the unlooked-for coming of your scepter's heir o'erthrows a rival hope, disturbs ambitions, which, perhaps, may soon—

Abd. Speak! What mean you?

Kor. Haste to the chiefs of tribes by your command assembled. Rally around you all your bravest, trustiest subjects. Let wisdom and decision crush the plots which treason may now meditate.

Abd. Prophetess! Your counsels shall be followed instantly. [*Departs with his warriors after having cast a glance of interest upon Mazeppa. Korella gives divers orders to the attendants for the service of the Prince. At a signal afterwards from the prophetess, they withdraw, guided by Zelos and Koskar. Left alone with Mazeppa, Korella, after having gazed on him an instant, glances carefully all around the tent, listens, and hearing no noise, half opens the curtains to examine whether there is aught outside to disturb the repose and safety of her charge. Satisfied on discovery of the sentinels pacing around the exterior, she returns to the side of Mazeppa, sits down near the stand and from deep thought sinks to sleep. After a moment of the profoundest silence Thamar appears. He steals forward and gazes all around. He discovers the intense slumber of Korella. The moment seems propitious to his plot. He makes a sign. Four ferocious warriors, devoted to Thamar, appear at the entrance of the tent. On a second signal they approach in silence. Thamar points them to the couch*]

Tham. [*In a low tone*] Comrades! Behold the traitress and the impostor youth! Fate puts them in our power! Both must perish. Advance in silence. [*The Tartars softly approach the alcove. Korella, still sleeping, makes a gesture which seems to express that she is in a dream. The Tartars recoil, surprised, their swords remaining uplifted*]

Kor. [*Her eyes not unclosed*] Aye, thou shalt reign, Mazeppa, thou yet shalt reign and make the people happy!

THAM. [*Low*] She dreams.

KOR. Traitor! In vain thou liftst a sacrilegious hand. 'Tis Heaven's decree. He triumphs o'er his foes. Aye, soon, thyself delivered up to death— [*She springs up*]

THAM. [*Raising his voice*] Thine first shall pay thy perfidy! [*Aiming at her heart, the blow misses her in rising and falls upon her arm*]

KOR. [*Shrieking*] Ha! [*Thoroughly awakening*] Murderers! Help! Save us! [*Thamar and his Tartars rush on her. Korella only strives to shield Mazeppa with her body*] Mazeppa, rise! Defend thyself, Mazeppa! [*The Tartars struggle with her, and she falls. During this bustle, which has for a moment withdrawn the assassins from the alcove, Mazeppa, starting from his sleep, feels in his peril a supernatural strength. He darts behind the couch, measures with one glance the extent of the danger threatening him, and, with the celerity of thought, catches from the open cofferet two pistols and levels them at the group surrounding the overthrown Korella. The Tartars quit Korella for their new adversary. He fires the two pistols. Two of his foes are shot and stagger off. Mazeppa grasps a saber, attacks Thamar, and at the same time defends himself against the two others as they seek to attack him on all sides at once, by planting his back against the alcove. After a considerable resistance in this unequal fight, he is just yielding to numbers, when Korella, having dragged herself to the back, strikes a shield which sends forth a startling sound. Violent tumult without. Trumpets sound. Cries are heard: "To arms!" The tent opens at the back. The great encampment of the Tartars, divided according to their tribes, appears with banners floating in the air and all the warriors under arms. Multitudes rush on in disorder, at their head, the Khan, environed by his chiefs. They rush on Thamar. Korella exclaims*]

KOR. The decrees of destiny are accomplished! [*Pointing to Thamar*] Behold the man who sought to gain the throne by sacrilege! Heaven, to confound his crime, has realized the oracle he dared to dictate for my utterance. The traitor then, arming 'gainst Heaven itself, with parricidal hand assailed his new found prince—

ABD. Be theirs the death they would have given! But, ere they go to execution, let them see his triumph whom they sought to humble: the triumph of my long lost son!

MAZ. Ha! Thou my father!

ABD. My son, my own Mazeppa!

MAZ. Mazeppa!

ABD. Come to my heart! [*Casts himself on the bosom of the Khan, who embraces him with transport. All the Tartars raise their arms around them and shout with joy*] Tartars! Behold my kingdom's heir, the warrior called by Heaven to be your prince! Already has he shown himself true to the blood which circles through his veins. Proclaim him instantly: Mazeppa, Sovereign of Tartary!

ALL. Long live Mazeppa!

MAZ. [*Whose surprise has been momently increasing, is violently agitated*] I, King of Tartary! Where am I? What has happened? After a doom beyond expression awful, bound to a wild horse, whirled o'er torrent, desert, precipices, on all sides danger and destruction, sinking beneath accumulated horrors, I ceased to feel—have I then passed the realms of death, and do I wake to a new life, another being? I find myself free, beneath a stranger sky, a prostrate people hailing me their king! Say, do I dream? Say, do I still exist?

ABD. Heaven has restored thee to thy native land and to the throne which thou wert born to fill.

KOR. Reign o'er thy land which welcomes thee, Mazeppa! Be powerful and be happy!

MAZ. Happy? I, happy—without my loved Olinska! Never, oh, never! I renounce glory Olinska shares not! If it indeed be true that Heaven, by some unwonted miracle, has brought me back into my native land, amid my brethren, that it has called me to *rule* o'er them too, I but accept the sovereign sway to right their wrongs and mine, to retrieve the honor of the nation, wrecked on the fields of Poland, to hurl swift vengeance on our foes, and rescue dear Olinska!

ABD. If she you love be worthy of your love, then head our tribes and tear her from your rival.

MAZ. Aye! Set her free or perish!

KOR. Haste thee, Mazeppa! [*To the armed Tartars*] To arms, ye warrior tribes! Fly on the traces of your prince to victory!

MAZ. Away! [*Abder Khan conducts his grandson to a white courser, richly caparisoned, which is led on from the back and which none but Khans have a right to mount. The youth springs on the courser. The aged Prince, satisfied, points to his successor. The arms and banners are bowed before Mazeppa. He is hailed Khan of Tartary. During these movements in front Thamar and his accomplices are taken off at the back. Picture*]

ACT III.

SCENE 1: *A Gothic chamber in the castle of the Castellan in Poland. Olinska, pale and agitated, is discovered seated at a rich toilette, encircled by females, who have just terminated the putting on of her robes and are placing upon her head a veil and diadem. Sad and absorbed in thought, she rises, scarcely allowing time for the completion of her brilliant dress.*

OLIN. [*To one of the females*] Bid my nurse come to me. You may retire. [*To the females who retire*] The victim is adorned, not for the altar, but the tomb! This day is the last whose light will shine on poor Olinska! [*She approaches the toilette, uncovers a little cofferet concealed beneath drapery, opens it, and takes out a portrait on which she gazes with the liveliest emotion*] Casimir! My beloved—murdered—mangled! Can I, ought I, survive thy horrid death! [*Takes from the cofferet a poniard, which she pushes from her with a shudder*] Oh, my father! Oh, my father, your threatened curse! Father, I have given you my oath to be the bride of Premislas. My oath shall not be broken. The honor of our house exacts this sacrifice! [*Takes the poniard and hides it in her dress*] One awful means is left of obedience and fidelity. Yes! This night, this very night restores me to my lover—[*Placing her hand upon the poniard*] In the tomb! [*In agony flings herself upon a seat. Enter Agatha*]

AG. Lady, dear lady!

OLIN. [*Affecting calmness*] I sent for thee. Are we alone?

AG. We are. [*Olinska goes to fetch the cofferet*]

OLIN. Look there. [*Opening it*] That portrait—

AG. [*Eagerly*] The image of—

OLIN. Oh! Utter not that name within these walls! Barbarians! Should they but hear! Behold these letters too. They are all his! Oh, agony! Before a cruel duty drags me to the altar, I must put from me these remembrancers of love. Nurse, I have not strength to let them be destroyed. To thee I would confide them!

AG. To me?

OLIN. Aye, to be placed in an asylum, sacred to all the tenderest recollections!

AG. I do not understand you.

OLIN. Not far from the last precincts of the castle, and by the wood which borders on the Dnieper, there lies a gloomy valley—

AG. The Valley of the Tartars, as 'tis called?

OLIN. At the foot of the statue of St. Casimir, under the pedestal, thou'lt find a hollow dug into the marble. 'Tis there my lost one placed his letters; 'twas there in mystery I hid my replies. To that spot would I now consign this dear deposit, and when I am no more—

AG. [*Alarmed*] No more?

OLIN. [*Recollecting herself*] No more—my lover's—I would say. When given to another—

AG. [*With strong emotion*] Yes, yes, I understand—yes—right, right. Your purpose shall be accomplished—

OLIN. [*Markedly*] Would it were already! Farewell! Farewell!

AG. [*Kissing her hand*] It shall be presently; and then, I hope, you'll be more calm, dear lady.

OLIN. More calm? Yes, nurse, yes, more calm, more calm! [*Bustle without*]

AG. [*Going up the stage*] Someone comes!

OLIN. My father! Away! [*Agatha takes the cofferet, which she conceals in her dress, and goes out on one side as the Castellan appears on the other*]

CAST. Olinska, your imprudence might have caused the ruin of your father; but Count Premislas, restored to life, has deemed the act of Casimir merely a presumptuous vassal's crime, without your sanction. But the pretender has been punished.

OLIN. [*Low*] Horribly!

CAST. Death, alone, could expiate the crime.

OLIN. Death will!

CAST. And now, Olinska, I trust I may confide in your entire submission.

OLIN. Implicitly.

CAST. That pledge disarms my wrath. My child, the past is all forgotten. Come to thy father's arms, who now can call thee once again his daughter! [*As she is dropping on her knees, he catches her to his bosom*]

OLIN. Father!

CAST. My child, my dearest child, may Heaven's peace attend thee!

OLIN. May thy prayer be heard, my father. Ere long thy child will cease to suffer. [*Trumpets heard from without*]

CAST. Count Premislas comes to present to his bride the knights and lords of his Palatinate. [*Goes up the stage to meet the Count*]

OLIN. [*Apart*] Arm me with courage, Heaven! [*Premislas appears, attended by knights and lords. He is followed by squires and servants, headed by Rudzoloff and Drolinsko. Premislas has his left arm in a sling. Ladies and pages are on the stage*]

PREM. Lady, deign to receive the noble knights who come to hail you as their sovereign. [*The knights advance and bow respectfully*]

OLIN. [*Agitated*] Count, some other than Olinska might have proved more worthy of this honor.

PREM. In sanction of this bridal our king permits me to name the Castellan, your father, Vaivode of this canton.

Cast. You add a heavy debt of gratitude to all I owed before! [*Olinska sighs. Premislas offers his hand to the bride, who accepts it as a resigned victim. The father follows proudly. The knights and lords attend them. They enter an apartment at the back, right hand. Rudzoloff, Drolinsko, squires, and servants remain on the stage*]

Dro. So, here's the marriage all settled. Who would ever have thought an affair begun in such a bustle could have ended so quietly? A Tartar, who—

Rud. Can't you keep your tongue still? You know his lordship has forbidden the mention of—

Dro. Well, well. No more of that. Let us talk of fêtes, of weddings. There I am in my element, especially since my new dignities. [*To the servants*] You know what I mean, you gaping louts?

Ser. [*Gathering round*] Not we. What is it? Speak! Speak!

Dro. Sad, I thought everybody knew of the change in my official functions. Why, I quit the duties of chief of the huntsmen, to enter upon those of officer of the mouth. My lord has appointed me one of the kitchen staff.

Rud. Call you that promotion? To be degraded from a huntsman to a cook!

Dro. All men are born with some peculiar talent, which sometimes they are a long while discovering. Now that has been the case with me. Nature intended me for the spit, but I caught up the sword in mistake.

Rud. Poltroon! [*Contemptuously*] To cook dinners when thou wert already an apprentice squire and on a fair way to have become a corporal! But what use is there in talking to a man who has no relish for glory?

Dro. Hark you, godfather. You fight men; I feed them. Methinks there is more glory in keeping men alive than in killing them?

Rud. Mere coward maxims of a fellow who could never stand fire.

Dro. Well, at any rate, I am in a fair way to learn.

Rud. A man insensible to fame—

Dro. I always thought solid pudding better than empty praise.

Rud. Hence to your scullery! [*Vaingloriously*] While I, with my guard of honor, escort the bride and bridegroom to the chapel.

Dro. And I, with my regiment of cooks, prepare the banquet against they come out. Talk of your guard of honor! I've heard of many a prince perishing in spite of his guard of honor, but I never knew a prince to starve so long as his cooks stood by him. So long life to all jolly cooks, and may the spit flourish forever! [*Exit Rudzoloff on one side with the squires; and Drolinsko on the other with the servants*]

SCENE 2: *A picturesque valley. At the back, left hand, a group of isolated trees in the midst of which stands a statue of St. Casimir on a pedestal whence flows a fountain. Beyond, on one side, rocks; on the other, the entrance of a thick wood. Groups of Tartars, variously disguised, appear, looking out on all sides and advancing cautiously. Ozeb and Zelos are their guides, accompanied by Koskar.*

OZEB. Halt! Here let us pause!

KOS. Here?

ZEL. Is it prudent to approach the castle with so weak a force?

OZEB. Such is our young Khan's order. With the precautions he has made us take there can be nought to fear.

ZEL. Who *does* fear?

KOS. Not *you*, I'll answer for it; so don't put yourself in a passion for nothing.

OZEB. Mazeppa, reared in this neighborhood, knows every turn and winding of the forest.

ZEL. And the inspired Korella, who attends our chief, promises victory; so who the devil can be afraid after that?

OZEB. No more, Mazeppa comes. [*Mazeppa enters quickly, wrapped in a large mantle*]

MAZ. Friends, everything seems to favor us! Our warriors approach, led by Korella's self, while we have advanced even to the foot of the walls, those hostile walls enclosing all I hate and all that I adore!

OZEB. A mistress and a rival! One shall be the reward of love, the other a sacrifice to vengeance.

MAZ. [*Gazing around him with emotion*] 'Twas in this spot my father sunk beneath the weapon of the foe. In this spot my mother, who would not quit his side even in the midst of battle, was most basely massacred. 'Twas in this spot that I myself escaped from death but to be given to slavery! Ha! How slowly lags the moment when my oppressors' blood shall wash away the prints of the vile chains they made me bear! Gallant Ozeb! Have my orders been obeyed?

OZEB. All.

MAZ. Those I selected to attend thee, are they ready?

KOS. [*Pointing to a group headed by himself*] Look, my lord.

MAZ. And the disguises?

OZEB. Are in the neighboring grotto.

MAZ. 'Tis well. 'Tis well. Our secrecy and the foe's security enable us to combine stratagem with daring. [*To Zelos*] Zelos, remain upon this spot with those whom you command; observe the profoundest silence, and let nought escape your vigilance. I go to guide Ozeb, to show him the most secret pathways to the castle. I shall hasten back to lead you hence to where Korella comes. Our forces once united, victory is certain and Olinska free! [*He goes out with Ozeb, followed by Koskar and all the rest of his party. Zelos remains with his own band. A stir in the forest*]

ZEL.   Someone advances from this side. [*Looking out cautiously*] Ha! As I live, a woman! Let's see what she wants in this lonely place! [*Zelos and the Tartars hide themselves behind one of the rocks at the back, whence they watch intently. Enter Agatha, who comes forward timidly*]

AG.   Luckily I've not met a soul. Now let me execute the commands of poor lady Olinska. [*Approaches the statue*]

ZEL. [*Apart*]   Olinska!

AG. [*Stopping short, and startled*]   Hey? [*Listens, gazes, but does not discover the Tartars*] I thought I heard somebody repeat the name of Olinska. I don't see anyone. Oh, it must be the echo. I can't help shuddering when I tread this silent wood, the scene of so many bloody battles. Now to seek the— [*She goes around the pedestal seeking, then pauses at an angle*] Aye, 'tis here. This stone is loose. [*Raises a stone at the foot of the pedestal*]

ZEL. [*From the back, not being able to see all her movements*]   What does she there?

AG. [*Turning*]   Hey? [*Looks around, and her fears cease*] The groans of the Tartars who have been slaughtered here seem perpetually in my ears. I'll do what I was bid and get away as fast as possible. [*Advances in great affright, with the cofferet in her hand*] Oh, if the dead really walk, if I should see the pale-faced ghosts of those horrible barbarians—[*Turning, she perceives Zelos and the Tartars, who have approached softly and are by her side*] Merciful Powers! They're here! Oh, save me! Save me! Save me! [*Shrieks, drops the casket, and staggers back. The Tartars dart after her, as Mazeppa, attracted by her cries, appears*]

MAZ.   Whence those shrieks? [*Accidentally striking his foot against the cofferet*] Great Heaven! The very casket which—[*Takes it up and attempts to open it, in which, with the aid of his dagger, at last he succeeds*] My portrait! A letter to Olinska! What wonder's this?

AG. [*Breaking from the Tartars and falling at his feet*]   Oh, sir, in pity—

MAZ.   Agatha!

AG. [*Struck with the voice*]   Hey? What? Good Heaven! Can I believe my eyes? 'Tis—'tis—

MAZ.   Aye, Casimir.

AG.   Casimir!

MAZ. [*Violently*]   Answer. Is it by thee this casket has been dropped?

AG.   My lord, y—y—y—yes, my lord—

MAZ.   By whose command?

AG.   Olinska's.

MAZ.   Did she not swear, ne'er, but with life, to part—

AG.   Oh, my lord, be certain nothing but the last necessity would ever have induced her to sacrifice these pledges of affection. Poor lady! She has been forced to obey her father, and, at this very moment, when she is to be united to another—

MAZ.   Another! What other? Premislas? Does Premislas still live?

AG.   Ah! Do not find fault with her. Had you but seen her tears, her despair—

MAZ. [*Wildly*]   Alive and wedded to Olinska! Perfidious woman! But I will change the nuptial flambeaux to funereal torches! This night, this very night, the castle's flames shall light me to triumph or a tomb! [*To the Tartars*] Friends, haste to cross the stream! Our warriors must have reached the opposite shore. Yes! Midst the very festivity of the bridal I'll rush upon the foe, the false one shall perish in my rival's arms, shall perish in discovering him she has betrayed! [*As he is rushing out at the head of his Tartars, Korella suddenly appears before him*]

KOR.   Mazeppa, hold! Whither do you haste?

MAZ.   To seek revenge on perfidy.

KOR.   The perfidy of whom?

MAZ.   Olinska!

KOR.   Condemn her not unjustly.

MAZ.   She has pledged her faith to another. They now prepare the ceremony.

KOR.   Who can pronounce 'twill ever be fulfilled?

MAZ.   These letters, this portrait, unworthily spurned from her—

KOR.   Speak the resolution of a desperate, but not a faithless heart—

MAZ.   Ha! Can it then—

KOR.   Olinska, fancying thee dead, and forced to obey her father, has yielded to this bridal to save the honor of her house, intending then the last sad sacrifice which Heaven has left her power to make thy love!

MAZ.   What sacrifice?

KOR.   Her life!

MAZ.   Great Heaven! What horrid light now flashes o'er my mind! Olinska! Loved Olinska! And I have dared accuse her! Merciful Providence! How to arrive in time to prevent the blow?

Kor.   By hastening the attack. I have foreseen, provided against all. Away, away, Mazeppa! There still remains to us a moment. Heaven will point the means to turn it to advantage. Away! Away!

Maz.   March! March! [*General movement among the Tartars, who flock tumultuously after their chief. Agatha, who has stood in a state of stupor, seeing Mazeppa following Korella off, runs towards him for protection*] Watch o'er this woman, Zelos! See no harm befall her! [*All the Tartars, their sabers drawn, follow Korella and Mazeppa. Agatha, spite of herself, is swept off in the rush*]

SCENE 3: *Superb gardens. Everything in readiness for brilliant fêtes. Right hand, an elegant seat raised on a platform with several steps and overhung by escutcheons and rich draperies. Beyond, right and left, colonnades forming the entrance of the castle of the Castellan. At the back, a marble balustrade with a gilded gate in the center, bordering on a large trench, beyond which appears a vast extent of forest, with many practicable platforms. Koskar, with the rest of the disguised Tartars, cross <es> the forest in the distance, looks through the gate, but disappears a moment among the trees, on discovering Drolinsko, who comes out of the castle, full of bustle, gaping all around him.*

Dro.   Well, here's a fête which I think will do me honor. Dances, banquets, illuminations! All out of this! [*Slapping his forehead*] This night will be the grandest day of my life! And then the gypsy crew, who stroll through the land to sing, caper, and tell fortunes. I have settled it all with their leader. He's given me his word that he'll astonish everybody! [*Ozeb at this moment appears at the back, disguised. He approaches the gate and makes a sign to those outside, while Drolinsko, not seeing them, proceeds*] He has offered to supply me with a dance executed by young Tartars after the manner of their country; so, I think, I've contrived a way to give the company a grand surprise. 'Egad, I long to see what they're going to do. [*Ozeb comes down*]

Ozeb. [*Slapping him on the shoulder*]   You shall, presently.

Dro.   Hey? Bless me! I thought you were below in the kitchen.

Ozeb. [*Abruptly*]   Oh, I'm in twenty places in a minute.

Dro.   What gruff chaps these Tartar gypsies are!

Ozeb.   Come! 'Tis time to let in the companions I've got waiting.

Dro.   Right, right. I'll go and open the gate for them. [*At a signal from Ozeb, Koskar and the Tartars reappear at the gate, which is set open by Drolinsko. They all enter and gather round their chief, who makes signs to them as Drolinsko shuts the gate after them and comes down*] After all, these are only mock Tartars. There's nothing terrible in them. [*To Ozeb*] Well, my lad, you are to figure at the marriage festival. If your capers please, you'll get the chink. You may never have such another chance of glory.

Ozeb. I'll warrant we'll make ourselves remembered.

Dro. But where are the young girls, they who dance so merrily?

Ozeb. Oh, they are in the forest.

Kos. Aye, in our encampment.

Dro. Encampment?

Ozeb. Yes, encampment. Don't you know it's the gypsy way of life? Ours is the soldier's home, the tented field.

Kos. We live like birds, in the air.

Dro. I wish you'd brought the girls, though. We shall be at a standstill without them.

Ozeb. They will appear on our signal.

Dro. Oh, in that case, all's right. I'm particular because my reputation is concerned. This is my first attempt in a new capacity. I want to make a noise in the world, to astonish 'em all. I want the whole castle to be in commotion. I'd have the walls caper—

Kos. Caper? They shall fly!

Dro. The walls fly? No, no. I'd not have that, though. How can walls fly?

Kos. You'll see, ere long.

Dro. [*Gazing at him a moment*] Nonsense! [*Aside*] These gypsy devils are always doing something out of the way. I shouldn't wonder if they *have* some famous trick in hand to amaze us all. [*A flourish of trumpets and gay music heard. Drolinsko goes up the stage to look out*]

Ozeb. [*Low to his companions*] The moment is at hand. Attention to the signal. Hold yourselves in readiness.

Dro. [*Returning*] Quick! Quick! They're coming. Look! The young couple, the lords, and the ladies and all. Go you and hide at the entrance of the forest, and don't appear until I give the signal. [*The Tartars instantly disappear among the left-hand trees. The Castellan, Olinska, Premislas, encircled by lords and ladies, advance through the peristyle. Their presence is the signal for the sports. They place themselves upon the seats prepared, and the fête begins. Ballet. Among the figures of which it is composed, young Tartars, in disguise, presented by Drolinsko, execute a singular armed dance mingled with pantomimic action. Ozeb and Koskar, upon the watch, on one side of the stage, seem to await the signal for action. Suddenly the dances are interrupted by three shots from the outside, and presently after, an external*]

*tumult mingles with cries, "To Arms! Treason! Treason! To Arms!" En-
tirely at the back, through the forest, beams a sort of crimson colored light.
Rudzoloff and soldiers rush in, in disorder*]

RUD. To arms! To arms! A horde of Tartars rush upon the castle. They
are already masters of the heights. Their purpose seems to set the forest on
fire!

ALL. To arms! To arms!

PREM. [*Drawing his sword*] Aye. Haste to meet these barbarians and
make them rue their daring! [*The Tartars suddenly fling off their disguises
and appear completely armed. The Polonese, headed by Premislas and the
Castellan, surprised, recoil an instant. Confusion and general alarm succeed.
The Polonese rally and fight with desperation. Amid this bustle Olinska has
fainted in the arms of her women. The Castellan goes to her*]

CAST. [*To the women*] Watch o'er my daughter. Conduct her to the
stronghold of the castle. [*Departs with his followers to oppose the Tartars.
The blaze of the forest begins to appear at the back, and detachments of Tartar cavalry course through the wood on all sides with torches. Olinska revives,
is about to retire with the women, when she sees Agatha run in in consternation*]

AG. At last, I've got away from them. Where is my lady? Where is Olinska?

OLIN. What seek you here? What have you to disclose?

AG. He lives! Fear not. A miracle—

OLIN. What miracle? Who lives? [*Violently agitated, she turns and finds
herself facing Mazeppa, his sword drawn and surrounded by his officers*]
Great Heaven! Casimir! Can my eyes tell me truth?

MAZ. Aye, Casimir, thy lover, thy preserver, no longer the obscure, the
friendless Casimir, but now Mazeppa, King of Tartary! Come, then, Olinska,
come, my betrothed; come with me to my camp, there to be hailed at once
my wife and queen!

OLIN. Alas! New ties forbid our union!

MAZ. My sword shall break them!

OLIN. Nothing but death can break them! Oh, Casimir, art thou indeed a
chief of Tartary? Do not, oh, do not say so! Can e'er Olinska wed the foe of
Poland? The spoiler of her country? Never, never! I can die for thee, Casimir, but ne'er will die dishonored! Farewell! Farewell, forever! [*In agony,
almost in delirium, she attempts to escape. Mazeppa detains her, attempts to*

hurry her with him in spite of herself, when Premislas and the Castellan spring upon him with their followers. Premislas with uplifted saber plunges on Mazeppa, who is forced to defend himself. Olinska, set free by this action, runs to her father, who, as well as Premislas himself, starts back with astonishment on recognizing Mazeppa]

CAST. What! Casimir!

PREM. My assassin!

CAST. Escaped the jaws of death!

MAZ. Barbarian! Your cruel sentence led me but to triumph. The wild horse bore me to the throne of Tartary. Mazeppa, now victorious, claims his bride!

CAST. A Tartar chief wed with a child of mine? Never! [*Pointing to Premislas*] Behold my daughter's husband!

PREM. And know him ready to defend his right.

MAZ. [*Furious*] Thou hast pronounced the sentence of thy death! [*Rushes on Premislas, who defends himself gallantly, and they fight off. The battle is renewed all over the stage. Amid the confusion the Castellan seizes his daughter to drag her from the danger. The tumult is at its height. The whole forest is in a blaze. The fight proceeds amid the flames. Groups of combatants are driven back by the conflagration. The front of the stage is left for a moment empty. Amid the disorder Olinska reappears alone, pale, wild, her hair dishevelled, a poniard in her hand*]

OLIN. My father! Casimir! My native land! No, nothing is left Olinska but to die! [*Lifts the dagger to stab herself. Korella appears at the back, darts towards her, and takes the poniard out of her hand*]

KOR. Hold. Renounce despair. It is a crime. Premislas has fallen, and Mazeppa triumphs. Thy death would now become thy nation's ruin. The Tartar hosts would devastate all Poland. 'Tis thou alone can be the pledge of peace! [*Olinska gazes astonished on this extraordinary woman, and, overpowered, allows herself to be guided by Korella as by a superior being. A violent explosion heard. The stage fills from every side. The Castellan enters, fighting with Ozeb, by whom he is about to be overpowered, when Olinska, seeing the peril of her father, precipitates herself before the blow as it is falling, just on the instant that Mazeppa, beckoned on by Korella, reappears*]

OLIN. [*To Ozeb and the Tartars*] Hold! [*To Mazeppa*] Mazeppa, save my father and take Olinska as the pledge of peace!

MAZ. Tartars, the war is over. Behold the only recompense I hoped from victory. Olinska's mine! [*Shouts. The whole picture changes. The conquerors*] *give their hands to the conquered. Korella has set free the Castellan, who, constrained by events, allows her to bring him to Mazeppa. Mazeppa makes the conqueror's pride stoop to respect for the father of his beloved, bends for the Castellan's blessing, and from his hands receives Olinska]*

TABLEAU

CURTAIN

THE SPANISH HUSBAND;
or, FIRST AND LAST LOVE

THE SPANISH HUSBAND;
or, FIRST AND LAST LOVE

THERE are four different manuscripts at Harvard representing four different stages of composition of *The Spanish Husband; or, First and Last Love*: first, *The Painter of His Own Dishonor*, a tragedy (TS 4501.-319); second, *The Spanish Husband*, a transformation of the tragedy into a tragi-comic opera, dated December 17, 1824 (TS 4637.32); third, a revision of the opera with the same title (TS 4637.32.3); and fourth, an alteration of the opera into a tragi-comedy with the full title (TS 4637.32.5). *The Painter of His Own Dishonor* is in an unknown hand, perhaps that of a professional translator, as Payne had been commissioning work off and on for some time to at least one, a man named Sullivan to whom he wrote on February 7, 1825. In the three versions called *The Spanish Husband* textual revisions in various hands besides Payne's are evident; it seems possible, however, to identify two of the hands, those of Washington and Peter Irving in the first version (see F. P. Smith, *Washington Irving and France*, a Harvard thesis, unpublished; Cambridge, Mass., 1937, p. 196, n. 1). In the British Museum (L.C. 5/22/1830) is the copy, in an unknown hand, submitted to the licenser for acting; this, which is much like the last of the Harvard texts, is reproduced here. In place of illegible readings in the licenser's copy, legible ones have been added from the last Harvard text.

The play, which was brought out anonymously at Drury Lane, May 25, 1830, was revived about half a dozen times during the year. Several months later, on November 1, it appeared in New York at the Park Theatre. According to the reviewer in *The Theatrical Observer*, May 26 (who incorrectly conjectures that Theodore Hook is the author), the London performance attracted a small house that nevertheless received the play more favorably than it deserved, for only the acting of Wallack, Cooper, and Miss Phillips "carried it."

The life of the play was too short to repay Payne for his long labor. He began work soon after the source, La Beaumelle's *Le Peintre de Son Déshonneur*, a prose translation of Calderon's tragedy *El Pintor de Su Deshonra*, appeared in *Chefs-D'Oeuvre des Théâtres Étrangers*, Paris, 1822. Intermittently during the next eight years Payne, aided by the general criticisms and, at an early stage, by the textual revisions of the Irvings, reworked the play at least four times. The first version, *The Painter of His Own Dishonor,* is a close rendering of La Beaumelle and, as the interpolation of a good many French phrases indicates, merely a rough draft. By December 17, 1824, he changed the tragedy into a tragi-comic opera, *The Spanish Husband,* with songs added and with the prose recast into blank verse. It is probably this version which Irving, in his letter to Payne, January 20, 1825, says that he and Peter are shortening; he adds that if necessary it can be altered into a play. Soon afterwards Payne rewrote the opera but failed to find a producer, as his letter to Irving, June 10, 1825, and that to Fawcett, January 7, 1826, show. Finally Payne changed the opera back to drama.

Although *The Spanish Husband* is treated with considerable originality the reviewer's opinion is correct: its language is "commonplace" and only "occasionally poetical," and the intrigue plot, "wild and improbable," as the characters are swayed erratically by the "heroic" motives of love and honor.

[CHARACTERS

Don Carlos

Don Alvar

Don Salerno

Don Hyppolito

Benedetto

Lissardo

Celio

Cardenio

Another Spanish Captain

Thomaso

Jeronymo

An Attendant

A Masquerader

Sailors

Bianca

Julia

Cariola

Flora

THE ACTION TAKES PLACE IN NAPLES AND BARCELONA]

ACT I.

SCENE 1: *Naples. A state apartment in the castle of St. Elmo. Servants preparing the decorations of the room, Lissardo superintending.*

LIS.   Hum! Ha! Very well. The roses here, the plate there! Ho, Antonio, order those musicians to be ready to strike up on his Excellency's approach. Ha! Paulo! Is the fellow deaf? A head like yours should have no lack of ears. Hurry! Hurry! [*Shouts and trumpets in the distance*] It would be well for some of you that I were Governor of his Majesty's castle of St. Elmo for half an hour. There are half a dozen of you that I should send to keep guard in the dungeon for the next century. The Signor Magnifico, Don Alphonso Alvar, is arrived this moment. [*Shouts and trumpets again. The Count Salerno enters, meeting Alvar, who is magnificently dressed*]

SAL.   Welcome, most noble lord, to Naples. Welcome, too, your lovely bride. A soldier's hearty welcome!

ALV.   Thanks, my good lord. My bride will thank you too,
        When she has first embraced her early friend,
        The lady Julia. I have left them now;
        Like doves long parted they have flown together,
        Though mine's the caged one.

SAL.   In a golden cage
        From which the prisoner longs to break no more.

ALV.   I'll make it so, if most unwearied love
        Is worth her liberty.

SAL.   I'm glad your travels
        Have ended thus in triumph. Little dreamed you
        When love for painting lured you to our land,
        To bear so fair a picture with you hence
        To witch the wonderers of Barcelona.

ALV.   Aye, noble sir, till now the brighter half
        Of this world's bliss to me was in eclipse.
        Study, the arts, and more than all, that art
        By which the pencil, like a wand, detains
        All nature's beauties, making them our own,
        And whiled my spring of life away, and left me
        In every treasure but affection, rich—

SAL. Without which treasure even the rich are poor.

ALV. I found it so. I felt the void
Which makes the empty heart an aching heart.

SAL. And so at last you took my friend's advice
And saw and loved his daughter?

ALV. To see her and to love her were but one.
But there's a waywardness in our affections
Which shrinks from loving where 'tis wished we should.
And when besought to meet Fabritio's daughter,
My stubborn will disdained to be thus forced;
I fled from Naples, wandered three long years,
Hating the sex, and most of all her name
Whom they would thus have bound upon my heart.
My pencil was my mistress; till one eve,
Wandering amidst the rose and vineyard bowers
That tissue Etna's side, I heard a voice,
The silver rival of the nightingale's—

SAL. Aye, the old tale, your freedom for a song.

ALV. I turned and saw a vision by a fount,
A form of bending beauty like a nymph,
The guardian of the stream. My hasty step
Disturbed the leaves. She raised a lightning eye,
A cheek to which the glow of western clouds
Were earthly. In that glance I felt my fate.
I followed, found her noble in her soul
As in her beauty. Aye, the paragon.
My fancy had conceived of female charms.
Oh, then I thought how hopeless is late love.
I writhed with jealousy when blithe eighteen
Smiled with its ruddy lip upon the fair,
But who can tell my sudden rapture when
I found the wonder I had scarce dared dream of
Was the self-same my friends had chosen for me
The Count Fabritio's daughter, the Bianca
Whom I had scorned so long.

SAL. 'Tis a shrewd proverb, there's a fate in marriage
And I'll be sworn now you yourself are yoked.
You'd preach the singly blest into bonds
As earnestly as e'er you hated wedlock.

ALV. Oh, could I make the bliss of chaste love felt
      Youth should never skulk in shame from bought embraces.
      Oh, could I make young luxury but feel
      The secret comfort which steals o'er a man
      Reading love's truth in a wife's honest eye
      The grass should grow before the wanton's dwelling.

SAL. Once more I give you joy.
      You've stolen a gem from our Italian mine
      That will flash living luster mid the pomps
      Of your proud Barcelona.

ALV. No, she still loves the shade. Her sunniest smile
        Seems touched by nature with sweet melancholy,
        Like that which tints the maiden's lip for love,
        Lost in the tomb. But no. She is too young
        To know an earlier love. I'd hate the heart
        Were it an angel's, that could have a thought,
        An image, but my own within its shrine.

SAL. I long to greet this wonder love, my lord;
      We'll find them in the alcove. How years will fly!
      It seems but yesterday, since on this knee
      She sat, a rosebud. My Julia's playfellow,
      My son Hyppolito, ill-fated boy,
      I now remember spoke of her as one
      On earth unrivalled.

ALV. My young lord
        Hyppolito, no evil as I hope?

SAL. No, sir, he sleeps where evil cannot come.
      This day, 'tis three long years of bitterness
      Since my boy sailed for Spain. I was to blame.
      He called it exile. I was stern.
      He went in agony. The winds
      Were up that night. The mountain waves
      Covered our shores with wrecks; and from that hour
      I never saw him more.

ALV. What! Lost at sea?

SAL. I know 'tis nature's law that all must die
      And would have bowed my head to meet the blow
      But for remorse. I drove him to that death.
      He pressed me with solicitings that seem

Like warnings of his fate against that voyage;
And thus we parted sternly, and forever!

ALV. Yonder they come, my lord: your lovely daughter
And my fair bride. [*Enter Julia and Bianca*]

SAL. Welcome, fair flower of Sicily, and take
An old man's blessing. May your years be smooth
As is your noble brow; your moments bright
As is the sparkling of those azure eyes!
Your path be roses, and your thoughts be joy.

BIAN. My lord, all praise to me is flattery;
And yet I thank the noble Count Salerno.
Heaven grant I ever merit it. [*Aside*] Poor Hyppolito!
[*Cannon without*] What means that fearful sound?

ALV. Be calm, my love—a signal gun.

BIAN. Its sound was strange. Death's herald! 'Tis
Of what I know not. But my heart is chill.

JUL. [*Apart*] The color leaves her cheek; her hand is ice.
[*To Alvar*] The voyage has overpowered her, but, begone!
I'll take her to her chamber.

SAL. Come, my lord.
I'll lead you through our city. We have sights
Well worth an artist's eye!

ALV. Lead on, my lord. Nay, cheer thee up, my love.
Repose thee for awhile. This bustling voyage
Has worn thy spirits out. Thy charming friend
Will bring them back. Adieu. Rest ye both well. [*Exeunt Alvar and Salerno*]

JUL. Look up, Bianca love!

BIAN. Thank Heaven, we are alone.

JUL. In tears, Bianca?

BIAN. Alas, my Julia, even the sight of thee,
Linked with the fatal story of my love,
Raises the lost one from his watery grave!
Thou, the companion of my early thoughts,
Who knowest the first fond feeling of this heart,
Can pardon all its weakness.

JUL. From my soul;
For mine has suffered—

BIAN. Thine? What? Carlos false,
Or has he perished?

JUL. He lives; yet lives to torture me.
      Gallant and gay and fond, yet each new face
      Threatens to lure him from me. Fickleness
      Is his delight. The gilded butterfly
      Roving from rose to rose is constancy
      To my light lover.

BIAN. But he comes again.
      He has not perished.

JUL. Then his princely rank
      Forbids the open knowledge of his love.
      Son of a haughty father, matched from childhood
      To Spain's proud daughter, thus my heart is filled
      With hidden doubts and fears.

BIAN. Oh, such concealments
      Are like a serpent nursed within the breast.
      There gnaws that serpent! Julia, chide me not.
      True love's a deathless spirit. Its gaze
      O'erlooks time's gulf to seek its home in Heaven.

JUL. I deemed thee happy with the noble Alvar.
      He was your father's choice, as I remember,
      When you and I and poor Hyppolito
      Lived in the fairy land of untold love.

BIAN. Are any happy? Ah, the healthiest face
      May wear a nearer death beneath its bloom
      Than the pale cheek which has looked out its tomb.

JUL. You talk in riddles. Tell me all; be plain.

BIAN. I gave Don Alvar all I had to give:
      A trusting spirit but a bankrupt heart.
      When my heart was with your brother drowned,
      For three long years I mourned for him in <vain>,
      Then meekly yielded to a father's will.
      I valued Alvar, knew him full of honor,
      Generous and gentle, though I could not love him.
      A—more than gratitude—a soft esteem,
      A twilight of affection dawned within me;
      I felt the delicacy of his suit
      That nothing urged, though ardent was his love,
      And by a father's sovereign will enforced
      Fondly, but silently, he gazed upon me
      And waited till my eye should turn and bless him.

We wedded, and a tender friend he proved;
And day by day I found new cause to prize him,
And day by day was softly wearing out
Remembrance of the past, till, seeing you,
With fearful power it rushed back on my mind.
Oh, when that signal gun—

JUL.   Our constant music.
    Forget it, dearest.

BIAN.   'Twas to me the voice
Of the death angel, calling me to turn
From my own bridal to behold my love—
[*Cannon again*] Again! It comes again.
Oh, hide me from it!

JUL.   'Tis nothing. Some newcomer at the port—

BIAN.   It shrieks, "Hyppolito!" Such sounds are heard
In nights of storm. Oh, such a sound it was
That sent its roar above the sinking ship
That down the billows bore Hyppolito! [*Enter Celio*]

JUL.   Ha! Celio! The Prince's page.
What has befallen? Speak! Is your lord dead?

CEL.   The Prince is well and on his way to Naples.

JUL.   Comes he today? Have you no letters, sir?

CEL.   Lady, I have letters,
But was commanded, ere I gave the letters,
To ask a word in strictest privacy.

BIAN.   I'll leave you to confer. I'll walk awhile
About the garden. I am better now.
When you have heard this page's news, you'll seek me.
[*Apart*] Yes! I'll seek the scenes so much endeared in youth,
Then close my heart forever to the past!
This is the final hour! Eyes, look your last
On the sweet spot you loved from infancy.
Here's not a statue, shrub, nor ancient tree
But seems to me like a beloved friend
With whom to part is sorrow! Yet one thought
Deeper than all throws beauty o'er ye all:
First love! First love! Earth has no stronger spell.
I've struggled with thee, driven thee from my dreams,
Weighed thee against a husband's noble heart,

<blockquote>
And thought I conquered thee; but here, one chance
Has shaken all my wisdom, sunk my heart
Into a hypocrite, made all my vows
Empty as air! First love! Thy fatal flame
Is quenched but with the grave! [Exit]
</blockquote>

JUL. But how is this?
  You say the Prince has news of my lost brother?
  You say the Prince knows that by Algerines
  Hyppolito was from the floating mast—
  How knows he this? Was't then in slavery
  My brother died?

CEL. If you can bear to hear—

JUL. I can bear anything but this suspense—

CEL. These letters will acquaint with the rest. [Kneeling]

JUL. Oh joy! Oh happiness! A thousand thanks,
  Carlos, for this! He lives! Hyppolito,
  My brother lives! Go, rouse the castle, sir—
  Tell all the news: my long lost brother lives!
  Now to my father, to Bianca—Heavens!
  Wretched Bianca!

CEL. Lady, I am gone.
  The tidings shall be spread through Naples.

JUL. Hush!
  Breathe not a word of it. The sound is death to
  Wretched Bianca! Well, thy prophet heart
  Beat at the signal gun! Go, tell your lord
  To keep the tidings secret as his soul.
  [Aside] Bianca sails tonight. A few short hours
  Of secrecy may spare her agonies [To Celio] The Prince
  When does he land?

CEL. Impatient to behold
  Your grace, he has already landed.

JUL. Joy!
  I hear his chargers trampling at the gate
  And sounds of many voices. Hark! Hyppolito. [Flourish]
  They see them and all's known! What's to be done?
  Fly to the Prince and stop them! Carlos! Brother.
  Undone Bianca! [Exit]

SCENE 2: *The garden of the castle. Enter Hyppolito.*

HYP.   Welcome, bright Naples!
       Thy airs all perfume and thy sounds all song!
       Thy skies all beauty and thy sounds all song!
       What's exile when it ends in hours like this!
       How be content Hyppolito! One joy,
       One rapture more would fill thy cup to the brim
       Were dear Bianca here to welcome me
       Where we were wont to meet when both were children.
       No matter, while nor chains, nor dungeon part us
       I feel, did even oceans intervene,
       She'd still be near me, still must be my own [*Bianca advances from
a bower in meditation*]
       Vision of ecstasy! Oh, Heavens and earth!
       'Tis she, Bianca's self! My love! My life! [*Rushes to her. She shrieks
and faints in his arms*]
       I was too sudden. I have slain my love!
       Saints guard her precious life. Nay love, look!
       Ha! She stirs, her eyes unclose, her lips begin to move.
BIAN. It was a lovely vision, though most fearful. [*Sees him*]
       Ha! There again! The phantom of my dream
       Has taken the form it lived in, and stands there.
HYP.   Her senses sink beneath the sudden joy—
BIAN. It speaks! It speaks! His spirit from the grave
       To haunt me for my broken faith. Look! Look!
       Nay, chide me not with that unearthly frown.
       I was thy widow ere I was his bride!
HYP.   Speak not thus wildly. Be thyself. Look, love,
       'Scaped from the waves, thy own Hyppolito.
BIAN. He lives! He lives! My own, my early love!
       But madness! Hate me! Scorn me! Fly me!
       I have undone thee and undone myself!
       [*Mournfully*] Poor, wronged Hyppolito! And dost thou then
       Come back to drag away long years of woe?
HYP.   To live long years of bliss in those dear arms.
BIAN. My arms! My arms!
       Avoid them like a pestilence!
HYP.   How, why is this? Thou in whose heart
       All the whole treasure of my life was locked—

BIAN. That treasure have I scattered to the winds;
And now the shipwrecked voyager returns
To find his hopes a desolation. All,
Trusted to one, that, a most faithless steward
Squandered them all for vanity!

HYP. What desperate words are these? Nay, cheer thee, love;
Thou knowest I live once more, am once more thine.

BIAN. Living or dead, 'tis now all one, all one!
Or dead or living, to Bianca lost!

HYP. Lost! Lost! Who shall dare part Hyppolito
From his heart's own betrothed?

BIAN. Her husband!

HYP. What do I hear? Or am I wild as she?
This is the ground I tread. Yonder's the sky.
I stand in Naples. [*Furiously*] Woman, speak!

BIAN. [*Wildly and anxiously*] Hyppolito!

HYP. Come, lightnings! Launch your burning arrows here.
I laugh your power to scorn, for here's a blow
Deadlier than all your fires: it strikes, yet kills not.

BIAN. Calm thee, Hyppolito!

HYP. Calm me? Ha! Ha! Ha!
Calm me? Deceiver, guilty, fickle, cold!
Toss the gashed sufferer from knife to knife
And bid him in his agony be calm.
Go to thy paramour, thou false one, go;
And leave me here to misery and despair!
But no! There's yet revenge! Thou fatal thing,
Tell me the villain's name. An honest sword
Shall search his heart.

BIAN. [*Rushing out*] Terror of terrors!
My husband's life at stake! Saints, pity me! [*Exit*]

HYP. Gone! Gone! She must be mine! She's mine by all
That's holy in the laws of early love!
None less than angel's arm shall fright me back
From my true Paradise. I'll seek her lord
And hang my cause upon my saber's edge.
Then Heaven defend the right. She shall be mine. [*Exit*]

SCENE 3: *An alcove in the gardens of the castle. Enter Julia and Carlos*]

JUL. Carlos, no more of this. What, fly with you?
      Bring down my father's curse, your father's scorn?
      Has two months' travel taught this truantry?

CARL. Two months, my beauty! Why, 'tis twenty years,
       To reckon by the lover's calendar,
       Since last I kissed your hand.

JUL. A gallant speech!
      Pray, to how many pairs of Spanish eyes
      Has that same speech been made?

CARL. 'Faith, not to one.
       The Spanish dames are handsome, but I passed
       Through all their blaze—

JUL. A salamander, Prince!

CARL. Yes, quite unscorched. I see the sex
       As one who sees the stars: most heavenly things
       But much too far for me to pluck them down.
       I'm all constancy.

JUL. Then I'll believe you.
      Then all vain fears and fretful jealousies
      Go to the idle winds. I'm thine forever.
      But hush! My father's here. Now, fly; yet stay—
      He brings Bianca with him.

CARL. Some beauty I'll be sworn.
       I love you more than ever,
       For trusting thus my constancy; aye, now
       I'm paid—

JUL. As yonder weathercock?

CARL. As fate,
       The great matchmaker. Were the queen of beauty
       To come in smiles, I could not see her smile
       So rapt is my fond heart in love and thee! [*Enter Salerno, leading
in Bianca*]
       [*Apart*] By Jove! A paragon! Is this Bianca?

SAL. Julia, I'm come to try if your light tongue
      Is stronger than your father's prayers. Beseech
      This gentle lady to prolong her stay.
      Your birthday fête comes in a week—

JUL. Stay even that week, Bianca.

BIAN. Sir, with all thanks for your high courtesy
    I must not stay. My husband's heart is set
    Upon his country, and his will is mine.
CARL. [*Aside*] She shall not go. She must not. [*To Julia, aside*] Make her stay.
JUL. My lord!
CARL. Not that I care, not I; but, keep her.
    [*Aside*] Can earth boast such a wonder? 'Tis some spirit
    Of beauty sent down from the skies to teach
    Humility to those the world deems beautiful.
SAL. [*To Julia*] Who's that cavalier?
JUL. Don Carlos, sir,
    Son of the Duke Palermo.
SAL. He who saved
    My boy, Hyppolito! Sir, I have longed
    To meet and thank you for my winter day
    Turned into summer. Lady Bianca,
    This is my boy's preserver. You well knew
    My wild Hyppolito.
BIAN. [*With emotion*] I—did—my lord!
JUL. [*Aside*] This talk will torture her. [*To Salerno*]
    Sir, it grows late.
CARL. [*Aside*] She's beautiful, a most delicious shape,
    An eye of sapphire—eye—no, faith, a star!
    Foot like a nymph's. I must see more of her!
JUL. Don Carlos, come. [*Aside*] He's deaf. The fickle one,
    He roves again. Bianca has his glance
    And with it goes his heart. This must be checked
    Or I'm undone! [*Aloud to Salerno*] The banquet waits.
SAL. My child,
    There is a time for all things, and this time
    Is for our gratitude. [*To Carlos*] You broke his chains.
CARL. 'Twas nothing. 'Twas to leave him heavier bound
    With passion's fetters. Some Italian dame
    Had flung her chain upon him. All night long
    He'd pace the deck and gaze on Italy.
    He questioned every breeze for tidings sweet
    From Italy. [*Aside*] She blushes deep. She likes my style
    Of painting passion. I'll make sure of her.

BIAN. Most noble friends, farewell! This night must hear
        My prayers for you upon the distant sea—
SAL. [*Speaks to and sends out attendant*] Lady, I have one favor still to
ask
        Before our parting. [*To Carlos*] Prince, you saved my son!
CARL. No, 'faith, not I. The hero saved himself.
        He was our wonder. As my galley neared
        The Algerine, he burst his iron links,
        Plunged o'er the side, and once upon our deck,
        Became our leader, darted on the Moor,
        And by the sudden havoc of his sword
        Gained us the victory.
SAL. My brave Hyppolito,
        Who but most love him, and when truly loved,
        Who could forget him?
BIAN. 'Tis the truth, my lord.
        He is a noble being, formed to win
        The people's heart, to be his house's hope,
        His glorious country's buckler. May his life
        Long be an honor to himself, his house,
        And his proud country. May all brighter hope
        Dwell in his soul, all sadder dreams be past;
        And all earth's woes be scattered from his face
        As clouds before the sun!
CARL. [*Aside*] Spoke like an angel!
        Where was she hid but now! I'll stop her course,
        If serenades and sighs can stop her!
JUL. Wretch! [*Aside*]
        He'll run away with her before my eyes.
        I've done with him forever. [*Aloud*] Come, Bianca.
SAL. [*Who has spoken to attendant*]   A moment yet. I sent him for a jewel,
        Which I would pray this noble lady's hands
        To hang upon the Prince's neck in thanks
        For his high service; but Hyppolito
        Insists on bringing it himself, to pay
        His gratitude with ours.
BIAN. [*Aside*] Hyppolito!
        I must not meet—[*To Julia*] Save me, or I die!
        [*Aloud*] My lord, pardon me. Don Alvar waits.
        Spare me awhile—

CARL. Fair lady, take my arm!

JUL. [*Aside*] He woos her to my face. [*Aloud*] No, sir, *my* arm
Is safer. [*Aside to him*] She can live without your sighs.
See me no more. I scorn and banish you. [*Exit with Bianca*]

SAL. It grieves me, Prince,
Your ceremonial duties should prevent
Your joining us at table. Good spirits guard you.
Farewell, my lord. [*Exit with attendant*]

CARL. So! Julia sends me into banishment!
Ungrateful woman! Frown amid my vows
Of constancy! I only show my generosity
And I am scouted if I scorn to lock
My heart up as a miser locks his dollars,
Scorned and have Julia calling me a traitor!
And why the devil now did nature give us
Two eyes, two hands, two legs, wer't not to show
How much she loves variety? Yet after all
My Julia *is* a most bewitching creature.
I'll after her and say so and implore
To be forgiven. Gad then, perhaps I may
Behold her friend once more. I'll fly to her.
Julia, beloved Julia, I am yours.
I'll never say a civil word again.
I'll never look on any other woman. I'm yours,
Unalterably yours, yours, yours for ever. [*Enter Cariola*]
Ha! A nice creature this—uncommonly!
I never saw finer pair of eyes!
Say, by what prettiest of names
You call yourself, my dear?

CARI. I don't call myself your dear at all. But pray, sir, who are you that
dare be thus familiar at first sight? But I can guess by your wandering about
here by yourself while all the house are carousing: a fop of a servant out of
place.

CARL. 'Faith, I have lost my place just now, I own.

CARI. Discharged for—

CARL. Too much gallantry.

CARI. I thought so. Aping lords and ogling ladies.

CARL. You've hit the mark. Aye, ogling was my crime.
But had I found a face like yours to ogle,
Oh! such temptation would have borne me harmless.

CARI. [*Aside*] La! How prettily he talks! How prettily he dresses. I should like to be of use to the poor fellow. I say, I'm in an excellent family. I'm lady's maid to the Lady Bianca—

CARL. A lucky mistress with so fair a maid.

CARI. Now it must cost you something to keep up your finery; and as you seem a sort of person of whom something might be made with a little attention, I'll take you under my patronage.

CARL. The patronage of beauty! 'Tis for that
   Alone I live! Make of me what you like!
   I care not what attention you may pay me,
   I will return it tenfold. She's a darling!

CARI. Then come and show me a specimen of your taste. I'm going to gather a bouquet for my lady.

CARL. Aha! Have with you. I'm a very bee
   Among the flowers. I know where to look
   For those which give the most delicious honey—

CARI. Indeed. Which are they?

CARL. Tulips, dear, like these! [*Kisses her*]

CARI. Fie, sir!

CARL. Nay, nay, no pouting. Come along with me.
   And you shall chide me as we gather more. [*Exeunt*]

SCENE 4: *The Mole of Naples. Boats and galleys. Enter Alvar and Benedetto.*

ALV. This gale breathes life! Welcome, ye dashing waves.
   Welcome ye birds that with your hurrying wings
   Dip on the ridgy foam! I love the sounds,
   Wild as they are, that tell me of the time
   When I shall see the mountain shore of Spain.
   Blow on, fair breeze! Ho, Benedetto, haste!
   Go tell my noble lady that we wait—

BEN. Lud, this reminds me of the story of a traveller
   Who once upon a time—

ALV. Ha! She comes! She's here! [*Enter Bianca, Julia, Salerno, Cariola, and attendants*]
   Aboard, aboard, my life! The anchor's weighed.
   Aboard! Aboard! or the impatient wind
   Will frown reproach to us by sudden change
   For slighting thus its favor with delay.

SAL. Lady, my blessing and my prayers are yours.

JUL. Remember Julia!

BIAN. My heart is sadly grieved! Farewell! Farewell!

Chorus:

Farewell! Farewell!
Gently wave your seas,
And a stormless breeze
Your white sails swell!
Farewell! Farewell! [*They embark, all but Julia,*
Salerno, and attendants]

ACT II.

SCENE 1: *Apartment in Don Alvar's palace at Barcelona. Busts, statues, an easel, swing glass, painting apparatus. Cariola and Benedetto are arranging the room. Cariola stands opposite the mirror and looks at her dress.*

CARI. Benedetto, isn't Barcelona a charming place? It gives one such spirits! One can't move a step without seeing something prodigiously well worth looking at.

BEN. No doubt you are of that opinion at this moment, Signora Cariola; but, for my part, I see nothing to admire in it.

CARI. [*Turning to him*] What a savage!

BEN. Except when they have some public rejoicing, and then they *may* be endured. At all other times I never saw such a drowsy set as these Spaniards are. Not a laugh to be squeezed out of a hundred thousand of 'em. Compare 'em to the people of Naples, of merry, junketing Naples; why, unless they've something vastly uncommon to stir 'em up, you'll see a whole street of 'em yawning like an oyster bed at the turn of the tide.

CARI. You ungrateful varlet! Have we had anything but delights and shows of all sorts since we came? A concert in the morning, a ball at night, a banquet the next day, a play the day after; if they ever yawn, 'tis from the mere weariness of pleasure.

BEN. Then I should think master and mistress would do nothing but yawn. How much they do make of 'em here! This comes of being a rich old man's new young wife! It is not enough that they're to go to the grand national masquerade in the public square tonight, but there's the fine bridal supper at Don Diego de Cardona's, where all the rest of master's kinsmen are to be assembled to do honor to his choice. When they are tired of walking about, they'll have a capital view of the show from the windows. There they can fill their eyes and their stomachs at once! Ah!

CARI. Have you seen 'em in their new dresses? What a glorious figure they cut! They quite do us credit.

BEN. By the bye, Carry, what dresses are you and I to wear?

CARI. Look like a sensible person, and nobody'll know you.

BEN. Talk like a civil one, and if anybody knows you, they'll swear they are mistaken.

CARI. La! We shall have rare doings! All sorts and ranks mingle in these public masquerades here. People may do as they like on holidays of this kind in Barcelona, and nobody has a right to be offended.

BEN. [With a grimace of alarm] May they? Ah, this reminds me of a story, a capital one, by St. Agnes! of how once upon a time a tailor from Valencia married a pretty girl from Ca<diz>. She was as lively as cherry bounce, but had a tongue as hot as cayenne pepper. On the marriage day, says the tailor to his bride—

CARI. Poh! you chattering wretch! Hold your tongue!

BEN. "Hold your tongue! Poh?" No! He had too much sense to expect anything of the kind. So, says the tailor—

CARI. Nonsense! Don Alvar will be here in a moment. Quick! Throw the drapery over that chair. Put this bust upon the stand. But hark ye, Benedetto, what can be the reason my lady takes the trouble to sit for so many copies of her face on canvas?

BEN. Because a beauty thinks she can never see her face too often. I should think nobody knew that better than you, by your ogling your mirror so.

CARI. No; it is because master thinks nobody can make her half beautiful enough. He tried his own hand at it, till, only think! he who never failed before! Since he failed himself, of all the artists he has been trying all over the province, none has yet succeeded. I wonder how the one he has just chanced upon will make out. He expects wonders from him. I'm dying to see him.

BEN. What is there about him so strange? You're always dying when cavaliers are expected.

CARI. He is a Don of Dons among the painters, bustling through Barcelona in such a hurry that he can only spare an hour or two for a candlelight sketch before the masquerade this evening. Master takes it as such a favor that he stops at all! So mistress is to be painted in her fancy costume, in some wild, mysterious scene, I suppose; but we shall see.

BEN. This affair is so like—la! you never heard such a story since you were the size of a squirrel. Once upon a time four or five little children—

CARI. Whip the little children! Here they come! [Alvar enters, leading Bianca, both sumptuously habited in masquerade dresses, Bianca as a Sultana.

Hyppolito follows as a painter, completely disguised. He takes his colors and pencils from an attendant, while he arranges them and reconnoiters the room. Alvar and Bianca converse apart at the front]

BIAN. [*To Alvar, aside*]   Who is this painter? Wer't not well, my lord,
  That he should come tomorrow, not tonight?
  His look is strange. You must not leave me here.
  I know not why I feel a sudden dread.
  His countenance is wild. What is his name?

ALV. And why so fanciful, my gentle love?
  The signor's name is Manso,
  Sent to me by my friend the ambassador,
  As a most famous artist. He has come
  To Barcelona but this morn; and flies
  Tomorrow, Heaven knows where! [*To Hyppolito*] Sir, is this place
  The one that suits your art? Sit here, Bianca.
  [*Aside to her*] How your hand trembles. I'll stay with you, love.

HYP. [*Preparing to paint*]   A little from the light—a little more.
  [*Aside*] His glance is keen. Those lights will show my face.
  [*He tries to sketch and stops*] Pray you, my lord, a little farther back:
  The lights fall on your robe. Or, take your place,
  Your pardon, lord, behind me, till the sketch
  Is made. [*He tries and flings down his pencil in vexation*]
  Corpo di Giove, wrong! This crowd of lights—[*Pointing with a fretted gesture to the lamps on the table*]

ALV. [*To Cariola*]   Go, carry off those lamps. Their varying blaze
  Will mar the pencil. Benedetto!
  Order the train to hold themselves prepared
  To wait upon your lady to the fête. [*Benedetto and Cariola go out, carrying the lamps and leaving but one light beside the easel. Hyppolito paints*]

HYP. Please you, fair lady, cast your eyes above.
  Ha! So—as if you gazed upon some star!
  [*Looking at her*] Now press your hand deeply upon your heart,
  As if you vowed the heart's fidelity.

ALV. [*Aside*]   A most romantic painter! But his art
  Or finds men mad, or makes them so. That touch
  [*Looking at the picture*] is life. I see the master hand. How fine
  The power to fix the hue of beauty's cheek;
  The sparkling of the diamond eye; the look
  That speaks without a tongue, yet speaks the soul

Quicker than tongue's e'er uttered. Glorious art!
That with the power of miracle defies
The truth of time, the blight of worldly woe,
All earthly trouble. On its tablet smiles
Beauty unsullied, cheeks washed by tears,
Lips that will ne'er grow pale with anxious sighs,
Youth, love, and loveliness, alike immortal!
[*He looks at the picture*] Magnificent! Divine!
The artist does you justice, my Bianca.

BIAN. My lord turned flatterer! Nay, I fear I'll shame
The Signor Manso's pencil.

HYP. 'Tis but honored
Too highly in its subject. Now look down.
Heavens, what a rich possession! [*To her*] But one smile—
[*As in soliloquy*] The arching of that brow; that dazzling eye;
That lip to which the budding of the rose
Were colorless and chill. Thou paragon!

BIAN. [*Agitated at half overhearing him, aside*] What words are those
Tell me there's evil nigh! [*Aside to Alvar*]
Stay by me. Will the Signor soon be done?

ALV. Disturb him not, my love.
[*Looking over the sketch*] Bravo! Signor! A Titian were outdone
With that delicious coloring. That glow
Is worthy the Venetian.

HYP. I was his pupil:
An idle one; but worshipped at his feet
For some wild years, enamored of the fame,
The glory that he threw around his land!

BIAN. [*Aside*] He gazes on me strangely. If on earth
There's magic in a glance, delusion wild,
Or dangerous spell, 'tis in that fiery eye.
Would that his work were done!
[*To Alvar*] How goes the hour, my lord? Your noble friend
Will think his banquet scorned by our delay.

HYP. [*Gazing on her*] One look, but one look, gentle lady, one,
And all is finished. Pray you, draw aside
That tress which hangs upon your brow.
[*Aside*] There's a living smile,
A glance that strikes the soul like sudden flame.

ALV. [*Gazing on the picture*] It grows in light and beauty.
  Signor, your task is finished for tonight,
  And richly finished.
HYP. One moment more. This *must* be done tonight,
  Or may be never. By tomorrow's dawn
  I leave the walls of Barcelona.
BIAN. [*Urging him*] Nay, Alvar, come. 'Tis finished. Lose no time.
  We must not fail in courtesy.
HYP. Fair lady, look again.
ALV. Yes, rest awhile.
  I will but go a moment, to command
  That all be ready for our cavalcade.
  [*To Hyppolito*] Signor, the moment that you sought is given.
  I shall return—[*To Bianca*] as swift as thoughts of love! [*Exit
Alvar*]
HYP. [*Aside, looking after Alvar*] He's gone!
  [*Throwing off his disguise*] Bianca!
BIAN. [*Terrified and springing back*] Hyppolito!
  [*Recovering her firmness*] Why this offense, Count?
  Why this base intrusion?
  Thus in disguise to enter, thus insult
  The noble master of this palace! Count,
  I tell thee now, begone, before his scorn
  Shall crush thee. Must I call my menials in
  To drive thee from my presence?
HYP. [*Gloomily*] Aye, upbraid me.
  Taunt and revile me. After thou hast broke
  The faith we pledged so deeply, one more scorn
  Is nothing. I have come, Bianca, thus
  To tell thee what thou'st done and die before thee.
BIAN. Lord Alvar will be back,
  And thou be slain. I put to endless shame,
  And all undone. Fly!
  He moves not, hears not. Then I leave thee
  To sorrow o'er the wreck that thou hast made. [*She turns to pass
him. He holds her and shows a dagger*]
  Is't for my heart? [*She struggles*]
HYP. No! for thy husband's! Curses on the name!
  Aye, for your Alvar's heart. He won my prize,
  Poisoned my life, has drained me drop by drop

Of my heart's blood. His payment shall be here.
This hour, the traitor dies!

BIAN. [*In terror*]   Murder my husband! Oh, Hyppolito!
If ever human feeling touched your heart,
If all your vows of love
Were not an idle mockery, spare my husband.
I love him, honor him. There's not on earth
A nobler spirit. He has bound my soul
By his stronger than marriage bonds. In life,
In death, I'm his.

HYP.   Tell me you were a traitress, that your heart
Even when I thought it mine, had played me false,
That in the very hour when most it wore
The garb of love, 'twas guilty, hollow, cold.
But I have sworn an oath before your Heaven,
I, or your husband perish.

BIAN. [*Shuddering. Hyppolito seizes her. She grows faint*]   Strike your
dagger in my heart!
Strike! [*She looks to the door*]
Oh, this is agony! Spare me, Hyppolito.

HYP.   Bianca—woman-traitress—tremble now
And thank thyself for this. The hour is come
When love is turned to poison and the draught
Shook through the veins in death. Yet no.
[*Gazing on her in his arms*] How lovely guilt can look when it's
disguised
<In> such a countenance. Look up, Bianca. [*Sounds of voices at
a distance. Short flourish*]

BIAN.   Hyppolito,
If you have mercy, if you have a heart,
Go from this place. Leave me. Your secret's safe,
I pardon all.
Go and be happy! Heavens! Alvar comes!

HYP. [*Looking at her*]   Here will I stand. Defy him to the teeth;
Tell him my wrongs;
Then, strike home
And pay the great account at once.

BIAN. [*Throwing herself upon her knees to him*]   Have mercy,
Have mercy on me, kneeling at your feet.
Look on me, spare my husband, take my life,

Or is there duty, service, task of pain,
Though 'twere a pilgrimage around the world,
Ask and it shall be done!

HYP. [*Rapturously*] Swear by yon stars,
No, I'll make chance secure. My brigantine
Lies at her anchor by the city gates.
Fly with me. In one little hour our sail
Will make pursuit. We'll dash the whirling waves
Where all the lazy fleets of Spain would chase
Our flying speed in vain. Here, let this cloak
Hide thee from prying eyes. [*He flings the cloak over her*]

BIAN. Let me die here!

HYP. But once on board,
Come, lean upon me, love!
Now for eternal triumph!

BIAN. [*Struggles and feebly cries out*] Alvar! Help! My lord! [*As he is carrying her off fainting, Cariola comes in hastily at the other end of the apartment*]

CARI. My lady! Ha! A man here!
That handsome young Count we saw at Naples.

HYP. [*Suddenly perceiving her*] What devil starts to thwart me! Silence, wretch,
Or die. Aye, gold, there's gold for thee. Nay, take it. [*Cariola makes some difficulty, but he forces a purse upon her*]
Let that be dumbness, deafness, blindness to thee.

BIAN. [*Recovering, sees Cariola and clings to her*] Help, help, awake the house!
Summon my lord! He comes—I hear his voice!

HYP. [*Draws the dagger*] Remember!

BIAN. [*In terror, aside*] Murderer!
My husband's life! [*To Cariola*] Go, Cariola, fly!
Keep back my lord.
Go, wretch, deceiver! Go, Hyppolito.
Think of my misery,
This spot's my grave
If you and Alvar meet.

HYP. [*Aside, looking forward to the casement*] The courtyard's full. Lights on all sides. Escape

Is now impossible. My prize is lost.

Yet here I'll stand to have at least revenge. [*Alvar's voice is heard outside exclaiming*]

ALV. [*Without*] Order the horses round. Your lady's escort
Will wait her bidding. I shall follow her.

BIAN. [*Listening in terror*] He comes and both must die! Begone! Begone!

HYP. Never!

CARI. [*Running up to Hyppolito*] Sir, you must leave the room this minute. There—go, sir! [*Hyppolito resists*] I insist upon it, sir. Hide yourself, sir. I know my business, sir, as well as any lady's maid in Italy. What! Not a closet! Not a nook to hide a mouse in! What savages those Spaniards must be to build such houses: no provision for the necessities of high life! My lady, haste and meet my lord and stop him, if you can. And you, sir—but where the deuce shall I stuff you? Ha! The easel! You managed so well before it, now try what you can do behind. Come, sir, come. [*Urging him*]

HYP. What! Must I basely cower? Well, well, for her sake, to save her. I go. 'Tis done!

CARI. [*Dragging him*] Behind the picture!

HYP. [*As he goes, his eyes bent to the last on Bianca*] Would it were my grave!

CARI. [*As she returns from concealing him*] It may prove so, if you don't keep quiet!

BIAN. [*Apart as she goes*] He's safe! And now to lure my husband hence!
Oh, hard dissembling! Wear a face of falsehood
To blind him who—support me, conscious honor! [*Totters out*]

CARI. [*Alone, looking after Bianca*] There she goes! Though the lover's rather a surprise to me. But why should she not have a cicisbeo as well as all our ladies? At all events, I know my duty, and it is to take my mistress's part in spite of all the husbands in the world! [*Going to the easel, in a low voice to Hyppolito*] Now, Signor, now for your life! The coast's clear now! [*Looking out*] No, not yet. Now—[*Looking again*] There is the Don standing in the portico! You have to go out by that staircase, down the garden, over the wall, and then all's safe as a cardinal's conference, or a secret, or a ring or any other trifle [*Significantly*] entrusted to your honorable servant. [*Hyppolito moves out and gives her a ring. Benedetto at that moment comes to the door and cries out*]

BEN. [*At the door, half entering*] Cariola!

CARI. [*To Hyppolito, apart and hurried*] That Benedetto here! Out, spy! [*She catches up the candle light, dashes it upon the floor, and exclaims*] Oh, what an accident! Is any body here?

BEN. Don't be afraid. It's only I. How unlucky that you dropped the light. I came for a peep at the picture.

CARI. Then take this candle, light it for me quickly. [*Aside to Hyppolito*] Glide by him as he goes, escape! [*Hyppolito comes out*]

BEN. Where is it? [*Feeling about, he catches the hand of Hyppolito, and exclaims, delighted*] My pretty Cariola! [*Presses it*] Mother of Cupid! What a hand for a wife! [*Feels his face*]

CARI. Hush! [*Trying to make her way, rushes against him. Hyppolito disengages himself and gropes about*]

BEN. Two of them! It's a man! Help! Help!

CARI. It's only me you caught.

BEN. You! By this hand. But there's a man in the room—a bearded man! It's a robber. It's a lover. Stop—Surrender! [*In groping about, catches the cloak of Hyppolito*] Aha! I have him! Help! A robber! Help!

HYP. [*Disengaging himself dashes him on the ground; in the tussle dropping his dagger*] Scoundrel, let go my cloak! Out of my way!

BEN. [*Roars*] Thieves! Murder! Robbery! Housebreaking!

CARI. [*Tries to restrain him*] Hold your tongue, you fool! [*Alvar, with his sword drawn, hurries in, followed by an attendant with a light*]

ALV. What means this outcry?

BEN. It means, my lord, it means—

ALV. Explain.

BEN. Coming in, my lord, I ran against—

CARI. No, my lord, going out I ran against a chair, and stumbling, the light went out as Benedetto came in.

BEN. My lord, there was a man here!

ALV. A man!

CARI. My lord there was no man here—there was nobody here but Benedetto.

BEN. A man with a beard. I ran against him.

CARI. 'Twas against me he ran, my lord.

BEN. 'Twas not, my lord. I tell her to the beard 'twas not!

ALV. Are ye both mad?

CARI. He's not much better, I fear, my lord. I am afraid something very unfortunate has befallen the poor creature. It's after dinner with him, my lord. He has no head, my lord.

BEN. Yes, my lord, but I have, and a broken one, too.

ALV. Then silly varlet, take up the blockhead, take him to his bed. [*The attendant lifts him and gives the light to Cariola*]

BEN. My lord, I'll swear I felt a man's hand as big as mine and as hard as a flint stone.

CARI. Yes, my lord, I believe he felt mine on his face. [*To Benedetto*] And I hope it may teach you better manners for the future, Signor Benedetto. [*The attendant tries to draw him away. Benedetto attempts to remain*]

BEN. My lord, I have more to say than you can imagine. My lord, I could tell you such a story—[*Enter Bianca, cautiously*]

BIAN. [*Apart to Cariola*] I see him not. Speak—Is he gone?

CARI. [*The same to Bianca*] Not yet.

ALV. [*Perceiving her*] Ha! My Bianca! And in terror, too. [*To Benedetto*] See what this rioting has done. Disturbed your lady. Spread confusion through the house! Your life deserves to answer it. [*To Bianca*] My love! 'Tis nothing but this fool! [*To attendant*] Carry him off or fling him in the dungeon.

BIAN. [*Aside to Cariola*] Where is he?

CARI. [*Aside, pointing*] There!

BIAN. [*Apart*] Should he be perceived. [*To Alvar*] Come forth, dear Alvar, come!

ALV. One moment—but one glance—bring the light nigh. One look but on thy picture. Why, my love, such sudden paleness? I would fill my eyes with the deep beauty of that portraiture as with thy thought, my soul. Give me the light. [*Cariola withholds it*]

BEN. [*In the attendant's grasp*] I tell you, I'll go quietly enough only let me just say one word. My lord, don't let 'em take me till I have told my guess. By St. Agnes, my lord, I speak the truth. There was a man in the room and by the cut of his beard which these hands felt, I have a guess.

BIAN. My lord, Don Alvar! Leave this room. The air
    Is deadly to me. All your friends will blame
    Our tardiness. Nay, I beseech you, dearest.
    Give me your arm and come!

ALV. [*Aside*] Her deep emotion and the menial's words
    Whom I have found still faithful. This strange painter
    So wildly come and gone. Here is a depth
    That I must fathom.

BIAN. Will you not heed me, love?

ALV. [*Tenderly*] Heed thee?

CARI. [*Aside*] I have it! [*Runs up to Benedetto and whispers*] Will you be ruin'd, fool?

There was a man in the room. It was Don Alvar
Making fierce love to me. He must be screen'd.
Help me to keep the secret or you'll be kicked out,
And without mercy.

BEN. [*Knowingly, aside*]   Oh! Well done, my lord.
See how he fixes both his eyes on me.

ALV. Fellow, you saw a stranger in the room?

BEN. Did I my lord? I must have been asleep,
Or mad, to say so.

CARI. Perhaps simply drunk.

BIAN. Let me beseech you, Alvar. Night's far gone.
I love to see the festival. [*Aside*] I die!

ALV. [*Aside*]   All this is darker still. [*To Benedetto*] No falsehood, sir.
You told me that he grasped your hand, nay struck you,
And with harsh language, too.

CARI. [*Aside to him*]   Now, for your life,
Deny it every syllable. If you betray
Your master, you might better hang or drown.

BEN. My lord, a thousand pardons! If I said
That I'd seen any man, much more your lordship,
It was the wine, aye, my good lord, the wine
That got into my brains! *You* grasp my hand?
'Twas Cariola!

ALV. Pshaw! The man's a fool!
Vex me no more, sir, with your idle stories—

BEN. [*Aside*] Mysterious idle stories!

ALV. Go. Carry off that portrait, for its sight
Seems to disturb your lady. Leave me, love! [*He approaches to move the picture*]

BIAN. [*In terror, aside*] Great Heavens! Fate, do thy worst!

ALV. [*Striking his foot against Hyppolito's dagger*] Ha! What's here!
[*Takes up the dagger*] What may this mean? Whose weapon's this,
Bianca?

CARI. [*Darting across between Alvar and the picture*] Oh, sir, I did not
dare mention all his wickedness, but Benedetto, in his drunkenness, sir—in
his drunkenness he took such a fit of jealousy, sir—of unreasonable jealousy,
sir—I wouldn't mention it before for fear of—He was actually going to put
me out of the world when your lordship saved me. That was the reason I
struck him. In his jealousy he fancied 'twas a man; that was the reason I
pushed him down on the floor as you found him. Oh, the exertion was too

much for me! The sight of that weapon—monster! I think I see the blood on it already. My lord, I feel so faint—support me—I die. I am going—now—now—take me out of this room. I'm gone! [*Flings herself in Alvar's arms. He attempts to get rid of her, but she clings to him, feebly pointing to the door*]

BIAN.   Hasten, dear Alvar. Bring her to the air. [*Aside*] Oh, Hyppolito!
        [*Aloud*] Soft—let me aid you. Take her hand. [*To Benedetto*] Fear not,
        Now she is calmer. Draw her gently off.
ALV.   Go, dearest,
        Make ready for the festival; forthwith
        I will be with you. [*Alvar and Benedetto take Cariola out on one side. Hyppolito, when the stage is clear, comes from his hiding-place*]
HYP. [*Aloud*]   And so will I!
        Aye, for the moment, triumph! Soon will come
        The hour of retribution. Look for it;
        It comes in silence, but it comes with swiftness.
        Fierce eyes are on the watch! Rival, beware! [*Exit Hyppolito*]

SCENE 2: *A public square, terminating in a quay which borders on the sea-shore. Left hand, splendid mansion of Don Diego de Cardona, magnificently illuminated. Right hand, on the seashore, a headland surmounted by a light-house. Same sides, galleys moored. In the offing, a galley, all sails spread, lying to. At the quay, a boat with sailors in it. A group of sailors come to the front with the captain. Huzzas, laughing, and sounds of music heard outside.*

CAPT.   Come, boys, bear a hand! Are ye all ready? In the name of St. Agnes, what can keep that mad signor who has chartered our galley for some mysterious voyage? He sent all in a hurry for us to spread sail and stand out. We've got the galley off, the wind blows fair, but our admiral lags, drumming after some woman in this carnival masquerade, I'll be sworn!

2ND SAILOR.   Ah! When a man begins to run after a woman, he runs after a will-o'-the-wisp—

1ST SAILOR.   And if he misses it, he tumbles neck-deep into a ditch.

2ND SAILOR.   Or, if he catch it after all, 'tis only to burn his fingers.

3RD SAILOR.   Well, 'faith, I don't much care for being obliged to stop. This is a famous show tonight. [*Huzzas and loud laughing outside*] Hark! Hear how they laugh and shout yonder? The crowd of masquers who roared off a while ago to see the monkey quadrille yonder is bearing this way again.

Capt. Stand back, then. No doubt we shall find our signor in the wake of some petticoat. Bear away and keep a sharp look-out in case of sudden orders. [*They fall back. Groups of masqueraders enter and among them some who dance a Spanish dance, while others sing the following rondo*]

> Love in a mask
>> Flings o'er our revels his favoring shade,
>> Guides through the gay dance the blithe Spanish maid,
>> Who, smilingly clicking her quick castanet,
>> Will ne'er from this soft hour of rapture forget
> Love in a mask!

> Love in a mask
>> Sees eyes of beauties with ecstasy glisten
>> As to his whispers with blushes they listen!
>> And bounds of young bosoms keep time with the beat
>> Of steps lightly springing which twinkle to greet
> Love in a mask!

[*As the dance ends, enter Alvar and Bianca, attended. Hyppolito follows them at a distance in a white domino, and while they are speaking, is engaged with a mask dressed as a Devil in Blue*]

Alv. Does this gay scene divert thee?

Bian. I ne'er beheld a gayer
And thank thy love for granting me its pleasures—

Alv. I should enjoy thy mirth; yet a dejection
Stands o'er my spirits which I strive in vain
To conquer or account for. [*The mask of the Blue Devil comes*]

Mask. [*To Alvar*] Signor Mask! Didst thou complain of low spirits?
I am Prince of the Blue Devils, and will tell thee the cause.
Signor, cross my hand with silver and then come with
Me into a corner—

Alv. There's silver for thee! Prince of the Blue Devils,
I marvel much to see and feel you here
And should be glad to have your ingenuity
Account for your intrusion—

Mask. Come with me, then. [*Going*]

Bian. [*Smiling*] May I be of the party?

Mask. Nay, lady, seek not devils. They come to thy sex without the seeking.

BIAN. A merry fiend! [*The mask and Alvar retire to the side. Hyppolito advances. Alvar turns and seems frequently disconcerted by the eager gaze of Hyppolito on Bianca*]

HYP. [*Aside*] She is alone. Now for a word with her.
[*To Bianca*] Fair Mask! May I hope that the privilege
This festal hour confers may make me happy
In being honored with that lovely hand
As partner in the dance?

BIAN. Nay, gentle mask,
You come too late.

HYP. Wherefore, too late?

BIAN. That hand is not my own. I *have* a partner.

HYP. Partners may be changed.

BIAN. My partner comes. Leave me, gentle mask. [*Alvar comes up on one side, as Hyppolito bows and falls back*]

HYP. [*Aside*] Evermore foiled!

ALV. [*Observing him, aside*] That mask ne'er turns his gaze from my Bianca!

BIAN. What said the fiend? [*They converse, low*]

HYP. [*Aside*] Hold! There's a minstrel boy I heard
Among these revels. I will sketch a ballad
Upon my tablets, give it to the boy,
And he shall sing reproof to her. [*Hyppolito goes out*]

BIAN. [*To Alvar*] Indeed!

ALV. Most true! And then he scattered random words to make
Me almost fancy he *was* what he feigned.

BIAN. Oh, 'tis the trick of these fantastic revels
To play upon our fears and make us wonder. [*Hyppolito, having returned with the boy and given him the tablets, at the same time pointing out Bianca, goes to the opposite side to watch. Alvar, almost at the same moment, sees the boy, without observing Hyppolito*]

ALV. Come hither, pretty page. What hast thou there?

BOY. A rhyme I learned but now from a lorn lover.

ALV. Thou hast a voice attuned to rhymes of love.
[*To Bianca*] Wouldst hear the music of the minstrel boy?
Just now I heard him, and, of all the lays
Of elder and more practiced minstrels, never
Heard I a strain more sweet.

BIAN. You make me eager to partake the pleasure
　　　　His strain has given thee. Let me hear thee, boy.
　　　　　　　　Ballad, "Minstrel Boy"
　　　　Adapted to French air, "Le Jeune Troubadour"
　　　　　　　　　　　1.
　　　A youth who loved Italia's fairest flower
　　　　Was forced by fate to leave her;
　　　One moonlight eve he sought his lady's bower
　　　　With his farewell to grieve her!
　　　　　　He said with fond emotion,
　　　　　　"While I brave the ocean,
　　　　　　"Think upon my last farewell!
　　　　　　"Oh, be constant, Isabel!"

ALV. [*Aside*] That mask still gazing! How my heart beats!
　　　　There's Benedetto! I'll set him to watch
　　　　The movements of this stranger! [*Exit Alvar. Ballad continued*]
　　　　　　　　　　　2.
　　　'Twas said the youth in the wild wave had perished!
　　　　She seemed by sorrow blighted!
　　　But soon forgetting him whom once she cherished,
　　　　Her faith anew she plighted!
　　　　　　The shipwrecked youth returning,
　　　　　　Found nuptial torches burning;
　　　　　　And his dismal funeral knell
　　　　　　Followed fast her bridal bell!
　　　　　　Faithless, faithless Isabel!

BIAN. Enough! Enough! [*She bursts into tears. Hyppolito, who has ob-
served her increasing agitation, advances while she is speaking*]
　　　　[*Apart*] Oh, memory, memory! What a host of woes
　　　　Storm the weak citadel of woman's heart
　　　　At thy wild summons!
HYP. Lady, you seem moved—
BIAN. [*Faltering*] There's a strange magic in that minstrel's voice.
HYP. And in his story? Has that no magic
　　　　To call up images of hours long past?
BIAN. Such images should pass with the hours.
HYP. But do they?
BIAN. I say they *should*—
HYP. Not that they *do?* If Bianca's love
　　　　Is writ in air, Hyppolito's—

BIAN. My fears are true, then. Then thou art Hyppolito!

HYP. Ever Hyppolito, if thou art not
Bianca who was plighted to Hyppolito!
But do not tremble thus. My frenzy's past;
I could not harm thee now, for now I know
Thou art the same I knew in happier days.
Your tears have told the truth and quenched my fury:
Those tears with which you heard the minstrel boy
Sing your lost first love, of those dear, dear hours—

BIAN. The memory of such hours should be buried
In their own grave. Were you no more, Hyppolito,
I might weep both for them and you; but now
To weep would be a crime!

HYP. And yet you wept?

BIAN. Those tears you misinterpret.

HYP. If tears can be commanded, teach me how.
What power can dry them?

BIAN. Honor! Shall the agony
Of the racked bosom triumph o'er its virtue?

HYP. You grant your bosom suffers then?
And whence the suffering? That—you are—another's?
Thence may I not infer—

BIAN. Thence infer nothing. These are words of madness—

HYP. Hereafter—

BIAN. Make me not hate you, curse the hour we met—

HYP. Some change—should give you—freedom—

BIAN. Away! Away!

HYP. This hope shall still sustain me; in this hope
I'll hover near thee, like a guardian angel,
Love thee unseen and be thy shield in peril.

BIAN. Would you be my murderer?
I am another's—

HYP. But thou shalt be mine!
If early faith then sworn when heart to heart
Responded as the echo to the lyre;
If early passion, burning through long years
With but a brighter flame; if memory
Writing as with a pen of adamant
All true love's vows upon the living soul;
If all can give a right to woman's heart,

I am thy husband; and the haughty lord
That bears the name's a stranger.

BIAN. Shame! The love
Of which you talk's unworthy of that name!
Respect my peace of mind, respect my honor,
If you would have me think I do not err
In once believing you deserved my love.

HYP. That word again! In that, there dawned a ray
Of happier moments and of kinder feelings!

BIAN. My thoughts and feelings are as they were ever,
But still, as ever, virtue rules them all.
I loved you, would have been yours, Hyppolito,
But you and virtue were so blended in
My heart, that when I saw you swerving from it,
It seemed as though Hyppolito were dead,
Dead as our fears had deemed him.

HYP. Oh, no more!

BIAN. I placed an iron hand upon my heart,
Repressed its weakness, till Heaven smiled upon me,
Called up a tenderness responsive to
The strong affections of my worthy lord,
And made what first was duty, end in love!

HYP. Oh, virtue! Agony! And am I doomed
To see all crushed at once? Even hope? Even hope?
The love of years a day cannot destroy.
You would deceive me, or else, you yourself
Are, by yourself, deceived!

BIAN. Say I deceive myself,
You should confirm my error!
Say you cannot master
Your own affection; oh, how noble then
Your sacrifice to that affection!

HYP. [Aside] Her words are angels' pleading! I'm disarmed!

BIAN. My husband comes!

HYP. Farewell Bianca! [Enter Alvar with Benedetto]

ALV. [Apart, to Benedetto] Watch that white domino. Discover who
And whence he is, nor quit him, on thy duty!

BIAN. Oh, my dear lord! Come, let us quickly hence.

ALV. Who is that mask, Bianca?

BIAN. [Flurried and faltering] One—who—who—come, husband, come—

ALV. [*Advancing to Hyppolito*]   It is not civil, Sir Mask, to press your suit
thus—

HYP.   Signor!

BIAN. .[*Agitated*]   Nay, my lord, do not—do not *you*
      Accost him—

ALV.   Wherefore not I—

BIAN.   You—know—it—is—forbid
      To make the unmeaning gallantries of scenes
      Like this the cause of anger.

ALV.   Only when they *are*
      Unmeaning. Sir Mask, I am this lady's
      Protector—

HYP.   Rather, she is *yours*.

BIAN.   Oh, hence, hence, hence! [*Enter Cariola*]

CARI.   My lady, they're all waiting for you at Don Diego de Cardona's.
There's the house! Only see how beautifully it is illuminated! And what a
light it sheds over the sea! They're all revelling and laughing and dancing
so! Lord, lord! How I wish I were in the midst of 'em! [*She goes among the
masks, and Benedetto watches her jealously and greatly perplexed by the
necessity of also watching Hyppolito at the same time*]

BIAN.   Come, dearest husband, come—let us go in.
      Make not yourself and me the gaze of strangers.
      Oh, come away! Come, come!

ALV.   [*Aside to Hyppolito*]   Signor, the time
      And your disguise are now your guardians. But,
      Mark me well, signor! should we meet again,
      Or one or both of us may mourn the meeting! [*Exit with Bianca*]

HYP.   His words seem prophecies! How it would glad me
      To write their consummation in his blood!
      Hold, hold, Hyppolito! He has not wronged thee!
      He knew thee not. The prize was in the chances;
      And he has won it. By thyself, Hyppolito,
      Dismiss this love! One glance more at Bianca,
      Then back to Naples! Whither is she gone? [*Goes among the masks
as Cariola comes down followed by a mask*]

CARI.   [*To the mask*]   I tell you it cannot be. Get out of my way. It is impossible you should ever have known me, and I'll take good care you never
shall.

BEN.   [*Fidgeting and alternately eyeing the two*]   What a deuce of a task
they've set me! To watch the mask gliding about there like a will-o'-th'-wisp,

while my sweetheart is so beset on all sides, 'tis as much as I can do to watch *her*.

CARI. [*To the mask*] The beauty of my hand indeed! It has *one* beauty that you must take care I don't convince you of—

MASK. What's that?

CARI. Strength to give impertinence a good box on the ear. [*Boxes his ears. Exit Cariola*]

BEN. [*Fidgeting*] I shall contract an everlasting squint from being obliged to divide my eyes in this way.

HYP. [*Advancing*] I do not find them. Doubtless they are gone
To the festivities at the Cardonas'. [*Retires up*]

BEN. How that white domino moves about! I say, Cariola! My situation here makes me envy the cook in the story that once upon a time had such an accommodating obliquity of vision that he could keep one eye up the chimney and the other on the pot. Cariola, I say!

HYP. [*Advancing*] It shall be conquered! To my fate I yield!
The bark I've chartered waits in readiness
To waft me back to Naples at my bidding.
Yes, yes, Bianca! Now I feel at last
There's a protecting spirit o'er thy head
That guards thy beauty from all ill. I yield,
I war no more against thy noble heart.
[*Flings off his disguise*] Away, vile robe! Aye, all that brings to mind
Bianca and these hours, away, away!
Now for my sea cloak; now once more for Naples! [*Throws off his masquerade robe and rushes out. Benedetto, while Hyppolito is casting off his disguise, is peeping about after Cariola and loses him*]

BEN. The jack-o'-lantern has dodged me, and hang it, so has Cariola, too. Hey? La, there she is going to join her mistress at old Cardona's; and— [*Stumbling on the domino*] what have we here? As I'm an honest man, if one wouldn't swear this was the strange mask's domino. I must find out first, though, before I go off duty—pray, whose cloak is this? Anybody own this cloak? Who's lost a cloak? Anybody lost a cloak? You? You? You? [*Disappears among the crowd, seeking an owner for the domino and looking after Hyppolito. Enter Hyppolito, dressed in the same fashion as the sailors and accompanied by the captain and several sailors*]

HYP. And ready, all, you say?

CAPT. All sails set and a spanking breeze, my commander. She's only lay-ing to for you, signor. The boat's at the quay, there, and we only want you in it to shove off.

HYP. 'Tis well. I'm with you. [*Captain and sailors retire up*]
[*Apart, gazing on the mansion*] Yonder is the mansion
Where my love revels! Now, farewell forever!
I shall stand presently upon yon deck
With my gaze planted on that hallowed spot,
Swept past by winds whose merriment mocks my love!
Farewell, Bianca! Farewell, hope, love, life! [*Turns to go to the boat, as 1st Sailor runs down, stops him, and points at the illuminated mansion whence a thick smoke is seen to issue*]

1ST SAILOR. Hey, my commander! What's yonder? [*Captain and others come down*]

CAPT. What a devil of a smoke there is coming out of that house.

1ST SAILOR. By the beard of Neptune, I think we shall be obliged to pipe all hands to the pumps. [*Voices heard within. Benedetto rushes in alarmed, and runs about the stage, exclaiming*]

BEN. Help! Help! The illumination has set fire to Don Diego de Car-dona's house! Run and put it out! Help! Help! Help! [*Voices heard within*]

VOICES. [*Within*] Help, here, help! The house is all in flames!

HYP. [*Who has stood as if petrified, starts suddenly from his stupor*] In flames! Bianca's life in peril! [*Rushes to the building. Cries heard from within the house again*]

VOICES. [*Within*] Help! Help! Help!

BEN. The fire increases! The danger draws nearer! Let me draw farther off! [*Voices heard on all sides*]

VOICES. Fire! Fire! Fire! [*During these last speeches Hyppolito has at-tempted to enter the building, but the flames have rapidly increased, and as he attempts to pass the threshold, a crash, succeeded by an overpowering glare and rush backward of all the crowd, repels him*]

HYP. [*Recoiling*] A flaming rafter tumbled as I rushed. Again I'll tempt the blaze. [*Darts forward. Part of the front tumbles. As he springs forward, Alvar is seen amid the blazing ruins, with Bianca fainting in his arms. He rushes down with her. Sailors, with Hyppolito in the midst, are grouped op-posite*]

ALV. Friends, ye are mariners! By the sailor's
Honor, hear my appeal! Some of ye receive
This rescued loveliness! Guard, revive her—

HYP. [*Deliriously*] To me, to me, aye, give her to my arms—

ALV. Thanks, friend! I'll trust thee—

HYP. [*Wildly and hysterically*] Wilt thou? Wilt thou?

All earth shall never wrest her from my grasp!

ALV. It is my life I trust to thy protection!

The rest follow me! I have a sister

And other kindred in that blazing pile.

Sailors, stand by me!

'Tis woman and in peril calls your aid! [*Alvar rushes out, followed by those of the sailors who are not in the boat. Exeunt, shouting, over the ruins into the blazing mansion*]

BEN. The devil! I won't be a coward. I'll not leave Cariola in the lurch. If I'm not roasted for my valor, I shall be sure to get roasted for my want of it, so here goes! [*Runs out*]

HYP. Bianca in my arms! Bianca here! Fate smiles!

The wind that fans the flames bears off the ship.

'Tis my good stars have thrown her in my grasp! [*Cannon from the vessel in the offing*]

Ha! A signal gun to urge me quick on board!

The boat is manned. There's but a moment left.

'Tis done. I am resolved. Bianca's mine! [*Rushes with her into the boat*]

Up, oars, away! [*The sailors row them off. Enter Alvar, preceded by other sailors, by masqueraders, and by Benedetto, pulling along Cariola*]

BEN. Thank Heaven, I've saved you, Cariola! [*Wiping his forehead*] But I had a hearty tug of it! This will be a story to tell!

CARI. A story indeed! The brave sailors saved me from the fire, and you have nearly pulled my arms off dragging me away from them.

BEN. Oh, if you were but worth your weight in gold!

ALV. Thanks, gallant friends! Ye have shown how bravely the sons of the ocean merit their high fame! Not one has perished! Now ador'd Bianca —where is she? Bianca!

CARI. [*Looking out*] Oh, my lord, my lord! Do you see that boat which flies the shore so quickly?

BEN. [*Looking out*] By the mass, there's my lady in the boat!

ALV. Great Providence! [*To the sailors*] Who was the man to whom I gave her?

1ST SAILOR. A disguised cavalier who had hired our ship to take him to Naples; he wore a white cloak and a mask just now.

ALV. It is—it must be so. I see it all—All bursts at once—She's false—I am undone! Duped—ruined—lost! Myself to give the charge of my heart's treasure to a traitor's hand. This—this is he who haunted all my steps; this the wild painter, this the cunning mask.

CARI.   The boat has reached yon vessel. Merciful Powers! The vessel puts to sea!

ALV.   Stop—stop them. What—will none? Oh, agony! My brain is whirling; tear this iron off that tightens round my brow; I shall go mad! [*Bursts away. During the whole of this scene the bustle of the fire and the consternation of the guests must be kept up. The action of the boat and the brigantine passes as described by the characters. At the close of the scene the brigantine should be quite in the horizon, riding rapidly over a sea somewhat agitated. At that moment some part of the palace should fall, so as to fling a full, rich, crimson blaze over the waters, by which Bianca may be discovered on the deck, with gestures, imploring succor*]

ACT III.

SCENE 1: *The dressing room of Lady Julia's apartment in the house of Salerno at Naples. Flora discovered arranging her ringlets at the mirror on the toilette table of her mistress.*

FLOR. [*Alone*]   Pretty, *very* pretty; yes, that will do—well! Commend me to the man who first invented looking-glasses! They never quarrel with me, always smile at me, keep all one's cabinet secrets, and, in short, are the safest and most agreeable companions for single ladies in the world. [*Lissardo steals in and peeps over her shoulder. She screams affectedly*] Ah! What monster—

LIS.   News! News! I have a story as long as our friend Benedetto's.

FLOR.   Then carry it to some one with ears as long as your own.

LIS.   The Prince is going to be one of our family!

FLOR.   Oh, the horrid coxcomb! He makes love to every pretty woman he sees, and has not the sense to know where he should stop. I might have been Princess of Palermo myself, but I scorned him.

LIS.   You were so desperately in love with me, that accounts for everything. The Lady Julia is not so fortunate. She will have to put up with the Prince.

FLOR.   The Lady Julia! That's shocking! What! A mistress manage a love affair unknown to her maid! It is really quite out of rule.

LIS.   Ah, she thought she had done it unknown to her father too, but the old fox was too sly for her. He detected the stolen interviews and called the Prince to account. A peppery old boy, that master of ours! This is the reason they have not met lately.

FLOR. But I thought the Prince was engaged to a high lady in Spain.

LIS. True enough, but news is just come that the high lady is laid low.

FLOR. Dead?

LIS. As dead as could be desired; and with her, all objections to the avowal of Don Carlos's passion for the Lady Julia! So there is to be this very evening a small party of friends to the amount of five hundred or a thousand at his palace to witness the ceremony of his throwing himself at her feet.

FLOR. Well, wonders will never cease. I am astonished!

LIS. Are you? Then be amazed; for there are greater wonders yet: an illustrious stranger is arrived.

FLOR. Hey?

LIS. No less a personage than our mad runaway young master, Count Hyppolito. He is just returned from his mysterious expedition to nobody can guess whither; and no sooner did his father set eyes on him, than, in a fury of a passion he ordered him from his presence instantly under the care of as fast-trotting and ill-looking a troop of dragoons as ever took the guardianship of a gentleman not come to years of discretion. If he ever again shows his face abroad without leave, he is threatened with his father's curse—

FLOR. But whither is the young count sent?

LIS. To rusticate at our rural castle at Terra Nuova. And now, if you are sufficiently amazed, I'll petrify you. Here is another illustrious stranger for you: Enter—[*Benedetto comes in, melancholy*]

BEN. Ah! Once upon a time, four or five little children of Barcelona—

FLOR. Benedetto!

BEN. [*Sighing*] Even he, Signora Flora, is much surprised to find himself at Naples as you can be to see him here.

FLOR. But how comes this?

BEN. I will e'en make a story about myself. I can rival Sinbad the Sailor or the Wandering Jew. What a subject! What adventures! My mistress is carried off by a pirate. My master jumps into the sea to swim after her. I remain upon dry land to bewail their loss.

FLOR. And *is* this true?

BEN. What! Take me for a story teller? Oh, fie! Hear me out: a boat brings my master ashore. He stares like a madman about the beach. "Where is yon flying bark bound?" says he. "For Naples," they say. Upon which, what does he do but jump aboard of another galley, takes me with him and I take Cariola with me, and away we come wife-hunting across the sea! Such storms as we have had! But nothing to the storm we shall have if we come up with the lady, for if he overtake her, whew! But soft, here comes Cariola, as usual, just to cut short my story—[*Enter Cariola*]

FLOR. Ah, Cariola! Ah, my dear, I am delighted to see you. And is this sad news true? Your poor lady gone—carried off?

LIS. Helen is strayed. Well, I have heard of such accidents before, particularly when the gentleman was about twice the age of the lady.

FLOR. What a gallant speech, and particularly before ladies. Have you no fears, wretch?

LIS. None *before* marriage and even after, not much, particularly where, as in our case, the lady happens to be about twice the age of the gentleman, my dear!

CARI. Flora, you must marry him, to be revenged.

BEN. Oh, the malice of the sex! That reminds me of the story—

LIS. But where have you left the haughty Don Alvar?

CARI. Hush! You must not breathe his name—

BEN. Yes, even I am not to know there is such a being in existence.

CARI. And the truth is, as for me, he did not know I came. I was stowed in a secret corner of the ship—

BEN. Among the lumber!

CARI. For, being thrown by this sad affair out of my place, I thought the only chance for me was dear Naples—

FLOR. Well, you have come just in time. If Lissardo's news be truer than is usual with that exquisite gentleman, I shall require an addition to my establishment as first femme-de-chambre, and I shall put you on my list for the next vacancy.

BEN. Spoken like a first lord of the Treasury!

LIS. Hang it! Can't she stay, in the meantime, at Terra Nuova? Fiametta wishes to go and see her sick brother and is anxiously waiting to find someone to supply her place for a week or two.

FLOR. The very thing!

BEN. Then will I hasten back with a light heart to my duty. [*Aside to Cariola*] He's to meet me at a little inn between Naples and Terra Nuova, but there's my duty! [*Aloud*] Ah, Carry! You see what it is to have the patronage of the great! Now this puts me in mind of the little barefooted boy, who, when they bid him begone to the dark, dismal wood—

LIS. Let us begone to a Perigord pie and a flask of champagne—

BEN. Spirit of hospitality, the thought makes me smile. Just so it happened once upon a time—

ALL. Come along! [*Exeunt Omnes*]

SCENE 2: *An apartment in the palace of Don Carlos at Naples, during a fête. Enter Salerno, leading in Julia and Don Carlos.*

SAL. Prince, she is yours. Julia, no words. My will
      Is law. Aye, she shall be your prisoner.
      Once let her out, my Prince, and she's as wild
      As the gazelle.

CARL. My lord, I'll weave a chain
      That, wore my Julia wings, she'd ne'er escape
      The chain of faithful love!

JUL. [*Laughing*] Oh, constancy!
      To hear such lips pronounce thy praise!

SAL. Nay, girl!
      Do him but justice. He has loved a month,
      Borne a week's absence, won a father's will,
      And now is ready to submit his neck
      To slavery for life; but I'll go in
      And give your guests a welcome, Prince. Farewell. [*Exit Salerno*]

JUL. And so I *must* believe you, sir?

CARL. Rail on,
      My prettiest of prudes, I'll bear it all.
      I've been a very butterfly, I grant,
      But when I turn my eyes into my heart,
      I find but one name there, although my head
      Has been a sort of drawing room for beauties.
      That name is: "Julia."

JUL. [*Archly*] Still I think you cheat me.
      You are a knave with women—

CARL. Call me all things
      That wit e'er taught to beauty, beauty spake,
      A true love welcomed—

JUL. Well, I may forgive;
      But 'tis on one condition: from this hour
      I must preside o'er that same drawing room
      You talk of in your head! Yes, from this hour
      You swear ne'er to look
      The way a beauty passes, send no sigh
      To woo her back. Swear but this,
      And I'll perhaps forgive thee.

CARL. [*Kneels*] With thy hand
 For my white altar, on my bended knee,
 And with as suppliant lips as ever wooed
 The wicked prettiness of woman, here
 I vow to be thy sport, thy mock, thy slave,
 All in one word, thy husband!

JUL. [*Touches him with her fan*] Thus I knight thee.
 Now rise, most puissant, valorous, noble Prince,
 And be upon thy shield, the marriage,
 Thy motto, "Constancy." Thy bosom's queen,
 My sovereign self—Sir Hymen, rise!

CARL. [*Rising*] Thanks, Queen!
 But I must kiss the book! [*He kisses her. A knocking heard and the voice of Bianca exclaiming within*]

BIAN. [*Within*] Unbar this door!

CARL. [*Aside, confused*] Hang women's tongues!

JUL. [*Startled, shrinks from him*] What voice was that, sir? Ha!

BIAN. [*Within*] Release me! [*Knocking*]

JUL. 'Tis a woman!

CARL. [*Affecting unconsciousness*] What dost say?

JUL. I knew your fickleness. Farewell. [*Knocking again*]

CARL. [*Aside*] Confusion!
 [*To Julia*] My love, 'tis nothing. 'Twas some passing sound,
 Some of the rambling minstrels that surround
 All palaces on nights like this. Be calm. [*Listens*]
 Gad there was *no* sound—'Twas all your mistake. [*Knocking again violently*]

BIAN. [*Within*] Open! Help! Open!

JUL. Mistake, was it, sir?

CARL. [*Aside*] What evil genius made Hyppolito
 Send his strange capture here? Shall I disclose?
 Yet, no. My honor's pledged. [*To Julia*] My love, but hear. [*Knocking again*]

JUL. I hear too much—

CARL. But let me speak one word—

JUL. [*Aside*] Now for a tale as plausible yet false
 As e'er fooled woman's ear. [*To Carlos*] My lord, say on—
 Nay, you're confused! Take time, collect your thoughts;
 'Twill make the tale run smoother. [*Knocking*] Hark! Again!

BIAN. [*Within, knocking more violently*] Open the door, or I will break it down!

JUL. Your gentle minstrel serenades most sweetly!

CARL. The truth is, love, a luckless friend of mine,
Names must remain untold, brought here this morn
The partner of his flight, and craved my leave
To find her shelter. Love, I saw her not,
And know not whence she came. But two hours hence
My friend should have conveyed her from this place—
Why he delays, I know not.

JUL. Know not, sir!
Why stoop to this? Why not speak out at once?
Unlock that door!

CARL. It is impossible!
Trust to my faith. [*Knocking. Aside*] Confound this confidence.
I will—no—honor—faith, forbid the deed! [*Knocking*]
[*Aloud*] Julia, but hear me. By my solemn truth,
By every tie that binds us heart to heart,
I'm wholly guiltless here!

JUL. [*Indignantly*] Unlock *that* Door!
Show me that—"minstrel!" Tell me who has brought
That wretch beneath your roof, if not yourself,
Or, by all solemn things, I, from this hour
Discard you, hate you, tear you from my heart.
Unlock *that* door! [*Knocking*]

CARL. [*Aside*] Confusion! Here's a strait!
But—break my promise? Aye, and hear the taunts
Of liar, coward, slave! on all men's lips!

JUL. Prince—[*Aside*] Ha! He's guilty! I'm undone! [*Aloud*] One word:
But yes—or no—

CARL. You yet will do me justice!
But what you ask's impossible.

JUL. Then sir, begone!
All's at an end between us. From this hour
Our hopes are separate, our hearts are twain,
I scorn and hate you, drive you from my sight—
Leave me!

CARL. [*Retiring*] 'Tis your will.
But, lady, this mistrust is death to love.
Once gone, I'm gone forever.

JUL. *'Tis* my will.

Be gone and gone forever! [*He bows and retires*] Now I'll have
The secret out, or die for want of finding it! [*Reaches the door*]
No lock! No hinge! This cunning cabinet
Shall not elude me! Ha! A secret spring! [*She touches a spring, the
door sinks, and Bianca, in astonishment and terror, rushes out into her arms*]
Bianca!

BIAN. Julia here! Oh, save me! Save me!

Where am I? In whose house? What sounds are those?
My eyes are dim with weeping, my heart wild;
A blight has fallen upon my life. Oh, save me!

JUL. [*Aside*] This is true anguish. Yet, in Carlos's house—
[*To Bianca*] How came you here, Bianca?

BIAN. I have to tell

A long and desperate tale. But now let's fly.
Your brother's furious passion haunted me.
Threats, tears, prayers, fraud, and frenzy all were vain,
Until, one night of Spanish festival
Some madman fired the palace. I was borne
Fainting and senseless through the burning ruins.
I woke to find myself upon the deck
Of a felucca—with the midnight sea
Flashing around me—

JUL. And Hyppolito?

BIAN. With his wild eye fixed on my dying face,
That look told all the mystery—

JUL. Was it he

Who bore you from the flames and his the ship
That swept you from your husband?

BIAN. There he knelt

And dared to ask my heart. I cast him off
Even as a serpent. From the ship last night
I was brought here in secret. How to 'scape
I knew not; but I prayed, and help has come,
And in an angel's form! [*Flinging herself into Julia's arms*]

JUL. [*Embarrassed and looking towards the distance, aside*] He will be
back. There is no time to lose.

But how to save her? Ha! There is one hope.
[*Aloud*] Bianca, love! You know our ancient house
Half-fort, half-palace, but a league or two

From Naples. You shall thence with me,
Unknown, unseen, and we will there confer
How best to meet the future.

BIAN. Thanks, thanks! And may your life's propitious stars
Turn all my griefs to blessings on your head.

JUL. Someone approaches. Come this way. We'll find
Our train beyond the garden. Now thou'rt safe—

BIAN. For Terra Nuova!

JUL. [*Aside, going*] Oh, my hasty heart,
How hast thou wrecked my happiness. He's yours.
Carlos is lost to me and I undone! [*Exeunt*]

SCENE 3: *An apartment in an inn on the road between Naples and Terra Nuova. Enter Alvar, in rude habiliments. He seems weary; takes a brace of pistols and a dagger from his coat and flings them on a table.*

ALV. [*Alone*] Still, he escapes me! Lie you there, my friends!
The only friends an honest man can trust
In this accursed Naples. Aye, this dress
Lets man into some truths that gold and jewels
Would never show him! Through what sullen haunts
Of vice and misery, what desperate tribes
Of bloody rapine, or of miscreant fraud
Have I not roved since morn! Yet one worse slave,
One more remorseless robber than the wretch
That cuts a throat i' th' streets for villain gold,
The murderer of my honor, has escaped me.
I would have stabbed him in the palace gate,
Within the halls of justice, at the foot
Of the high altar. But the miscreant fled
And mocks a husband's vengeance! [*Benedetto runs in*] Ha! What
news?

BEN. I've learned, sir, that Count Hyppolito was seized by order of the Governor immediately on his appearance in Naples yesterday, and sent off under an escort of horse in arrest for having gone to Spain without leave.

ALV. Whither is he sent?

BEN. That, my lord, I could not discover. It seems the old gentleman had ordered it to be kept a secret even from the Count's own sister; but, from the best I could make out, I think it must be to a place they call Terra Nuova.

ALV. [*Aside*] Ha!

BEN. A sort of country seat of the Governor on this road, but fortified against the Barbary pirates. But, my dear lord, your lordship looks pale and weary. I know you must be hungry by the forlorn state of my own appetite. My lord, pray be prevailed on to take a little refreshment.

ALV. Benedetto.

BEN. My lord.

ALV. Remember my commands. I have disclaimed
All titles and am now a traveller,
A stranger, what you will. [*Apart*] This low disguise
Will sooner lead me to my full revenge
Than grandeur's robes. [*Aloud*] See you betray me not.

BEN. Not I, my lord. I'm no blabber. Did you ever catch me in a story, my lord? But I was only thinking how much our voyage put me in mind of the story of—

ALV. Peace, babbler! Take those pistols up! And mark me—

BEN. Pistols, my lord! You make me tremble.

ALV. Take up those pistols—

BEN. Won't you go in, sir? Have you the heart to let the meat grow cold?

ALV. Obey me—

BEN. So I do; but as to these pistols, you don't mean to eat with pistols. I could tell you such a story about pistols—

ALV. No more! Away! [*Exit Alvar*]

BEN. [*Alone, following in a tremble*] Humph! Pistols and pudding! Ah, if anything should happen to me, so much the worse for the world. Nobody will ever hear how once upon a time four or five little children of Barcelona— [*Alvar heard within*]

ALV. [*Within*] Benedetto!

BEN. Coming, sir. I shall never get a chance of telling that story, no, not even to myself. [*Exit Benedetto. At the same moment, on the opposite side, enter Carlos*]

CARL. [*Alone*] That Celio comes not, and 'tis past the hour!
Hither I haste, half way to Terra Nuova,
To get my news thence sooner, and i' faith,
It seems as though 'twere twice the time in coming
It would have been had I remained in Naples!
Shame, Carlos, shame! Shall I be fluttered thus
By a weak woman's nonsense? I, whose life

Has been one round of sporting with the sex?
The empty jilts! They are not worth a feeling!
I care for them! What! I? Ha! Celio comes! [*Enter Celio. He runs to him*]
Well, you have been to Terra Nuova? What news thence?
What have you gathered? Speak. The worst at once.

CEL. I've bribed the servants and found all out. It *is* true, the Lady Julia is gone thither with the mysterious captive left under your charge by Hyppolito—

CARL. Go on, go on—

CEL. And what is more, not in the humor she was.

CARL. How so? Proceed.

CEL. I have discovered that ever since she has been there her time has been passed in scribbling letters to you and tearing them up, in weeping with her strangely found new acquaintance and about herself, and, were you now to show yourself—

CARL. I'm a changed man. I'll fly to her at once.
But no; she'll throw me off in scorn! 'Tis right
Her petulance should suffer. Shall my pride
Stoop to beg pardon, when I am, by miracle,
For once the wronged? Besides, if I should thus
Begin with her when I am innocent,
What shall I do if I should see occasion
To take a holiday sometime hereafter
And flirt a little for my recreation?
She must be punished! Now, could I but find
Some fair excuse for going to the castle,
Some reason in which Julia forms no part—[*A bustle heard without and Alvar's voice*]

ALV. [*Without*] Stand back, I say.

CARL. What noise is that? [*Celio goes to listen*]

ALV. [*Without, the bustle growing louder*] Stand back!

CEL. A stranger struggling to come in. Ha! I caught something about Terra Nuova, and he says he *will* enter. He is here! [*Alvar bursts in wildly, eyes both, and starts away, disappointed*]

ALV. [*Aside*] Confusion! [*To the Prince*] Pardon, sir, I was mistaken.
They said someone was here from Lord Salerno's
And would not let me see him, though I fancied
It was a person whom I knew, aye, well,
And one to whom I owe no trifling debt.

CARL. 'Tis rare to find men, so very ready
      To seek their creditors.
ALV.   Once more, your pardon.
      Perhaps the want of courtesy with which
      The boor would fain have forced me back might chafe me
      Into abruptness, and I crave your pardon.
CEL. [*Apart to Carlos*] This man, my lord, has seen some better days.
CARL. [*The same, to him*] 'Tis evident he has. [*To Alvar*] And where-
fore, sir,
      Were they thus rude in their repulse?
ALV.   Oh, sir,
      The cur will ever bark at rusty robes—
CARL. Your bearing, sir, is noble.
ALV.   I—I've lived
      Among my betters. My pursuits have led me
      To talk with great men, taught me to be proud,
      Too proud, perhaps.
CARL. What are you?
ALV.   What?
      Oh, sir—a—an artist, sir, only an humble artist.
CARL. I love the arts, and more than all love painting.
ALV.   And I, sir, 'tis my idol. That's a love
      Which will endure. Aye, aye, no treachery there,
      For painting gives a life to history
      And makes the visions of the poet real.
      It triumphs over time, restores the dead,
      Sustains the rose which time or sorrow withers,
      Comforts fond hearts when they are torn asunder;
      And in this silent monitor old age
      Sees what it was and scarce believes the change!
CARL. [*Aside, to Celio*] Ha! Now it dawns! I'll turn this strange adventure
      To good account. This will be a pretext
      For my intended visit. Is't not so?
CEL. [*The same*] Nobly contrived, sir, a most lucky thought.
CARL. [*To Alvar*] Your eloquence enchants me, sir, and I
      Would be your friend—
ALV. [*Bitterly, and half aside*] My friend!
CARL. There is a picture
      In old Salerno's place at Terra Nuova—

ALV. [*Eagerly*]   Well!

    [*Apart*] Let me but get within those walls! [*Aloud*] Go on, sir, well—

CARL.   For which a certain female friend of mine

      (I' faith a little of a jilt) once sat

      As the chief figure. She has wandered from me—

ALV. [*Wildly*]   Wandered! All tortured in their turn. [*With a delirious laugh*] Ha! Ha!

CARL.   Insult!

CEL.   What means this fellow?

ALV. [*Not hearing them*]   Woman, woman!

      She's the grand riddle, beautiful illusion!

      Why were ye formed so fair and yet so false?

      As light as air, uncertain as the wave—

CARL. [*Apart, to Celio*]   The man is mad—

ALV.   And so you're stung, good sir.

      The serpent has been twining round you, too,

      Until the fangs were buried in your heart.

      [*Recovering, aside*] Madman! I shall betray myself. Down! Down!

      [*To Carlos*] Pray, sir, forgive me. 'Twas some memory,

      Some bitterness of other times, that wrung

      This passion from me. But you're in the right:

      One moment can extinguish all the love

      Won by a life of tenderness. Oh, woman!

      Well, sir, the picture. Come, the picture, sir—

CARL.   I blame no man for writhing, when his heart

      Is torn by man's falsehood, sir. The picture

      Is one that gives the moral to a tale

      Told from the birth of mankind.

ALV.   How is't named?

CARL.   'Tis Hercules and Dejanira:

      He who could strangle lions at a grasp,

      Yet could not cope with the deceit of man.

ALV.   Aye, he who madly gave the wife he loved,

      The treasure of his soul, to the vile hand

      Of a smooth-spoken robber. Fool, fool, fool!

CARL.   The picture's finely painted. There you'll see

      The centaur springing on the further bank,

      His arm flung round his prize, his visage hot

      With furious triumph—

ALV. [*Apart, writhing*]   Damn him, damn him, damn him!

CARL. While the husband stands—
ALV. Aye, what of him?
       The great, the demigod, turned to an idiot?
CARL. Ah, the sad fate of husbands! *Who* would marry
       To see his wife borne off before his eyes—
ALV. [*Violently*]   *He* had his great revenge! The monster fell!
       He had revenge! Ha! Ha! Nor man nor devil
       Can cheat him there. The husband had revenge!
       I see him grasp his bow, I see the shaft
       Dipped in the hydra's poison. Now it twangs—
       'Tis in the robber's heart. He has revenge!
CARL. Sir, you seem moved by this—
ALV. 'Tis passed. 'Tis nothing—fancy's dream, no more!
CARL. We must be speedy. 'Tis of such high dreams
       That genius builds its world. Art's miracles
       Are but the transcript of the fiery mind.
       [*Calls*] My horses there! Follow me, sir. An hour
       Will bring you to the picture.
ALV. [*Apart, violently*]   And revenge! [*Exeunt*]

SCENE 4: *A picturesque garden in the château at Terra Nuova. A wing of the villa seen partly over trees in the distance. Right hand of the audience and in front, a pavilion with bars from the ceiling to the floor, running the whole length of the side facing the audience; or else, full-length French windows standing open. At the side, steps leading up to the entrance of the pavilion, which opens on the garden. In the pavilion, a large painting with a curtain before it, a table and chair. Opposite the pavilion, a beautiful bower. Enter Bianca, led by Julia.*

JUL. My heart is lighter, love. The Prince is here.
      Now we can meet, now all can be explained.
      Flora, the maid we brought, found out the secret:
      He comes pretending 'tis but for the copy
      My father promised of the noble picture
      In yon pavilion. With him comes some artist—
BIAN. And have you seen him?
JUL. No, not yet, my love;
      But when true hearts are near as we are now,
      The rest is easy. We shall both dissemble
      For yet a little while; then both be fonder

Than we have ever yet been. 'Tis the history
Of all love's quarrels. [*Enter attendant and whispers to her*] What!
Father come!

My father's just alighted with Lissardo.
Pardon me but a moment, dear Bianca.
He is incensed to find me gone o' th' sudden;
He comes to scold me and to know the reason,
Which 'tis not fitting that he yet should know.
I must begone to soothe him with excuses.
A moment and I'm yours. [*Exit Julia*]

BIAN. [*Alone*] Oh, gentle girl,
Bright be your hours with the sweet smile of love!
Your name ne'er torn, like mine, by bitter malice!
But what is malice to the consciousness
Of an untainted soul! There's but one scorn
By which we should be shaken: 'Tis the scorn
Of the accusing heart! The world may hate,
Virtue o'ercomes the world! What lethargy
Is this that darkens o'er me? On my eyelids
A weight is pressing, as upon my heart.
Hyppolito, 'tis you have made me what I am;
Yet I forgive you all, I pardon you,
Aye, as one pardons on the bed of death!
I feel the world's passed from me! To my lord
I shall return no more to bring a stain
Though innocent upon his stainless name!
Let me rest here awhile! The air is soft.
Would that this couch were but my last retreat,
Were but the cloister where the hours shall pass
That lie between me and my early tomb!
Come, sleep! Sleep! Sleep! Oh, would thou wert repose! [*Sinks to
sleep in the bower. Attendant enters the pavilion, deposits something upon
the table, then beckons on the Prince and Alvar, and retires*]

CARL. [*Pointing to the picture*] This is the picture, sir; and hence, perhaps,
You may behold, ere you complete your work,
The Dejanira of the noble artist.
She often roams this garden. For the moment
Farewell, good sir. I leave you to your labor. [*Exit Prince. Alvar dis-
tributes the painting implements and takes out the pistols, placing them on*

the table by the side of the painting things. He then sits down for a moment, exclaiming]

ALV. [*Gloomily*] No news of this Hyppolito. No clue—[*At this moment Hyppolito cautiously steals in, wrapped in a mantle, from the side where the pavilion stands. He comes between the window and the bower, his back being turned to the window, so as to intercept Alvar's view of Bianca, while unseen himself*]

HYP. [*Advancing, says low*] It was Bianca whom I saw.
　　　All's still—'Tis she.
　　　[*Low, observing her*] But how did she come here?
　　　What miracle—Her sleep seems troubled—Hark!

BIAN. [*In her sleep*] I'm wronged! Death if thou wilt, but hear me ere I die!

ALV. [*Springing from his stupor*] That voice—can it, no,
　　　No, my ravished fancy
　　　In every voice of woman hears but hers! [*Drops back in his chair again*]

BIAN. [*Writhing*] Spare me—oh, spare me till you know the truth!
　　　Then kill me and I'll bless you! [*Springs from the couch, rushing down the stage, and falls on her knees before Hyppolito, still unseen by Alvar*]

ALV. Ha!

HYP. What means this madness? Speak! You're safe, most safe.

BIAN. [*Seeing him, recoils*] You! Is it you! The man's here, then—tremble!

HYP. What man? What?

BIAN. Oh, such a dream, so full of horror.

ALV. [*Apart, wildly*] Am I in sleep or mad?

BIAN. I thought I was once more upon that wave
　　　Which makes me such a wretch, when suddenly
　　　A tempest shook me from my sleep. I started,
　　　Sprang to the deck, black clouds encompassed me.
　　　A voice amid the fearful darkness howled,
　　　"Traitress, I come! In death I claim my bride!"
　　　And I saw hovering o'er me a fierce spirit,
　　　Half wrapped in cloud. I recognized the face
　　　Though changed to fury 'twas Don Alvar!

ALV. [*Who has remained as if petrified, and unconscious, shrieks*] 'Tis she! It is my wife with her betrayer! [*Both start*]

Bian. [*Shuddering, involuntarily clings to Hyppolito*] Hark! Heard you not a voice? A voice like his?

Hyp. [*Trembling violently*] I—I—but no, it cannot be.

Bian. [*Loosening her grasp of Hyppolito and with calm decision*] As I am living, 'twas his voice I heard.

Hyp. [*Flurried and faltering*] Your husband is no more. The news arrived
    But now at Naples.

Alv. [*Confusedly pacing the back of the pavilion*] Like the pent lion must I pace my cage,
    Denied to dart and crush them at a bound?

Bian. [*Recovering from a burst of tears, mournfully*] No more? 'Tis well. Life were to him a curse,
    Doomed to endure the scoffs of an unjust world
    Which turns the husband's wrong into his shame!

Alv. [*Who has, in the meantime, been feeling wildly for his pistols, now grasps them, but trembling violently*] Now, ministers of justice!

Hyp. [*Hurrying Bianca away*] Come hence with me. I feel there's danger here.
    I know not why, but here I'm sure there's danger.

Bian. [*Struggling*] Whither? Where would you drag me? I'll not leave!

Hyp. You stand upon a precipice. Your next step
    May be—perdition!

Bian. [*Struggling*] Oh, whither? Whither?

Alv. [*Tremblingly and wildly points the pistols*] Now—now—

Hyp. [*Seizes her*] To—to—[*She throws off Hyppolito, and the struggle forces her out of the range of the shot*]

Alv. [*Fires and shrieks violently*] Death! [*The Prince, Julia, Salerno, Flora, Cariola, Lissardo, and Benedetto instantly run in from different sides. Julia receives Bianca, who is yet staggering from the struggle by which she has been withdrawn from the grasp of Hyppolito. Hyppolito falls. The Prince and Salerno rush to him*]

Carl. [*Raising up Hyppolito*] What murderer has done this?

Sal. Shut all the gates!
    Let search be made. He bleeds.

Hyp. [*Faintly*] Look to the lady.

Ben. [*Low*] Run to your mistress, Cariola. [*Bianca sinks on Cariola's shoulder*]

Sal. Bianca! Can it be Bianca?

Carl. Whence came the shot?

BIAN. [*Feebly, pointing to the pavilion*]   There! There!

CARL.   She points to yon pavilion. Burst the door. [*As they approach, the door flies open, and Alvar appears wildly on the steps with pistols*]

ALV.   'Twas I who did the deed! 'Twas I!

BIAN. [*At hearing his voice, springs towards him*]   Alvar! [*Suddenly stops, overcome by recollections, and falls back in the arms of the attendants*]

ALL.   Alvar!

ALV.   Aye, the wronged husband, Alvar: it was I!
I saw them twining in each other's arms
And swore revenge on both. Are they both slain?

SAL.   Oh, my unhappy boy! Bear him away! [*Carlos resigns Hyppolito to the attendants, who bear him to the house*]
He bleeds! Don Alvar, this was fierce revenge
And shall be sternly recompensed.

JUL.   Bianca is unhurt, murderer, unhurt!

ALV.   What! Has my traitor arm refused to right
Its injured master? Thus then let me end—[*Alvar dashes down the pistols and starts forward with his dagger. The Prince disarms him; Julia throws herself before Bianca, and Lissardo and Benedetto go to Alvar*]
'Tis well. Yes, yes! Enjoy the spectacle
Of injury unredressed. Smile as scorn's finger
Points at the husband who has twice stood by
And seen the traitress with her paramour.

JUL.   Bianca, speak! Give tortures to his heart
By telling him that thou wert pure as Heaven!

CARL. [*To Alvar*]   Sir, this was frenzy. She is innocent.
Sweet lady, wake and tell thine own proud tale
To him who would have drained thy generous veins
In wild suspicion.

BIAN. [*Kneeling to Alvar*]   Alvar, by our love,
By plighted faith, by all my hopes of Heaven,
Your wife is at this fearful hour as clear
Of all offense as lisping infancy.
I have been made the prey of bitter tongues,
Of desperate chances, strange and evil days,
But still was true to thee. I ask but now
Thy leave to give the remnant of my days
To some sad cloister, there to pass my life
In prayer for thine.

ALV. [*Aside*] Can I believe all this?

    Yet truth seems living in her countenance!

    [*Aloud, bitterly*] Came she not here to meet her paramour?

JUL.   It was I

    Who brought her here to shun him, nor, till now

    Knew I that he was here, nor where he was.

SAL.   'Twas I that sent the Count Hyppolito—

    Sent him a prisoner, 'gainst his strong entreaties,

    Now, until now, had I a thought Bianca

    Was even in Italy.

ALV. [*Aside*] *All* cannot league against me!

SAL.   My boy revives. He strives to speak. Give way! [*They bring Hyppolito forward*]

HYP.   Lord Alvar, hear my words, as if I spoke

    The last these lips shall utter. She is pure.

    I loved her, sought her heart, and I was scorned.

    She told me that her faith was thine, Lord Alvar,

    And that her heart went with it. She is pure.

    Forgive her. If I shall survive this wound,

    Naples shall see my face no more. I go

    To fight the battles of the Holy Cross

    Against the Moor and live a penitent.

    Bear me away. [*Salerno and Lissardo lead him out*]

ALV. [*Apart*] Yes, yes, I've done her wrong.

    Oh, what a storm of undeserved woe

    Has poured upon that innocent!

    The cloud is gone from my benighted soul,

    My heart now owns thy virtue and o'erflows

    For having wrongfully suspected thee. [*Flings himself in a passion of tears at her feet*]

BIAN. Oh, rise, pray rise. You break my heart with joy.

ALV. [*With frantic exultation*] She's saved! She's saved! Virtue is ne'er deserted!

    Bianca's innocent! Bianca's here,

    Here in my arms! We part no more forever!

BIAN. [*Flinging herself on his arms*] Now, now to die were happy!

ALV.   Talk not of death, but rapture. No, sweet wife,

    We'll live and so be happy. From this hour

I'll scorn suspicion. Come to my arms!
Life may have pains and tears and agonies
Like sudden clouds that dim the summer skies;
But the true radiance stooping from above,
The sun that lights them all—is wedded love!

CURTAIN FALLS

www.ingramcontent.com/pod-product-compliance
Lightning Source LLC
Chambersburg PA
CBHW031936080426
42734CB00007B/713